Hugh Stowell, Charles Bullock

The Passover

And other Sermons

Hugh Stowell, Charles Bullock

The Passover
And other Sermons

ISBN/EAN: 9783337160975

Printed in Europe, USA, Canada, Australia, Japan

Cover: Foto ©Lupo / pixelio.de

More available books at **www.hansebooks.com**

THE PASSOVER,

AND

OTHER SERMONS

PREACHED IN CHRIST CHURCH, SALFORD.

BY THE

REV. HUGH STOWELL, M.A.,

RECTOR, HONORARY CANON OF CHESTER, RURAL DEAN, AND CHAPLAIN TO
THE RIGHT REV. THE LORD BISHOP OF MANCHESTER.

WITH A LIFE OF THE AUTHOR

BY THE

REV. CHARLES BULLOCK,

RECTOR OF ST. NICHOLAS, WORCESTER, EDITOR OF "OUR OWN FIRESIDE."

LONDON: WILLIAM TEGG.
1869.

CONTENTS.

SERMON		PAGE
	LIFE OF THE AUTHOR, BY REV. C. BULLOCK, M.A.	v
I.	GODLY REPENTANCE	1
II.	THE PASSOVER: ITS OCCASION AND IMPORT	7
III.	„ THE VICTIM	14
IV.	„ THE SHEDDING OF THE BLOOD	22
V.	„ THE APPLICATION OF THE BLOOD	30
VI.	„ THE EFFICACY OF THE SACRIFICE	38
VII.	GOD INCARNATE	46
VIII.	THE PROMISE OF THE HOLY SPIRIT	53
IX.	THE MARVELLOUS GRACE OF CHRIST	62
X.	CHRIST OUR PRECIOUS EXAMPLE	73
XI.	STUMBLING AT CHRIST	82
XII.	CHRIST SERVING HIS PEOPLE	95
XIII.	PARTAKING OF THE SUFFERINGS OF CHRIST	105
XIV.	THE SUPREME AFFECTION	116
XV.	SEEKING THE LORD THE GRAND DUTY OF MAN	125
XVI.	DIVINE TOKENS FOR GOOD	137
XVII.	ACQUAINTANCE WITH GOD	149
XVIII.	THE NOTES AND MARKS OF TRUE REGENERATION	159

CONTENTS.

Sermon	Page
XIX. THE INSPIRATION OF THE BIBLE	167
XX. VAIN SPECULATION	178
XXI. THE VISIBLE CHURCH	189
XXII. THE CHARACTERISTICS OF SPIRITUAL WORSHIP	197
XXIII. GOD'S BLESSING WITH RICHES	207
XXIV. GOD'S BLESSING WITH POVERTY	218
XXV. THE EDUCATION OF THE YOUNG	229
XXVI. THE WISDOM OF WINNING SOULS	237
XXVII. TREES OF RIGHTEOUSNESS	246
XXVIII. READY AND WAITING	256
XXIX. THE JUDGE AT THE DOOR	266
XXX. THE SOLEMN MESSAGE	276

SKETCH

OF THE

LIFE OF THE REV. HUGH STOWELL, M.A.

I.—EARLY YEARS.

HUGH STOWELL was born on the 3rd of December, 1799, at Douglas, in the Isle of Man.

His father, styled "the Apostle of the Church of Sodor and Man," the writer of the life of Bishop Wilson, was eminent for his fervent piety and simple eloquence; nor less distinguished for the primitive simplicity of his life, the sweetness of his disposition, and the refinement and courtesy of his manners.

Soon after the birth of Hugh, Mr. Stowell was presented to the vicarage of Kirk Lonan, situated in one of the most picturesque localities in the island. We are indebted to Mr. Howard, who succeeded him in the vicarage, for a very interesting account of the Stowell family during the period when Hugh was a child, and until the time when his education for college began.

"I remember," says this gentleman, writing to the sons of Hugh Stowell, "your dear father from the time he was between five and six years old. He was a sweet little boy, very social and friendly, and quite at home with everybody. . . . One day, when he was about six years old, I had lifted him on my pony for a short ride; and the animal coming to a piece of water by the roadside, stooped down to drink, and pulled the little fellow over his head into the water."

However, no harm followed, and his father seems to have been rather amused at the adventure of his hopeful son. He writes thus: "I was extremely sorry that you had so much trouble with the young horseman. He was not in the least hurt, but seems ashamed of his awkwardness. I feel much obliged to you for your tender attention to him on the occasion."

When Hugh was about twelve years of age he had outgrown his strength, and looked so delicate that consumption was feared. Change of air being thought desirable, he spent some weeks at the vicarage of Kirk Braddon, with his father's friend. They took long rides together in the parish, and, says Mr. Howard, "Very pleasant rides they were. His natural, friendly manner made him a great favourite amongst the people, and after he left us there were many kind inquiries concerning him."

This short visit was of great benefit to his health; his cough left him, and he returned home almost quite well.

It must have been to this period of his life that the following anecdote, frequently told by himself, refers: "When I was a boy, I was fond of the simple Manx eloquence, and sometimes strayed, something I fear to my dear father's displeasure, into the Manx chapels, to listen to their own preachers in the native language. Once I remember the preacher, inviting the flock to the Gospel feast, exclaimed, 'Come, for all things are now ready; there you will *find mountains of porridge and rivers of new milk!*'"

Amidst these tranquil scenes, young Stowell was being prepared for loftier service and for his Master's work. When he was about thirteen years old there was a young cottager residing in his father's parish who was suffering from a tedious illness, which ended in his death. Hugh took a great interest in this young man, and lent to him religious books, and taught him to read; and great was the joy of the poor sufferer when he could read a little in his Bible; and his eyes used to brighten, it is said, when from the little window of his bedroom he saw his youthful instructor coming to the house. In his last interview with him, the dying youth, feeling that he was drawing near to his end, exclaimed to him in Manx, with looks of joy, "Glory and praise to God; I am going home, I am going home."

"Never," says Mr. Howard, "have I beheld a more beautiful picture of domestic happiness than the little Vicarage of Lonan presented. It was indeed the abode of harmony, peace, and love. Mr. and Mrs. Stowell were of one heart and mind, and what was known to be the wish of one became immediately the will of the other. Their religion was brought into every part of their daily conduct. Mrs. Stowell was a very superior person, and had remembered her Creator from the days of her youth. She was a lovely looking woman. There was a striking feminine delicacy in her appearance, and her manner was gentle, cheerful, and kind. But along with this there was great firmness and decision in her character, in doing what she believed to be the will of God. She was one of the tenderest and best of mothers, but at the same time required from her children strict obedience to the commands of their parents. It was the great desire of both her and her dear husband to bring up their children in the nurture and admonition of the Lord, and to train them up for heaven."

Young Stowell was only about fourteen years of age when the first and heaviest affliction of his life fell upon him; he lost his mother. Never afterwards did he know a sorrow greater than this; indeed, he seemed to be a stranger to those afflictions which in general fall heavily upon those who are called to eminent service in the Church of Christ. There was something that almost smote upon the heart of many of his dearest friends, when they saw playing upon his features the smile of constant happiness, such as an infant has while it lies basking in the full sunshine of a mother's love; and yet, if any grief were unburthened to him, none sympathised more deeply than he. He seemed without difficulty to make the sorrows of the sick and dying all his own. He could not only "rejoice with them that do rejoice," he could "weep with them that weep;" and his power of throwing himself as it were into another's mind, and especially into their sorrows, was something which must have been seen in order to be appreciated.

Long instructed at home by his father, he was thence sent, for a short time, to the late Rev. John Cawood, the excellent incumbent of Bewdley, an able preacher, as his published sermons testify, and a good scholar.

From Bewdley Mr. Stowell proceeded to St. Edmund Hall, Oxford. His earliest and warmest friend, the Rev. Thomas Watson, now the Vicar of East Farleigh, speaking of his college life, says:—

"His course was characterized with a beautiful uniformity throughout; and yet it was anything but monotonous. Naturally he was blessed with great buoyancy of spirits, and no one enjoyed more than himself sallies of wit and humour on occasions which gave rise to innocent mirth. He had not a particle of asceticism in his composition. All approaches to that kind of levity which the Scriptures condemn he seemed always to have an instinctive dread of. Judging by what I observed in him, I should say that 'he feared God from his youth.' I cannot recollect a single instance, in our long intercourse, when he appeared to cast aside a filial, reverential, wholesome fear of God. The words of the Psalmist, in his case, were, if I may so express myself, stereotyped; they were engraven on his heart: 'Blessed is the man that feareth always.' And this salutary fear was accompanied with no morbid sensibility, slavish dread, or any depression whatever; on the contrary, it was a well-spring of joy which day by day overflowed his cheerful, happy soul.

"In Christian fellowship and love, it may be truly said of him, 'Once a friend, a friend for ever.' The sun of prosperity might set over you, and the cold winds of adversity beat on you bitterly and keenly in the lapse of time, yet you might always rely upon his fidelity and on his faithfulness,—unlike those men whose feelings, once ardently expressed, are only like the summer's brook, fed by no perpetual spring: so that their friendship and their feelings are soon dried up. He was ever ready to stretch out the warm hand of friendship; and the grasp of his hand was the interpreter of his heart."

II.—HIS MINISTRY.

WHEN at College, Mr. Stowell assiduously cultivated those powers of imagination and of eloquence which were afterwards so admirably employed in his Master's service. Mr. Watson gives this College reminiscence:—

"As at present, so in our day, there was in the University a debating society. It consisted of but few members, from different colleges. I well remember one of his first efforts at 'speechification.' The subject, I think, was the place the Bible ought to occupy among all classes of Christians, and in every relation of life. After some rather abortive attempts by others, he stood up, and with a commanding air, and a figure as erect as a dart, without other preface or introduction, he exclaimed in his deep-toned voice, 'What, I would ask, would be this our world *without a sun?*' You can imagine the rest. He rushed onward like an impetuous torrent, in a full flow of eloquence; and the outburst of feeling, when he threw the reins on the neck of his inward emotions, I can only compare to a burning volcano struggling with its hidden fires. At such times it was hardly possible to gaze on his finely-chiselled Saxon countenance—his noble features, his lustrous eye, his lofty brow, his well-formed, massive frame, and not admire the man. This *début* on the platform was a presage of his future almost unrivalled powers as a public speaker."

Mr. Stowell took his B.A. degree in 1822, and was ordained in 1823 to the curacy of Shepscombe, amid the beautiful scenery of the Cotswold Hills.

A friend gives an interesting record of a conversation with Mr. Stowell many years after, in which he described the first Sunday after his ordination, and the circumstances which led him to adopt an extempore style of preaching :—

"In a conversation with Mr. Stowell, I was once led to remark," says this friend, "that the power of extempore preaching greatly extended the usefulness of a clergyman, and relieved him from much severe toil, and to ordinary congregations gave more effect to the sermon." Mr. Stowell replied that he always felt thankful for being able so to preach; adding that he had never preached but one written sermon, and that was the first.

"I was," he said, "ordained by Bishop Ryder sooner than I expected, in order to take charge of the curacy of Shepscombe, having to go there the following day. I arrived late on the Saturday evening, tired and wearied, with one sermon written, and part of another; and found that I was to take the whole duty the next day—Sunday. I felt the solemnity of my position, and had made it a matter of much prayer. The Sunday morning came; I went to Church, read the prayers, and felt them too. I then ascended the pulpit to preach my written sermon. The congregation was a rural one; and as I glanced over it whilst preaching, my heart sank within me; and I thought I read their expression to be,—'What sort of a stripling have we got' (for I was then very youthful in my appearance); 'this may be all very good, but it is above our comprehension.' I retired to my lodgings, but had no appetite for my dinner. I offered up a heartfelt prayer, and on rising from my knees proceeded to finish my sermon for the afternoon. As I did so, my eye rested on a text which I thought very applicable to my then state of feelings and circumstances, and which I should like to preach upon. So after meditating upon it, and turning to parallel passages, I concluded to preach an extempore sermon on that subject. Much relieved, I went to Church, read the prayers, and then preached to the people in the fulness of my heart. I had not been long preaching before I observed tears trickling down an aged face. I felt that I was understood. From that time to this (about 1840), I have never preached a written sermon."

"He looked back," he added, "with interest and pleasure to his first rural flock, and even up to that time occasionally received from some of these simple people affectionate letters, which he prized much."

Shepscombe was an interesting field of labour, but it soon proved too narrow for his ardent spirit; and great as was the mutual regard and esteem subsisting between his incumbent and himself, he relinquished his curacy the following year, to undertake that of Trinity Church, Huddersfield.

Soon after he accepted an invitation to take the sole charge of the Church of St. Stephen, Salford. At that time Evangelical principles were held by a very small minority of the clergy in the vast parish of Manchester, of which Salford was but a chapelry; and it is a curious and painful illustration of the state of feeling which then prevailed, that the late Dr. Blomfield, then Bishop of Chester, hesitated at first about licensing one who had been represented to him as "an extemporaneous fire-brand." In a personal interview with the good Bishop, who always had the manliness to think and act for himself, this preliminary difficulty was readily overcome; and so acceptable did his ministrations prove, that his hearers, knowing how uncertain a curate's position is, and fearing lest he might be induced to accept an incumbency elsewhere, soon after determined to build a church, by subscription, for him, a little further out from the heart of Manchester, but still within the bounds of his overgrown parish.

Before this church was yet consecrated, Mr. Stowell's father paid him what proved to be a farewell visit. The venerable old man delighted all who were invited to meet him. He was quite aware of the dangers to which young men in general are exposed from early popularity, and did not live to see how thoroughly proof against them was, in this respect, his highly favoured son. When congratulated on the estimation in which he was held, "Ah," said he, "they are administering poison to my son out of a golden dish!"

Established in his new position, Mr. Stowell commenced a routine of labour which, with singular devotedness and perseverance, he continued with little alteration to the end of his life. His peculiar gifts necessarily opened many doors of usefulness abroad; but whilst ready to seize upon these opportunities to the extent of his powers (and possessing an iron frame which scarcely knew what illness was, those powers seemed as if they could scarcely be overtaxed), it may be truly said he excelled most in the usefulness which has its sphere at home. During his lengthened ministry in Salford, he was seldom absent for a single Sunday in the year, except when he took his autumnal holiday; and wherever he was, his heart seemed to yearn over his flock. Schools thoroughly well worked and sustained, district visiting, adult classes, libraries, mutual improvement society, clothing clubs, and other parochial institutions, indicated his anxiety to promote the welfare, temporal and spiritual, of his people.

In the pulpit, and on the platform, he was an Apollos in eloquence, and a John in love. In the pulpit his eloquence was especially adapted to move the hearts of his hearers, evincing a quick insight into the feelings and tendencies of human nature. His remarks were always perspicuous and pointed, his illustrations true to the subject in hand, but there was not any striking amount of deep thought. He made the pulpit as it should be, not the philosopher's desk, or the professor's chair, but the source of well-directed appeals to the conscience, and the deepest emotions of the heart. He studied simplicity as a matter of principle, making it his aim to reach the understanding of the poorest hearer. "I fix my eye," he said, "upon some poor man in the middle aisle, and when I perceive, from his attitude and the attention he pays, that I have interested him, then I proceed with comfort." Hence, while some leading men thought *for* the people, Canon Stowell thought *with* them; and the thoughts that passed through the minds of his hearers, and the feelings that surged through their hearts, were what he gave utterance to.

The style thus formed by a preacher who was a scholar and a gentleman, was pure and simple eloquence, such as fell from the lips of Latimer when he preached at Paul's Cross before King Edward, and king and "common people" equally "heard him gladly." Canon Stowell might have said with Baxter, "I never was ashamed to call a spade a spade; and yet, on the other hand, I never forebore a criticism in Greek or Latin, although I knew it would be above the range of some of my hearers."

On the platform he possessed remarkable power. His words came fresh from the anvil of the heart, and quickly kindled the enthusiasm of the audience. His mode of delivery was highly impressive, always in happy unison with the point he was arguing, or the appeal he was urging. He managed the tones of his voice with as much ease and propriety as the most consummate adept in elocution, never shouting or straining himself to an unnatural pitch. On one occasion, in a conversation on this point with the writer, Mr. Stowell gave the following laconic but useful counsel: "Never *try* to make yourself heard." It is very certain that the voice is *best* heard in its natural key, and the strained effort is not only ineffective, but painful alike to the speaker and the audience.

He was especially successful in gaining an influence over the working classes. He never seemed to condescend to them: never affected to *patronize* them. At a crowded public meeting he once spoke with the utmost contempt of the proud parson "who could not cordially shake the horny fist of the labouring man with his hand, and give it a hearty shake." At the same time, there was a becoming dignity about him, so that he could do this, and yet none would for an instant take unfitting advantage of the kindly familiarity encouraged.

Emphatically a man of action, he found but little time for literary compositions; but he nevertheless published two volumes on "Tractarianism," and another on "Nehemiah: a Model for Men of Business." Amongst numerous smaller pamphlets and tracts, one entitled, "I am a Churchman," has been exceedingly popular. As a hymnist, also, he deserves to be remembered, if only as the author of the exquisite hymn, "From every Stormy Wind that blows."

What he was as the Pastor of the flock may be gathered from the following testimony of one of his parishioners:—

"The absence from church of any member of his congregation, whose seat was not likely to be unoccupied, except from sickness, would be noticed, and affectionate inquiry made. The first person across our threshold under such circumstances was our Pastor. How loving, how affectionate, how full of sympathy and comfort were those visits, I can speak from my own experience. No fear of infection ever weighed with him, however contagious the disorder."

But perhaps the result of his labours in his own parish will best be estimated by the fact, that, during the first twenty-one years of his ministry, the communicants increased from one hundred and eighty to between five and six hundred.

III.—HIS PROTESTANTISM.

IN any sketch of Mr. Stowell's life, however brief, marked prominence must be given to his unflinching adherence to Protestant principles.

"A commanding sense of duty to my country, my faith, and my God, constrained me to make Protestant truth the polestar of my public conduct."

"The struggle with Rome has only begun. It waxes, and *will* wax, closer and closer. Spiritually, ecclesiastically, politically, she must be withstood. Meekly, but manfully, with all charity, yet with all determination, let us gird ourselves for the battle. *The battle of the Reformation has to be fought again.*"

"Emphatically, let all your doings be done in a right spirit—in a spirit of prayer. Let there be no resentment, no retaliation, no asperity. Leave personalities and slanders to those whose cause they befit. 'Be not overcome of evil, but overcome evil with good.'"

So spake and so acted Mr. Stowell, the faithful and devoted champion of our national Protestantism.

His was no spirit of intolerance or bigotry. On the contrary, it was *because* he regarded Romanism as the very essence of intolerance, that he avowed himself a Protestant—truly tolerant, truly Catholic, truly Christian.

"We are simply intolerant of intolerance, jealous of the most insatiable spiritual despotism. We protest against caressing our most implacable adversary; against furnishing her with weapons to destroy us. It is not religion we are resisting, but a system which, under the name and guise of religion, masks a huge sacerdotal conspiracy against the liberties of mankind—a system whose essence is exclusiveness, whose duty is persecution, whose passion is universal domination—a system, one of the greatest advocates and expositors of which, Cardinal Bellarmine, says, 'when heretics are strong, we commit them to God; when weak, to the executioner,'—a system which converts the cross into a scaffolding for the erection of an illimitable pyramid of priestly power, and transforms Christianity itself into a stupendous stalking-horse for hierarchical ambition to bestride, that it may ride rough-shod over the consciences, the liberties, and the lives of the whole human race."

Such an unfaltering and uncompromising testimony against intolerance, in all its shades of development, could not fail to make the witness himself obnoxious. On the one hand he was opposed and vilified by those who were identified with the Romish system, and on the other hand he was regarded as a disturber and an enthusiast by those who, as nominal Protestants only, were sufficiently indifferent to Revealed Truth to be disposed to "tolerate any error," however dishonouring to God, and however dangerous to civil and religious liberty, so long at least as it did not immediately threaten to interfere with their own personal rights. Genuine Romanists and indifferent Protestants were thus united in one rank against the faithful champion of God's Word, as the Charter of the Church of the Reformation.

It may be regarded as an axiom, none are so intolerant of individuals as those who are in error themselves, or tolerant of error in others. The Romish and mediæval spirit of persecution is in close alliance with the equally persecuting spirit of worldly indifference. Religious earnestness and faithful adherence to the Divine Word, which tolerates no error in doctrine or life, but demands the implicit recognition and acceptance of *absolute truth* as the alone standard of faith and practice, without any reference to human opinions—whether those of the sceptical disciples of science falsely so-called, or the devotees of superstition giving heed to the voice of a fallible Church as if it were the voice of the infallible God, or the worldly-minded who can only endure a religion that brings with it no cross of spiritual discipline and conflict—will always subject men to the penalties which the toleration of error in a sinful world necessarily involves, (St. John, xvi. 33.)

Mr. Stowell's experience formed no exception to this rule. Genial and loving, zealous and self-denying, buoyant in spirit and winning in manner, he might have been expected to disarm even intolerance of her weapons. But it was far otherwise. He had to count and pay the cost of faithfulness. He was branded as "a dictating priest." Misrepresentation did its worst. More than once his personal safety was endangered; but he never shrank. "It was not in his nature to be timid, and over his grave might have been pronounced the eulogy once pronounced over the grave of Knox—'Here lies he who was never afraid of the face of man.'"

He received many anonymous and threatening letters. These he invariably burnt without reading them. His rule was neither to read anonymous letters, nor to notice them when they appeared in the newspapers. A friend once remarking to him that he never replied to the letters in the newspapers, especially to one writer who attacked him violently, he replied, smiling, "No, I treat him as I would a chimney-sweeper whom I might meet in the street with a sack of soot on his back: I give him as wide a berth as possible." All those who have felt it their duty to stand in the fore-front of the battle learn, after a while, how cheap is their remedy against the threats and taunts of anonymous adversaries —secret stabbers ashamed of their names—namely, by committing such things, unread, to the waste-paper basket.

At the time when the arrogant attempt was made by Cardinal Wiseman to place England under the Canon Law of Rome, and to establish a Roman Catholic hierarchy, Mr. Stowell was one of the first to protest against the insult, and his efforts contributed in no mean degree to bring about the passing of the Ecclesiastical Titles Bill. On that occasion he addressed a meeting of nearly seven thousand persons in the Free Trade Hall, Manchester, for nearly three hours, the vast assembly listening with unflagging interest. His concluding words may well be pondered by every Protestant elector in the anticipation of the new Reform Parliament of 1869 :—

"In all probability the time is not distant when we shall have a dissolution of Parliament. I never asked any man to give a vote, and I never influenced a man in giving a vote; I never took the remotest part in party politics; I have been placed as a politician when I have been merely a simple Protestant man. I have loved Protestantism from my mother's lap; I was trained in loyalty to it, and I should have been unfaithful to a mother's prayer and to a father's teaching had I not been a true-hearted Protestant. But a political partisan I have never been, and, God helping me, I never will; but for once in my life I think I may deviate, and at the next election I will ask every man in my congregation to vote for no man that will not resist Popish aggression, and uphold our common Protestantism. My friends, enter into an agreement among yourselves, and if Manchester will show a list on the Exchange of some four thousand voters pledged to the point, our representatives will become mightily Protestant; we shall have a great change in the tone of debates when Parliament meets; do it—it can be done. Is there a Protestant here not willing to enter into such an agreement? Every man of God will agree to this; it is no political thing. I don't care whether we have a Whig, Tory, or Radical representative, so that we have a sound-hearted Protestant man. I can say little more. Don't lose your temper; don't lose your spirit. Love the Romanists; pray for them, feel for them, show them kindness. Show them that you love them, though you hate Popery. Resist Popery—oppose it to the death; you are warranted in doing so—Scripture upholds you in doing it. Your glorious Protestant rights and privileges bind you to do good—defend the right, and we have no fear of the consequences."

In another speech at this same period, Mr. Stowell thus met the charge that he was "dragging politics into religion:"—

"We are *not* dragging politics into religion, but we are bringing religion into politics. To do the one is to *profane*, to do the other is to *honour* our faith. We are not *politically* religious—that were *hypocrisy*; we are *religiously* political, that is *fidelity*."

This discriminating and admirable definition bespeaks the watchfulness over his own spirit, the constant exercise of which preserved him from the perilous deadening influence which invariably creeps over the mere controversialist. Mr. Stowell was not a political churchman, and, however his conduct and principles were at times maligned and misrepresented, the abuse which fell to his share made no lasting impression on the public mind, and did his character no harm. His opponents styled him "the Pope of Salford," but he lacked not vindicators of the noble and manly course he pursued.

"Is there anything in such conduct," asks one of the leading Manchester newspapers, dealing with these assailants, "unworthy of Mr. Stowell as an Englishman or a Christian minister? They know very well that there is not, and therefore they represent him as aiming at personal aggrandisement, in the teeth of notorious facts, and the evidence to the contrary furnished by the acts of nearly a life-time. These perpetual assaults upon Canon Stowell are the most striking tributes to his merits and services. Great influence he undoubtedly possesses, and he has exercised it most beneficially in a thousand ways, and in none more conspicuously than in keeping up the tone of Protestant feeling."

The accusation of seeking "personal aggrandisement" advanced against Mr. Stowell, was indeed made "in the teeth of notorious facts." His income arose from pew-rents only, and never exceeded that of a professional man in ordinary practice. The Church of England, as a Church, contributed nothing to her distinguished son. "He was a lion in her defence, but she was always a heartless foster-mother—'*leonum arida nutrix.*'"

The generosity of his congregation on two occasions nobly supplemented the amount received from seat-rentals. In 1846 he received a present of £1,500; and in 1860 he was presented with a silver salver and the sum of £5,000, " in testimony of the eminent services rendered by him during a ministry of thirty-five years, and of the able and uncompromising manner in which he has on all occasions advocated the maintenance of the Protestant Institutions of this country."

This latter subscription originated with two friends, one of them a Churchman and the other a Wesleyan, and was raised without the slightest canvass, "*the only condition being that it should be applied for the benefit of Mr. Stowell and his family as he might think fit.*" This condition was not unnecessary, for Mr. Stowell " demurred to accept the sum of money for *personal purposes,*" and only yielded when he was assured that "the majority of his friends had contributed on the express understanding that it should be so applied," and that he " would occasion them much pain and disappointment were he to defeat their design." But in complying with their wishes, he added, " At the same time I hope

b

that the augmentation of my income will not only add to the comfort of my family and myself, but also to my resources for benevolent and charitable purposes."

That the pastor was truly worthy of these acts of generous consideration on the part of his flock, can need no additional proof, but an extract from a friend's letter may serve to set the disinterestedness of Mr. Stowell in a still stronger light.

"Although he had various offers of preferment with greater emolument elsewhere, nothing could induce him to leave his beloved parishioners. I recollect on one occasion, when taking tea at my house, he wrote a note, and took out of his pocket a letter to get the address. Just as he was putting the note in an envelope, he said, handing the letter and note to me over the table, ' I need not withhold this from an old friend.' On reading them, I found the letter conveyed the offer of a living worth almost three times the amount of his own; his reply was, as nearly as I can recollect, simply thanking the gentlemen for their kind offer, but adding that if they knew how happy he was in his present position, and, he trusted, useful likewise, they would not be surprised that he should decline accepting it. I have reason to believe, too, that he refused a canonry because it would have involved nonresidence, which he did not think consistent."

Such was the man against whom a censorious world, or rather an intolerant section of the professedly Christian Church, could urge the accusation of "aiming at personal aggrandisement."

But he lived long enough to silence even his detractors:

> "Assailed by scandal and the tongue of strife,
> He gave the answer of a blameless life ;
> And he that forged, and he that threw the dart,
> Had each a brother's interest in his heart."

Never was there a controversialist who more thoroughly combined the faithfulness of the ambassador with the love of the brother. He loved peace and union, but he loved purity and truth more dearly still; and this was the secret of his zeal against Popery, and of his faith and fervour in denouncing Tractarianism.

"He was a genuine successor of our best Reformers. His soul beat in true harmony with Hooper and Latimer, and Cranmer and Bradford. Against the fashion of the times—against the tide which was manifestly a rising tide of secular advantage and advancement—he maintained in simple dignity the integrity of his testimony for the Protestantism of the Church of England. While many were forsaking the standard—while many were lowering the standard—while many were mingling its noble inscriptions with mongrel mottoes, to make it pleasing to all sorts of people, Hugh Stowell, grasping the banner and holding it aloft—that banner of the Protestant Reformers and the liberties of the Church of England,—refused to lower his tone or to dilute his testimony; and peacefully, prayerfully, conscientiously, with his eyes open, he preferred honourable neglect—ay, and contempt and scorn—to any crooked management or disingenuousness, or even concealment of his convictions, in order to conciliate compromisers in high places."*

IV.—THE CLOSE OF LIFE.

In 1862, while visiting Bishopwearmouth, to deliver a lecture, Canon Stowell met with a painful accident, seriously injuring his knee-cap. He was very much shaken, and some who loved him well could perceive a decline in his vigorous powers from that time. He rallied, however, and still adhering to his oft-expressed opinion, that it was "better to wear out than to rust out," he was soon in full work again. We find him at one time lecturing in the Free Trade Hall, Manchester, on the Moderation of the Church of England; then preaching the Assize Sermon in Chester Cathedral; and in 1864 he again visited London, and addressed a vast congregation in the nave of Westminster Abbey. In one of his letters referring to this sermon, he speaks of "two hours' highly interesting but not quite satisfactory discussion with Dean Stanley." The Dean "yielded one or two important points."

But the wearied soldier of the cross was obliged at length to confess his almost exhausted powers. There is something very affecting in the following letter. Many a believer sinking into the grave, who finds, like Job, that sleepless nights and wearisome days are appointed unto him, will read it, and be comforted. No "strange temptation" befalls the most active and devoted servants of God when such an experience of the plague of their own hearts,

* Funeral Sermon by Dr. M'Neile.

even at the end of their labours, opens out more clearly the "comfort" that is to be found in Jesus:—

"Llandudno, July 4th.

"DEAREST SISTER,—You will like to hear from my own pen how I progress. Very slowly; but I hope, please God, surely. The hot weather sadly prostrates me, and my heart continues very languid. Pray for me, that I may be refined in the furnace, and lie as clay in the hands of the potter. Oh, how deeply do sleepless nights and wearisome days open up to us the plague and vileness of our whole lives. Were it not for Jesus, and for what Jesus is, what could we do?

"We remain here (all well) another week, and then I hope I may be moving about for some months. All are well, and send love to all. All grace be with you, prays

"Your affectionate brother,

"HUGH STOWELL."

After reading this letter we are almost surprised to hear of his rallying once more, but he appears to have done so; for we find him writing on April 8th—

"We are all in fair health, and compassed with mercies. I had the largest communion last Sunday I ever had during forty years' ministry; within 13 of 600 communicants. Oh, the goodness of Jesus!"

This, however, was only the flickering of the light of life. His strength was manifestly and rapidly failing, and the crisis was hastened by another fall at Matlock. A few months later his medical attendants advised him to desist for a time from preaching, and he proceeded to Grasmere for rest. While there he had a severe attack of diphtheria, and was obliged to return home. In a few days the disease seemed to abate, but the symptoms presently became unfavourable. Added to this, about a week before he died, congestion of the lungs set in, followed by a slight attack of paralysis. From that time he gradually sank, gently falling asleep, about noon on Sunday, October 8th, 1865.

The following record of his closing hours is from the pen of his son, the Rev. Thomas Alfred Stowell. Seldom have we read a more touching tribute of filial affection to departed worth.

"During my father's last illness—borne with exemplary patience and unmurmuring submission, it pleased God that the powers of his naturally clear and vigorous mind should be much impaired by the nature of his disease. For the greater part of his last week on earth he was suffering from oppression on the brain, which manifested itself either in semi-unconsciousness or mental wandering. Yet whenever he was able to speak, and so to indicate to those around what was passing within, his words most clearly gave evidence, even when that evidence was involuntary, that his mind was entirely filled with holy and heavenly things, nor even in delirium distracted by thoughts of earth.

"These utterances abundantly testify to *his love of and delight in prayer*. Almost every word was prayer, couched for the most part in the language of Holy Scripture or the Book of Common Prayer; and these prayers were characterised by the *deepest humility and most entire self-distrust*. It was indeed an affecting and, at the same time, solemn and instructive lesson, to hear one, of whom we might think that, like the great apostle, if any one had whereof he might trust in the flesh—he more, like him, confessing himself the chief of sinners. One of the passages he most frequently repeated, perhaps *the* most frequently, was, 'If Thou, Lord, shouldest be severe to mark what is done amiss, O Lord, who may abide it? But there is forgiveness with Thee that Thou mayest be feared' (Psalm cxxx., 3, 4); to which he invariably added, 'Let that forgiveness be extended unto me, for Jesus Christ's sake, Amen.' Short petitions, such as the following, were continually on his lips: 'Lord, have mercy upon me.' 'Christ, have mercy upon me.' 'Lord, have mercy upon me.' 'Lord, save, or I perish.' 'O Lord, I am like a little child, very meek and lowly; have mercy upon me, and help me, for Jesus Christ's sake, Amen.' Several times he repeated the well-known verse—

> "'Just as I am, without one plea,
> But that Thy blood was shed for me,
> And that Thou bidd'st me come to Thee;
> O Lamb of God, I come.'

And also that beginning

> "'Poor, weak, and worthless though I am.'

I may here mention that he appeared to listen with great delight to the following hymns, which had been great favourites in his life when read or sung to him:—

> "'Rock of Ages, cleft for me;'
> "'Come, let us join our cheerful songs;'
> "'Through all the changing scenes of life;'
> "'Nearer, my God, to Thee;'

And

> "'My God, my Father, while I stray.'

"Equally apparent was his *simple and firm trust in his Saviour*. The last night but one before his death, about half-past one, he awoke perfectly conscious, calm, and quiet, though much exhausted. I was sitting by his bedside, and asked him if he was happy. 'Yes,' he replied, 'and quite resigned to God's will.' To the question, 'Is Jesus with you and precious to you?' 'Yes, so that He is all in all to me,' was his answer. During his waking moments after this he frequently exclaimed, 'Very much peace,' and several times, 'No fear:' 'Abundance of joy.' More frequently still, sometimes in scarce audible tones, he breathed those words which told of his blessed experience, 'A very present help in time of trouble.' Another and remarkable expression was, 'Oh, the comfort and the support of the society of Jesus!'

"On the day before his death, he uttered the prayer, 'Come, Lord Jesus, and take me home;' and when his eldest son said, 'Even so, Lord Jesus, come quickly!' (Rev. xxii. 20), he rejoined, 'But when?' 'In His own good time; and is not that the best time, dear father?' 'Oh, yes, Amen.' When disturbed a little by an attempt to change his position, he said, 'Wait, wait a little.' When asked what for, 'Death,' was his reply. He had before prayed for help 'in this my last illness,' thus indicating his consciousness that he was standing on the confines of eternity.

"The morning of his death, the only articulate words that we could catch, uttered two or three hours before his decease, were 'Amen! Amen!'

> "'His watchword at the gates of death.
> He enters heaven by prayer.'

"At one o'clock in the afternoon, on God's blessed Day of Rest, without a struggle and without the shadow of pain crossing his peaceful countenance, he entered into rest—the 'Sabbath-keeping that remaineth for the people of God' (Heb. iv. 9)."

The day of Mr. Stowell's funeral presented a sight such as seldom, perhaps never, occurred at the obsequies of any private clergyman. The whole of the borough of Salford was in mourning, and the city of Manchester seemed to "sit solitary." The funeral procession was a mile in length. The Bishop of the diocese and more than two hundred of the clergy, with the representatives of leading dissenting communities, followed him to his grave. The whole road to the church was thronged with the multitude of people, and the indications of sorrow were deep and fervent. This, too, was not the result of pre-arrangement, but the spontaneous expression of public feeling. The Bishop read the service. At some parts of the solemn ritual his utterance was choked, and "few indeed were they who refused the tribute of a tear."

It was felt to be no mere private loss, but the removal of a pastor who had not only endeared himself to his own flock, but had left his mark upon his age—had stamped his sovereignty more widely and deeply upon the popular mind of the Church of England, than perhaps any other man living.

"And I heard a voice from heaven saying unto me, Write, Blessed are the dead which die in the Lord from henceforth: Yea, saith the Spirit, that they may rest from their labours; and their works do follow them" (Rev. xiv. 13).

I.

GODLY REPENTANCE.

"And I will pour upon the house of David, and upon the inhabitants of Jerusalem, the spirit of grace and of supplication; and they shall look upon Me whom they have pierced, and they shall mourn for Him, as one mourneth for his only son, and shall be in bitterness for Him, as one that is in bitterness for his first-born."—ZECHARIAH xii. 10.

CHRIST crucified is the centre point of eternity, Christ crucified is the centre object of the universe, Christ crucified is the soul of His Church, Christ crucified it is that bruiseth the hard heart, and Christ crucified it is that binds up the broken heart. Christ crucified is the spring of all godly sorrow, and Christ crucified is the source of all godly joy. If Christ be not fundamental to our faith, we may be Christians in name and form, but we are not Christians in deed and in truth. "What think ye of Christ?" may test our character. We cannot be right in the rest if we are in error here. Our Church has beautifully and scripturally, in the order of our Christian year, given to Christ crucified, the great, the grand, and the prominent place. The season of Lent; the week called Passion week, the week of Christ's agony, Good Friday, Easter Sunday, the Sundays following Easter, are all full of Christ crucified and of Christ glorified. It were well if those who call themselves members of our Church entered more into the spirit of the Church and her services. In entering therefore upon this week,* desiring to draw your hearts and affections towards the centre object of our common faith, how beautifully and how expressively is the subject brought before us in that grand piece of ancient religion, the Passover. In casting about for a subject that would fitly draw your thoughts and affections,—and it may be your sorrows and your deep sympathy,—on this Palm Sunday, the Sunday on which we commemorate the entry of Christ into Jerusalem to commence His awful anguish, and to accomplish His glorious triumph, the words I have read commended themselves to me as very appropriate. They describe, primarily, the deliverance of Israel, "I will pour upon the house of David, and upon the inhabitants of Jerusalem, the spirit of grace and supplication: and they shall look upon Me whom they have pierced." Yet, though the description is primarily of Israel, it is a description of all genuine repentance. It is a description of what it is that causes, and is the great object of true repentance, and it will lead us very briefly to touch upon these three points:—

The spring of true repentance:—*the object that occasions true repentance:*—and *the depth and intenseness of godly repentance.* May the Spirit of God accompany His word, that we may profit by it.

We have then, in these words, *the spring of true repentance.* "I will pour out upon the house of David, and upon the inhabitants of Jerusalem, the spirit of grace and supplication. *There* is the author of true repentance, the Spirit of God, the author and giver of all good, one of the first fruits of the Saviour's preparation. When He, the Spirit, "is come, He will reprove the world of sin, and of righteousness, and of judgment; Of sin, because they believe not on me; Of righteousness, because I go to my Father, and ye see me no more; Of judgment, because the Prince of this world is judged." He taketh of the things of Jesus, and showeth them unto us.

* Passion week, 1862.

He is called "the spirit of grace and of supplication." The spirit of grace, because it is the gift of sovereign mercy; He works graciously, freely, and sovereignly. If, penitent sinner, thy repentance be genuine, it is the act of the Spirit of God, and of God's grace. "By grace are ye saved." "By the grace of God I am what I am;" and grace only makes me to differ from the vilest of the human race; therefore "God be merciful to me a sinner," is my prayer. There is no true repentance but what is breathed by the Spirit in the heart of man, and no man pours out his heart in the spirit of truth, who does not do it in the help and power of the Holy Ghost. "Likewise the Spirit also helpeth our infirmities; for we know not what we should pray for as we ought; but the Spirit itself maketh intercession for us with groanings which cannot be uttered. And He that searcheth the hearts knoweth what is the mind of the Spirit, because He maketh intercession for the saints according to the will of God." "God is a spirit," and must be worshipped "in spirit and in truth." You may take it as a certain sign that a man has received the spirit of grace if it produce in him the spirit of supplication, for "He that searcheth the hearts," has marked it as genuine repentance. "Behold, he prayeth."

> " Prayer is the contrite sinner's voice
> Returning from his ways;
> While angels in their songs rejoice
> And say, 'Behold, he prays!' "

The spirit of supplication:—Blessed thing, one to supplicate in heaven as our Intercessor there, and one to supplicate in our hearts as Supplicator here. The Son knoweth "the mind of the Spirit, because he maketh intercession for us according to the will of God," and the Spirit knoweth the mind of the Son. And they that have the Spirit are in Him, and are one with Him and with the Father. Who can fail to succeed in prayer with such an Intercessor to help him, and to present his prayers to the throne of grace?

"A spirit of grace and supplication" I will *pour* out upon them. What a rich abundance! What an ample provision! "I will pour floods upon the dry ground,"—such is the beautiful expression of the richness of Christ Jesus. As He said Himself on the great day of the feast—"If any man thirst, let him come unto me and drink. He that believeth on me, as the Scripture hath said, out of his belly shall flow rivers of living waters."

Turn we to *the great object that produces repentance of heart* —that is, godly repentance. "They shall look upon Me whom they have pierced, and they shall mourn for Him as one mourneth for his only son, and shall be in bitterness for Him, as one that is in bitterness for his first-born." Here is another touchstone of genuine repentance. If a man's repentance does not lead him to the cross, and if the cross does not underlay his repentance; if the great source of his deep abasement be not the crucified Saviour, it is transitory. It may be worldly sorrow, "the sorrow of the world" that "worketh death;" it may be a superstitious sorrow, or it may be a natural sorrow, which is right as far as it goes; but it is not the "repentance to salvation not to be repented of." That always arises from grace, the spring of repentance, and the spring of godly sorrow; for, after all, what is sorrow if in it is not seen the exceeding sinfulness of sin in the sight of God, if it does not bring the sinner to arise and go to his Father, and say to Him—"Father, I have sinned against heaven, and before Thee?" Godly sorrow leads a man to take a view of the cross of Jesus, of the Saviour crucified for him, bearing his iniquity, and "travelling in the greatness of His strength" to make satisfaction for him. What can break the hard heart, if this cannot? The law may appal, but it oftentimes also hardens, and drives to despair; but it is the cross of Christ, and the sufferings of the Saviour, that lead the poor penitent to cast himself solely and simply on the mercy of God, through the merits of the Saviour.

"They shall look upon Me whom they have pierced." See the tenderness of that description. It is not a merely casual glance, it is not a mere admission of the crucifixion of Christ, but it is to look intensely, earnestly, and with a riveted attention on that dread sight which made the earth shake and tremble to the centre. Dear brethren, as the sinner goes up to that dread sight, he begins to say, *I* pierced Him, *my* sins wounded Him, they brought Him to the cross, the scourge, and the spear. I look to Him and say, I have gone astray like a sheep which is lost; the Lord hath laid on Him my iniquity, and the iniquity of us all. "Behold the Lamb of God," who taketh away my sins as He does the sins of the world. Look fixedly and abstractedly on Christ crucified, and you will be led to say, "Father, I have sinned against heaven, and before thee, and am no more worthy to be called thy son."

Look at the *depth and intensity* of the repentance:—"mourneth for Him as one that mourneth for his only son, and in bitterness for Him as one that is in bitterness for his first-born." I know that the sorrows and sufferings of Jesus are passed for ever. The "travail of His soul" is finished, for He said with His dying breath, "It is finished;" and now He lives, and "death hath no more dominion over Him." Where is the mother or the father who does not remember the deep suffering and anguish occasioned by the loss of a loved child, the first-born; who does not remember the intensity of the suffering? And do they not, when they think of it, feel the anguish again, though they know the child is beyond the reach of pain? There is still some recollection of the child, accompanied with deep sorrow, and it is natural and right that it should be so. It is meet and right, too, that we should never look at the crucified Saviour but with feelings of abasement, of self-humiliation, and agony, with the feelings of one who has lost an only son. This we should do in the privacy of the closet, in the presence of God, and at His holy table. There we should show contrition and humiliation, for we know that "they that sow in tears shall reap in joy;" and more, we "know the fellowship of His sufferings;" "if we suffer, we shall also reign with Him; if we deny Him, He also will deny us;" if we pledge Him in the bitter cup, He will pledge us in the cup of everlasting consolation and joy; and we shall at last live with Him, and the cross will be only the prelude to endless glory and ecstasy.

If you will have that godly sorrow, you must have the author and giver of it; you must seek from God "the spirit of grace and supplication." You must pray that the Holy Spirit will keep you, that you may no more forsake and depart from the great centre-point of your hope. Therefore, do not let this week pass away absorbed in the things of this life, but give attention to the great things of eternity. Redeem the time! regard the concerns of your immortal souls as your chief concerns, and not business, and pleasure, and fashion, and the follies of the world. Oh, they are nothing in comparison with a crucified Saviour. None can serve you as He can, none can do for you as He can do, none have your eternal interests at heart as He has; for if you have Christ, then "whether Paul, or Apollos, or Cephas, or the world, or life, or death, or things present, or things to come, all are yours; and ye are Christ's, and Christ is God's;" but Christ lost, Christ neglected, Christ slighted, and your great salvation is shipwrecked. God grant that we may be so looking upon Him, that when He comes in glory we may not be amongst those who quake for fear, but may we lift up our eyes with joy when we behold our salvation coming.

II.

THE PASSOVER: ITS OCCASION AND IMPORT.

"What mean ye by this service?"—EXODUS xii. part of 26.

IT is truly interesting, and it is at the same time truly instructive, to examine the etching as well as the finished picture, to examine the architect's outline as well as the completed structure, to examine the mould as well as the perfect casting. Comparing one with the other, we discern more fully the wisdom, the skill, and the beauty of the work. And so it is in the things of the Spirit of God. We are not to suppose that the etchings, and the moulds, and the architectural plans of the Old Testament are of no utility now; so far from it, we shall never have so clear and full an impression of the great work of redemption as when we study them, and by not doing so, we shall not only rob our own souls of much benefit and blessing, but we shall rob God of much glory and praise for His manifold wisdom. In this very solemn and, to the devout soul, very interesting week of Christ's passion, I have made choice of what we may not unfitly style the most beautiful etching of all in the Old Testament, the most beautiful architectural outline of the great temple of redemption, the most beautiful mould of the glorious casting of salvation, the tracing out in the shadow of the substance of that shadow. May the Spirit of God accompany us, that we may learn somewhat more of the length, and breadth, and height of the love, and the wisdom, and the greatness of the salvation that is in Christ Jesus, which He accomplished as at this time in "His agony," in "His bloody sweat," in "His cross and passion," in "His precious death and burial," and in "His glorious resurrection and ascension."

The passover is pre-eminently the prince of types. It is the one that is fullest of Christ, the fullest of the fulness of Christ. It is the one that gives us, as in a beautiful parable, the whole work of the redemption of the sinner through the sacrifice of the Lamb of God. Therefore we shall take it in detail, and we shall seek to lead you into all its admirable expressiveness, ordained to be a perpetual memorial till the passover should be accomplished in "Christ our Passover." "As often as ye eat this bread, and drink this cup, ye do show the Lord's death till He come." "Christ our Passover is sacrificed for us."

God ordained that when the children of Israel should ask "What mean ye by this service?" the explanation should be given—This keep as a perpetual memorial of the great redemption wrought for Israel. We ask the same question this evening with regard to the passover, "What mean ye by this service?" And we shall first of all bring out the occasion of the institute, and then, as briefly as we may, we shall refer to the import of the institute in its relation to Israel, and in its prefiguration of Christ. May the Spirit of God attend the word of God, and bring it home to our minds and hearts in love and power.

The occasion of the paschal feast. The occasion we are familiar with, and we shall do well to recall the circumstances, that we may be more impressed with the beauty of the type. All Israel, as you know, had been in bondage for centuries in Egypt. They groaned under the bitter yoke, and their cry went up to heaven, to God, who said, "I know their sorrows," and compassionate them; and the time came for their deliverance, and by signs and wonders vengeance was poured forth upon Pharaoh and upon the Egyptians. At the same time Pharaoh was infatuated, and God "hardened his heart," that He might show forth His great power and signal judgments, and he refused to let the people go. At last, the crisis came, and God declared that He would destroy the first-born of all the Egyptians; and the angel with his destroying hand went forth with the dread message of death to every family, "from the first-born of Pharaoh that sat on his throne, unto the first-born of the captive that was in the dungeon, and all the first-born of cattle." But this great destruction was not to come nigh to the house of Israel. They had been exempt from the former plagues, which were of a lighter character and dealt rather with externals, than with families themselves; but now that life, human life, was to be subject to judgment, now that men themselves were to be the victims, it pleased God by the ordinance of the passover to make it abundantly evident that it was not for their righteousness, not for their being by nature or practice undeserving of His righteous wrath that He spared them, but that it was all His grace and love that made the difference between them, and that they had merited the punishment of death, even as the Egyptians, should be clear and distinct and manifest to them.

The *occasion* then of this institution of the passover was to rescue Israel out of the bondage of the Egyptians by a last fearful visitation of Divine vengeance, and the *import* of it was to signify to Israel and to all men in every period, wherever the word of God's truth comes, that there is no difference, that Israel of themselves and in themselves merited the punishment of death even as the Egyptians did, that by their own deservings shall no flesh be ever saved, and there must be a method by which God can declare his righteousness by exercising His mercy, by which He shall punish sin and give it its deserts, whilst He passes over the sinner, and screens him from destruction. All this we shall see clearly brought out and made most emphatic by the blessed ordinance of the paschal lamb.

But our concern at present is with *the correspondence between the antitype and the type in the occasion and in the import*. The correspondence is very accurate and clear. The whole of the sinful race of man are by nature in Egyptian bondage; they are under corruption; they are under the power of Satan; they are "dead in trespasses and sins;" they are all under the thraldom and curse of God's broken law. The sentence is suspended, but it is recorded, and there is but the breath of their nostrils between them and death—the death that never dies. Such is the condition of man by nature. There is no difference between Jew and Gentile, between "Barbarian and Scythian," between "bond and free;" and from this fearful bondage and condition "no man may deliver his brother, nor make agreement unto God for him." But God, in His infinite grace and love, has devised means by which the exiled may return to Him, by which the enslaved may become emancipated, by which the perishing ones may be brought out from amongst the lost family. He has provided rescue for the captive, He has opened the prison door, and He proclaims liberty to the prisoner. He would put a difference, deep as between heaven and hell, and broad as eternity, between His people and His enemies; but He would do this in such wise—and now comes the *import*—as that He should make it clear to the universe that it was all of His own sovereign grace and mercy. But that it was so He did not set aside justice, He did not violate His own law, He did not connive at sin, He did not make light of transgression and iniquity, He did not expect anything perfect, or anything lower than the fulness that His law required; and in order to this, "Christ our Passover" has been "sacrificed for us."

and the design and the import—the glorious redemption that is by Jesus corresponds with the design and the import of the paschal ordinance. That was a kind of material representation and prophecy in things and in acts of the great method of human redemption and reconciliation, and the paschal feast was instituted that the Israelites might behold, as in a mirror, the grace that was magnified towards them in their desert of punishment, and in their salvation by substitution and intervention, the just suffering for the unjust, the sinless for the sinful, the guiltless for the guilty, the infinitely perfect for the utterly imperfect; that they might see in that ordinance as in a glass, foretold, anticipated, and proclaimed the great purpose of the passover. It was intended to be a perpetual memorial to recall their bondage and rescue, and above all, their exemption from the desolation that visited their enemies; and to recall it in such wise as that they should be perpetually affected with the deepest sense of their own unworthiness, and learn to give up themselves to Him who had so wrought mightily for them. No doubt this was one design of the passover, but so to speak, the lower design; for more momentous far than this inferior bearing was its bearing upon the mighty deliverance that was hereafter to come; for while it took back their thoughts to Egypt, it took forward their hopes, their faith, and their expectations to the infinitely mightier deliverance of which that was the mere shadow and type, the wondrous deliverance to be wrought at Gethsemane and on Calvary. And so it served this two-fold purpose. How beautiful, how eloquent, and how expressive a type, leading them back to that wondrous night when God brought them out with such "a mighty hand," and taking them forward with hope and joy to Gethsemane and Calvary! To Him they shall yet as a people look, even Him "whom they have pierced," when "the spirit of grace and of supplication is poured out upon them."

You see then, beloved, the answer to the question "What mean ye by this service?" You see the *occasion* of it, and you see the immediate *import* and design of it; what it was to express and convey, and what it was to represent, and you see how closely in all this it corresponds with the infinitely mightier deliverance of God's chosen people from the thraldom of sin, from the curse of the law, from the bondage of Satan, from the vestibule of hell. You see how in all this, as in a parable, we have Christ and His salvation set forth in the most beautiful and impressive manner.

We shall next have the victim of the sacrifice and of the ordinance to bring before you, and we shall in each step see the glorious correspondence opening up to us more and more fully and expressively.

Let us not forget that we should "look unto the rock whence we are hewn, and to the hole of the pit whence we are digged." Never let us forget what we were, and what we must have been for ever but for Jesus, had not God found "a Lamb for a burnt-offering," had not God in his own wisdom provided a stupendous method of reconciliation, which brings "glory to God in the highest, and on earth peace, good will toward men." We must ever have remained in the thraldom of Satan, and under the chains of our iniquity through time and through eternity, had it not been for this "great deliverance." Oh, what infinite grace it was that rescued us, and saved us when we were ready to perish!

But, at the same time, let us bear in mind that if such were our state, and if from such degradation we were rescued, it becomes us to "walk humbly with our God." May we keep before our hearts by His spirit that we owe all to His sovereign grace. "God forbid that we should glory, save in the cross of our Lord Jesus Christ."

And oh, how sad for those who love their chains, and will not leave their house of bondage even when the door is open!

The chains are ready to drop from them, the prison doors are open, and the Saviour cries to every one, come to me, "Look unto me, and be ye saved." Alas! that we love "darkness rather than light," that we love bondage rather than freedom, that we prefer Egypt to heaven—I had almost said Satan rather than Christ. Brethren, let us not neglect this our one and great salvation, but let it fill our hearts with the deepest love and gratitude; for if the love of the Father was infinite, was not the love of the Son infinite, to leave the throne of the universe to take upon Himself our human nature, and to bear the burden of our guilt, "travelling in the greatness of His strength," to make our peace with God. Dear brethren, let the language of our hearts then be—

> "When I survey the wondrous cross
> On which the Prince of Glory died,
> My richest gain I count but loss,
> And pour contempt on all my pride.
>
> "Forbid it, Lord, that I should boast,
> Save in the death of Christ, my God;
> I know no other hope or trust,
> Than the atonement of His blood."

III.

THE PASSOVER: THE VICTIM.

"And looking upon Jesus as he walked, he saith, Behold the Lamb of God!"—St John i. 36.

ONE of the simplest, one of the most touching, and one of the most comprehensive descriptions of the Christian passover, the holy Supper of our Lord, is that given by St. Paul, "As often as ye eat this bread, and drink this cup, ye do show the Lord's death till he come." How expressive is that description, how it makes the blessed Supper stand out amid the ordinances of Christ's Church paramount and pre-eminent, representing and keeping not only in constant memory, but as it were steadily before our very eyes, Christ crucified. We are to do this until His second coming in glorious majesty, thus taking our faith from Christ, and leading us to associate as we ever ought His infinite humiliation with His exaltation, and to connect Christ crucified with Christ glorified.

The paschal feast, the type of our spiritual passover, was similarly fitted at once to recall the past and to be prophetic of the future. It led the devout Israelite to behold through the form and shadow the reality and the substance; to not only commemorate with a grateful heart and mind the deliverance of his forefathers from the bondage of Egypt, but to forecast the infinitely more transcendent deliverance to be wrought in due time on the cross. We are, therefore, fully warranted in taking up this blessed type on this solemn week and in tracing step by step the beautiful correspondence between the paschal feast and the glorious Christian feast of Christ crucified.

We have showed you how the occasion of the institution of the passover most impressively represented the occasion of the ordinance of Christ's sacrifice—the Israelites' escape from the bondage of the Egyptians representing the rescue of Christ's people from under the bondage of hell; and how the import of the ordinance showed the Israelites that they were not less guilty than the Egyptians, but that grace alone distinguished between them and those that perished by the destroying angel. We have showed you that it was to represent by the offerings up of the paschal lamb, and the sprinkling of the blood upon the doors, that we are to be saved and passed over by the destroyer, thus signifying to us that "all have sinned and come short of the glory of God," that by reason of the law and by personal merit shall no sinner be ever saved, that all who are saved must be so through sacrifice and through the shedding of blood, and that those who have merited eternal death have redemption by blood.

We come now to that most important point in the great paschal type, the victim to be provided, and we at once fasten our attention upon that victim as setting before us "in the fulness of time" Jesus, and pointing out and preparing the way for Him who "was in the world," "and the world knew Him not," who "came unto His own, and His own received Him not." St. John exclaims as he looks upon Him, "Behold the Lamb of God!" May the Spirit of God be with us while we seek to behold that blessed and glorious Lamb that bore our iniquities and made our peace.

The Israelites were directed on this wise with regard to the victim that was to be sacrificed on the paschal occasion:

—" Speak ye unto all the congregation of Israel, saying, In the tenth day of this month they shall take to them every man a lamb according to the house of their fathers, a lamb for a house. .... Your lamb shall be without blemish, a male of the first year. .... Ye shall keep it until the fourteenth day of the same month: and the whole assembly of the congregation of Israel shall kill it in the evening." Thus we have a description of the lamb for the burnt-offering. We may just remark what special and what precise instructions the Lord God gave. There is an exactitude about this type, and a precision and particularity which are most significant, and these are intended to be a kind of parable of the cross of Christ, a kind of picture of our glorious atonement. It was to be " a lamb of a year old," it was to be " without blemish" and without spot. Jewish writers tell us that the utmost care was exercised by the priest lest a flaw or a blemish should be found, so that it might be abundantly evident that it was spotless; and if the smallest imperfection was discovered it vitiated the victim. Then it is interesting to see how it was to be set apart four days beforehand—kept in reserve. It was to be brought by the whole congregation, they were to be assembled at the slaying of the paschal lamb, and they were to behold the lamb. We need not dwell at large upon the more obvious and plain points of resemblance. The lamb is always considered the emblem of meekness, of simplicity, of purity, of patience, of submission. Hence we read, " He was brought as a lamb to the slaughter, and as a sheep before her shearers is dumb." It is deeply touching and interesting to see the meekness of the lamb. I have more than once watched the lamb led to the slaughter, and I have seen the little guileless animal lick the hand about to be imbrued in its blood, patient, meek, and free from all that looks like resentment; and in all this it is appropriate as shadowing forth that blessed "Man of sorrows" who came amongst us with the majesty of omnipotence and the meekness and gentleness of a lamb. He was never provoked to resentment, or to cavil, or to retaliation. How meekly He stood amidst His persecutors, as a lamb amongst ravening wolves! how He returned love for hatred, blessing for cursing, tenderness and kindness for mockery and hatred! What words of gentleness He answered when He was cruelly smitten by those who mocked His woe! "If I have spoken evil, bear witness of the evil: but if well, why smitest thou me?" Oh! what meekness was there! how He who could have spoken, and the earth would have swallowed them up as it did Koran, Dathan, and Abiram, displayed His meekness and patience in language that might have broken the hardest heart! Why smitest thou me?" And so, throughout the whole scene of His suffering. There could not therefore be a more fitting emblem and type of Jesus than the meek and gentle lamb. And how beautiful His patience and long-suffering. He never was provoked to unkindness. All that He ever said, though often tempted, was—" O faithless and perverse generation, how long shall I be with you? how long shall I suffer you?" Even when He rebuked for hardness of heart those that would not be saved by Him it grieved Him, and it was the language of sorrow, still beautifully tender and touching. And it was striking testimony to His holiness that when He was accused, it was not merely the law of God that pronounced Him spotless, but the princes of this world could find nothing against Him, for when the high priest, acting under the law, tried to entangle Him and overpower Him, and Pilate and Herod did all they could to bring Him in guilty, they could find in Him "no fault at all," and the blessed Lamb was pronounced spotless in the face of heaven and hell. No one could bring against Him one speck or flaw, He was made a sacrifice for us, and we were redeemed with "the precious blood of Christ, as of a lamb without blemish and without spot."

The glorious antitype is here fitted into the type; and how complete the harmony! It was mainly in its sacrificial character that the lamb was typical of the Lamb of God. The lamb was the special choice of God, and how worthy of Himself was the choice. He did not choose the lion, but the meek lamb, to be the great centre-point of the whole ordinance, as the representation of how the guiltless should be substituted for the guilty, to bear the transgression of the guilty, and to make expiation, so that the guilty should be taken as guiltless through the innocent bearing his guilt; the sin of the guilty imputed to the guiltless, the merit of the guiltless imputed to the guilty. The blessed doctrine of substitution is at the core of the whole gospel. It is the only foundation of hope to the sinner, and so it was beautifully represented in that type antecedent to the passover, when Abraham offered up his son Isaac, and the son is described as bearing the wood, in prefiguration of the only-begotten Son of God bearing His cross to Calvary. Isaac said, "My father;" and Abraham said, "Here am I, my son. And he said, Behold the fire and the wood, but where is the lamb for a burnt-offering? And Abraham said, My son, God will provide himself a lamb for a burnt-offering. . . . . And Abraham lifted up his eyes, and looked, and, behold, behind him a ram caught in a thicket by his horns: and Abraham went and took the ram, and offered him up for a burnt-offering in the stead of his son. And Abraham called the name of that place Jehovah-jireh: as it is said to this day, In the mount of the Lord it shall be seen." And so in the fulness of time God provided a Lamb, and now we can say to the whole universe,—"Behold the Lamb," "Behold the Lamb of God," that God hath chosen, that God hath accepted, that God hath magnified, that God hath exalted, and is now in the midst of the throne, and there the song of the Lamb wakes the raptures of those in heaven who sing :—" Salvation to our God which sitteth upon the throne, and unto the Lamb.".

This lamb was to be set apart four days before the slaying of the lamb in the presence of the congregation of Israelites, beautifully indicating how God is the God of order, and would have all things prepared, and nothing in His worship and service done hurriedly, but all according to His purpose. We find throughout the whole of the gospel the glorious line of time and order, "When the fulness of the time was come, God sent forth His Son, made of a woman, made under the law." We continually find such beautiful arrangements as this in the exact correspondence between the type and the antitype. The blessed Redeemer entered Jerusalem, in order to become Christ our Passover, four days before he was suspended from the cross; and during that time He was examined, and they could "find no fault in Him." God permitted that He should be crucified, the just for the unjust, and it was so ordained that He was crucified between the two evenings, at three o'clock in the afternoon. Now the ending of one day was held to be the beginning of another; and the ninth hour was three o'clock, so that God in the wondrous working of His providence ordered that that which was done by the passions and caprice of wicked men urged on by darkness, exactly fulfilled his purpose, and corresponded to the smallest jot and tittle with His own blessed design. Thus His providence is made to harmonise with His promises, and though foolish men think they are discordant and come into collision, it will be seen in the end that not one jot or tittle of all the good things He has promised shall be withheld from those that love Him, and not one of the evil things uttered against His enemies shall fail, but all shall be accomplished, and the whole universe shall be forced to confess that He hath done all things according to His purpose. Glorious is God in His ways and in His truth, and all things shall bear witness to His truth in the end.

Then, brethren, further, it was to be " a lamb of the first year," in all the vigour of youth, in all its fulness and maturity. And so the blessed Redeemer at His crucifixion was about thirty-four years of age—some think thirty-three. He was then in the fulness of His perfection as a man, indicating to all that while He was meek and gentle as a lamb, He was " the Lion of the tribe of Judah," " mighty to save," while meek, omnipotent. How beautiful to reflect upon a correspondence of this kind, and to " behold the Lamb of God, which taketh away the sin of the world."

Then we would say to every poor sinner, " Behold the Lamb of God!" look for Him, have an interest in Him. Thou hast wept for thy sorrows; thou hast wept for thy disappointments; thou hast wept for thy vexations; hast thou never wept for thy sins? Go then, poor sinner, into thy closet, and look at that great sight until thy heart melts, and tears of sorrow gush from thine eyes, and thou art ready to cast thyself at the foot of the cross, and feel that thou art not worthy to look up at that blessed sacrifice; and yet because He says " Look unto me, and be ye saved, all the ends of the earth: for I am God, and there is none else," the Saviour, and none other,—thou canst say, I will venture to look with trembling.

We would say to those who are broken in heart and know not where to find refuge, " Behold the Lamb of God!" look upon Him until hope springs up in thy heart and thou canst say, " Lord, I believe, help thou mine unbelief." And then you shall sing the blessed song, " O Lord, I will praise thee: though thou wast angry with me, thine anger is turned away, and thou comfortedst me. Behold, God is my salvation; I will trust, and not be afraid: for the Lord Jehovah is my strength and my song; He also is become my salvation."

And we would say to the believer, "Behold the Lamb of God!" Let thy light be kindled afresh, and say, "I am crucified with Christ." Behold, I live because He lives. "God forbid that I should glory, save in the cross of our Lord Jesus Christ."

And may we not say even of the angels and archangels, and the whole ransomed Church of God,—behold the Lamb of God! for even in heaven it is "the Lamb that was slain" that is the most magnified, and is the theme of the blessed song: "Unto Him that loved us, and washed us from our sins in His own blood, and hath made us kings and priests unto God and his Father; to Him be glory and dominion for ever and ever. Amen."

IV.

THE PASSOVER: THE SHEDDING OF THE BLOOD.

"And the whole assembly . . . . . shall eat the flesh in that night roast with fire, and unleavened bread; and with bitter herbs they shall eat it. Eat not of it raw, nor sodden at all with water, but roast with fire."—Exodus xii. parts of 6, 8, and 9.

The epistle for the evening begins with the memorable and solemn declaration:—"Where a testament is, there must also of necessity be the death of the testator. For a testament is of force after men are dead: otherwise it is of no strength at all while the testator liveth. Whereupon neither the first testament was dedicated without blood." It was of necessity, therefore, that "Christ our Passover" should be sacrificed for us. If He had not laid down His life, if He had not sealed the covenant of reconciliation with His blood, salvation could not have been ours; for as a testament is of no force while the testator liveth, the death of the testator is necessary in order that the will may come in force, and in order that those to whom the property is bequeathed may come into possession. And so, to speak after a figure, our Great Head, who came not only to give us an inheritance, but to give us that inheritance through His death, must Himself die ere His testament could have its full power and efficacy. It may be said, indeed, how many were saved who beforetime believed in Him as the Saviour? And the answer is that to the infinite and eternal God who inhabits eternity the future is as the present, the present is as the past, and the past is as the present and the future. He had respect to "the blood of the everlasting covenant," and as after and on the day of His crucifixion, so before, even from the beginning, Jesus is designated as "the Lamb slain from the foundation of the world," because the certainty of His sacrifice in due time was such that it was not more certain when it did take place, than it was certain that it should take place ere it came to pass. Hence the efficacy of the atonement stretched back to the first primitive period, and still the efficacy reaches downwards to the present moment, and it reaches onward and onward until time shall be no longer.

> "O holy Lamb, Thy precious blood
> Shall never lose its power,
> Till all the ransom'd Church of God
> Be sav'd to sin no more."

Thus, then, it was the certainty of Christ's death that made the covenant of effect before He died, and it is the fact of Christ's death that makes it effectual now, and will make it effectual until all His chosen ones are received into glory. "It became Him"—it was in conformity and consistent with His own perfections, it was in harmony with His own moral government—"in bringing many sons unto glory, to make the Captain of their salvation perfect through sufferings," in order to rescue them and lead them to victory; perfect as our Prophet, perfect as our Mediator, perfect as our Captain, perfect as our High Priest, and "perfect through suffering."

We are brought, then, to that beautiful stage in the great typical ordinance of the passover where this point is brought out in fulness and in force—the shedding of the blood of the lamb, pointing to the blood-shedding of the Lamb of God, and the mode of its suffering and sacrifice as designed to be typical of the glorious and most solemn and affecting agony and death of "Immanuel, God with us." May the Spirit of God calm and solemnise, and subdue and soften our spirits whilst we dwell upon this affecting and sanctifying theme.

We have touched upon the fact that the slaying of the lamb was to be by the whole congregation of Israel; not that the lamb was to be slain by the hands of all, but by the concurrence and in the presence of all. The priests and the Levites were employed in the slaying, but the whole congregation were *consentient* to the sacrifice. We have already touched upon this, and it is worthy of being dealt upon for a few moments again. It typifies that all believers alike are to be *consentient*, as it were, to the death of Christ, themselves being accessory to it. Many poor blind people think they do right in indulging in a kind of resentment against Judas, and against the high priest, and against the cruel Jews, because they crucified the Lord of glory, but that is blind unbelieving; for the believer, when he reflects upon the death of Christ, is led to say:—I was one who crucified Him, I look upon Him whom I have pierced and mourn for Him in bitterness. The high priest, Pontius Pilate, the Jews, could have had no power if it were not given from above—given from above for my sake and on my account. The Lord laid on Him the iniquity of all my sins. Where there is the deepest load there is the fullest pardon; myself I feel to be the chief of sinners, and my guilt were not pardoned if the crucified Redeemer in the garden of Gethsemane had not "sweat, as it were, great drops of blood," and agonised on the cross till He cried, "My God, my God, why hast thou forsaken me?" It is this I conceive that is most touchingly expressed in the whole of the congregation participating in the slaughter of the lamb. He was offered as a sacrifice by us all. "All we, like sheep, have gone astray; we have turned every one to his own way; and the Lord hath laid on Him the iniquity of us all."

This individual sense of our own participation in the death of Christ brings home the personal conviction, and we can indulge the blessed thought that He died for all, and that even those who never take the blood by faith sprinkling it on their souls, even those who never spiritually eat His flesh and drink His blood might have done so, for the sacrifice was for all the guilty of the world; and if He suffered for all, why should any perish with the blood shed that "cleanseth from all sin," with the bread which is the bread of immortality? All might be, but still will not be, cleansed and saved. Here is infinitely more than would furnish spiritual food and sustenance for all the beings in the world and all worlds. Who can limit that which is limitless? Jesus was an infinite Saviour, infinite while finite, God while man. The Lamb was to be slain, and the blood was to be shed. Alas, that it should be so! Some people speak as though they revolt at this mystery of our redemption; they say it is to them a source of distrust and distaste. God forgive them! for surely there is in this glorious provision of infinite wisdom something unspeakably solemn as well as mysterious. As by sin came death, by death came salvation. "For this purpose the Son of God was manifested, that He might destroy the works of the devil," "and deliver them who through fear of death were all their lifetime subject to bondage." What a glorious depth of wisdom, and triumph of power over weakness, that by dying death is overcome, that by stepping down to the grave He "led captivity captive," "subdued principalities and powers," and conquered death and the devil in their own region and dominion, and by His glorious resurrection restored to all His people everlasting life! Yes, the very core and kernel of the gospel of salvation is the shedding of the precious blood of Christ, the death of Him instead of our death. The death of God and our life is the blessed doctrine that all the countless sacrifices of the patriarchal times in the whole extent of the Levitical dispensation pointed to, all speaking one language, the language of the epistle of this evening—"without shedding of blood there is no remission." There must be expiation, there must be satisfaction, there must be representation to the whole universe of the justice of God, and that only the death of the Son of God can reverse the sentence, or blot out one stain or set any sinner free; therefore there is no other hope of any guilt being expiated except through the precious blood of Jesus "that cleanseth from all sin," and therefore the death of Christ stands as the great centre point of all salvation. The cross rivets the eye, and sustains the hope of all those who are saved.

The Saviour's death is typified in this most expressive ordinance by the lamb being "roast with fire." Much emphasis is laid upon this point again and again. They were not to eat of the flesh "sodden or boiled, but roast with fire," and the entire body. Now we cannot be at any loss for a key to this feature. We know that there is no agony greater than burning with fire, and no doubt this was designed to represent the death of the blessed Redeemer,—not simply His dying, and not simply the death of the cross—though that is the most agonising of all deaths, but that His soul should be scorched, as it were, with fire. I know the wondrous efficacy of Christ's atonement did not lie in the extent of His sufferings, though He suffered in a few hours of His agony more than the torments of eternity; but I do not conceive the Scripture bears out that this intensity of suffering gave any efficacy to the sacrifice, but it manifested that Jesus magnified His holiness and truth. He was infinite as well as finite, and therefore in His sacrifice there was a grandeur, a majesty, and a glory more than the human race could conceive. Therefore I do not think the efficacy of the sacrifice is owing to the intensity of the sufferings of the sufferer; but, at the same time, in order that the heinousness of sin might be made more fearful, in order that the justice of God might have its full display, we doubt not the sufferings of the Redeemer were such as none but Himself could have sustained. He would sustain the crushing load of guilt imputed to Him, He would endure the sense of Divine displeasure for all sin, and the fearful consequences of that sin such as only Himself could comprehend and sustain. We are not to explain away such expressions as—" The Lord hath laid on Him the iniquity of us all;" "He was made sin for us;" "Awake, O sword, against My Shepherd, and against the Man that is My fellow, saith the Lord of hosts: smite the Shepherd, and the sheep shall be scattered;" "it pleased the Lord to bruise Him, He hath put Him to grief." Nor are we to explain away, by any idea of the fear of death, that most awful and mysterious, and unfathomable mystery of Jesus in the garden, sweating as it were great drops of blood, and falling on the ground in the agony of His blessed spirit, when He prayed:—"O my Father, if it be possible, let this cup pass from me;" nor such expressions as—"My soul is exceeding sorrowful even unto death;" and "He began to be sore amazed;" or that awful and mysterious cry, "My God, my God, why hast thou forsaken me?" Doubtless His soul was consumed as it were, by a sense of sin and the wrath of His Father against sin; and though to us this is inconceivable, it is at the same time most manifest and impressive. Oh what it cost Him to make our peace, and to manifest God's justice in giving us peace, and to magnify God's law in setting us free from the curse; so that, in the beautiful language of the psalm in this evening's service, "Mercy and truth are met together; righteousness and peace have kissed each other!" Dear brethren, "is it nothing to you," says the Saviour, "all ye that pass by? behold, and see if there be any sorrow like unto my sorrow!" "Is it nothing to you?"

There is one feature more that we must not omit in the

sufferings of the Redeemer. "Ye shall not break a bone thereof." Who can doubt for a moment that we are not indulging in a mere fancy in tracing here a beautiful analogy between the passover of the Jews and Christ our Passover." When we remember these minute circumstances, and the minute fulfilment, we see how the Scriptures were fulfilled. When the soldiers came to break the legs of those that were crucified, in order that "their bodies should not remain on the cross on the Sabbath-day (for that Sabbath-day was a high day)," they found that Jesus was dead already, and they brake the legs of the two malefactors who were crucified with Him, that the Scripture should be fulfilled, "a bone of Him shall not be broken." Can any one doubt that the passover was in this respect a kind of material prophecy of Jesus, though none of the prophets foretold in so many words that Jesus should not have a bone broken? Nor was this without its mystic meaning. It signified that though the Lord Jesus might be crushed in the dust by the weight of our guilt, yet He triumphed in suffering, and that in vanquishing death, and gaining for us a victory, He bruised and crushed the serpent's head, and so the blessed Redeemer was "more than conqueror" over all His foes, even death and hell. Not a bone of Him was broken. May not this teach us that we are not to divide what God has united? We must receive the whole of Christ as our salvation and our desire, we must not dissever Christ as our Prophet, Priest, and King, but Christ must be all and in all."

The time allows us but just to glance at one feature more. What was to be done with the blood that was to be shed? It was not to be sprinkled upon the ground or to be trampled upon as a common thing, but it was to be received into a vessel. Is it too much to say that His precious blood is, so to speak, the consecrated vessel, for it is "the blood of the everlasting covenant," it is the blood of reconciliation, and beautifully is it signified in the cup of salvation, for Jesus when He instituted our Christian passover of the Lord's Supper said, as we have it in the gospel to-night: "This cup is the new testament in my blood, which is shed for you:" "the cup of blessing which we bless, is it not the communion of the blood of Christ? The bread which we break, is it not the communion of the body of Christ?" And so the precious blood of "the Lamb of God, which taketh away the sin of the world," is received as it were in the cup of the covenant that He still offers to all who come to Him in faith, and that draw near by the blood of Christ, that Great Shepherd of the sheep, through the blood of the everlasting covenant."

And now, dear brethren, let us in our closets to-night, and on our pillows, meditate upon these things. Let us not account this as a season that we should pass by unheeded and neglected, let us not neglect such opportunities and occasions, but let us seek that God may arouse and stir up our minds, leading us afresh to Gethsemane and to Calvary. Dear brethren, "is it nothing to you," who live in neglect of the Bible and the Saviour, that such sacrifice has been offered, and that the Lamb of God has died for our peace? "Is it nothing to you?" It must be something to you, either unspeakable loss or unspeakable gain, either condemnation or salvation, either deeper hell or glorious heaven; and "how shall we escape, if we neglect so great salvation?"

V.

THE PASSOVER: THE APPLICATION OF THE BLOOD.

"And they shall take of the blood, and shall strike it on the two side posts, and on the upper posts of the houses, wherein they shall eat it."—EXODUS xii. 7.

"Through faith Moses kept the passover, and the sprinkling of blood lest he that destroyed the first-born should touch them."—HEBREWS xi. 28.

THE Spirit of God tells us that it was through faith that Moses kept the passover, as ordained by God, and the sprinkling of blood, lest he that had destroyed the first-born of all the land of Egypt should come nigh the dwellings of the Israelites; and if it was through faith, then it had respect to that which was to come. "Faith is the substance of things hoped for, the evidence of things not seen," that which substantiates them with force and reality while yet unperformed. It is clear, then, that the believing worshipper in the feast of the passover had the eye of his soul directed forward to that which this most impressive and emphatic parable in words pictured, the shadow of good things to come; and therefore it was an exercise of faith, not only as regarded the past, but as regarded the future.

We come this evening to the most important and momentous point in the parable, one that concerns us individually more than all that has gone before, because it brings home to every sinner that great truth, without which he had better never have been born, and with which all things are his. May the Spirit of God accompany His word, that, at this solemn and affecting season, it may be brought home to our consciences and our hearts in all its touching power and efficacy.

We have seen that when the blood of the paschal lamb was to be shed, it was not to be shed on the ground or cast away. It was precious, and so typical, and therefore it was to be received into a vessel. Then the application of the blood was to be by dipping a bunch of hyssop in it, and then, with the bunch of hyssop, striking the two side posts and the lintel of the doors of the houses of the Israelites. Here we have that which is individually and personally made of interest to us, the atoning blood of the Lamb, that blood which was shed to make our peace and to declare God propitious and just in forgiving, exercising a righteous display of His justice, whilst exercising a righteous display of His grace and mercy to mankind. What profits it that the victim is slain, and that the blood is shed? What advantages it that "God was in Christ, reconciling the world unto Himself, not imputing their trespasses unto them; and hath committed unto us the word of reconciliation?" Of what profit, I say, would it be, if the individual sinner does not avail himself of the blessed propitiation, if he does not "fly for refuge to lay hold of the hope set before him," if he does not through faith in Jesus become sprinkled with "the blood that cleanseth from all sin" and death, if he is not "one with Christ and Christ with him," if he does not seek that Christ as a sure "hiding-place from the wind, and a covert from the tempest; as rivers of water in a dry place, and the shadow of a great rock in a weary land?" And therefore, brethren, the hinge and turning-point of the sinner's salvation is his being one with Jesus, and being made partaker of the cleansing efficacy of the blood of Jesus.

The blood was to be sprinkled upon the side posts and upon the lintels of the door. It was to be manifest; it was not to be behind the door, as if men were ashamed of the cross of Christ and of His reconciliation. "Whosoever shall be ashamed of me and of my words," "of him also shall the Son of man be ashamed," but "whosoever shall confess me before men, him will I confess also before my Father which is in heaven." Therefore, there must be the application as well as the reception of Jesus, by whom we receive the atonement; and there must also be a blessed avowal of it, "for with the heart man believeth unto righteousness; and with the mouth confession is made unto salvation." As an old divine said:—"The mark of the beast may be either on the forehead or on the right hand, but the mark of the lamb is always on the forehead." A man must therefore openly profess the faith of Christ crucified. The language of the believing spirit must be, "God forbid that I should glory, save in the cross of our Lord Jesus Christ, by whom the world is crucified unto me, and I unto the world."

Then, special care was to be taken that the blood was not to be upon the threshold, and it was not to be dropped upon the ground. It was never to be trodden under foot, and "of how much sorer punishment, suppose ye, shall he be thought worthy who hath trodden under foot the Son of God?" How shall we escape, if we make light of that great atonement and slight that precious blood, that only cleansing blood in the universe that can wash us clean? Therefore, "take heed, brethren, lest there be in any of you an evil heart of unbelief," in counting the blood of Jesus a light thing and of no efficacy.

The blood of the lamb, when sprinkled, was to be the stronghold, the castle of the believing captives; and if they went out at all on that eventful and fatal night, their protection was left behind, and the destroying angel had no warrant to pass over them, and God only knows what would have been the consequence. Even so we must abide in Christ, and Christ in us. We are not simply to receive Christ for a time, but we must cling to Christ. "If any man draw back," says God, "my soul shall have no pleasure in him." "We are not of them who draw back unto perdition; but of them that believe to the saving of the soul." And so we see the apostle's appreciation of the importance of being found in Christ, for he says, "I count all things but dung, that I may win Christ, and be found in him." Yes, in the great day when "the heavens shall pass away with a great noise, and the elements shall melt with fervent heat," and "we shall all stand before the judgment-seat of Christ," the question will be, Are we found in Christ? are we placed where judgment cannot reach us? for judgment is satisfied by that most glorious satisfaction, the atonement of Christ, and "there is therefore now no condemnation for them which are in Christ Jesus, who walk not after the flesh but after the spirit." "It is God that justifieth. Who is he that condemneth? It is Christ that died, yea, rather, that is risen again, who is even at the right hand of God, who also maketh intercession for us."

How beautiful, beloved, is the completeness of the picture. We are not only to have the blood of sprinkling, but we must abide in the blood of sprinkling, the temple and habitation of the Lord Jesus, the rock of our salvation.

Then the sprinkling of the blood was to be by a bunch of hyssop. That corresponds to faith, it is that which, so to speak, dips into the precious blood, and applies it to the conscience of the sinner, "having our hearts sprinkled from an evil conscience," so that He that taketh away the feeling of condemnation removes the sense of God's wrath, and it is changed into the apprehension of His favour and love. This is indeed having the blood by faith, through the Spirit, so sprinkled upon our hearts that the guilt is removed, and the soul rejoices in pardon and peace. "O Lord, I will praise thee: though thou wast angry with me, thine anger is turned away, and thou comfortedst me." He giveth us "beauty for ashes, the oil of joy for mourning, the garment of praise for the spirit of heaviness."

But then, brethren, this picture is not yet complete as to its application. There was a twofold application; first, the blood was to purify, to justify, to atone and to give peace to those that thus had the blood applied in order for their deliverance from the peril of death; and they were also themselves to have and to appreciate a direct spiritual life, and it was to come from the same source from which their rescue from eternal death came—Jesus, at once the author of our eternal life and rescuing us from the wrath to come, our aliment and our spiritual life, bringing immortality to the soul; so that, after the sprinkling of the blood, they were to partake of the flesh of the lamb, roast as it had been with fire, and it became their food and sustenance. Is not this a lovely type of how the Lord Jesus was willing to bring the souls of his people home? He himself said, "I am the bread of life; if any man eat of me, he shall never hunger." "Except ye eat of my flesh and drink of my blood, ye have no life in you." "He that eateth my flesh and drinketh my blood hath eternal life, and I will raise him up at the last day." And again, "for my flesh is meat indeed, and my blood is drink indeed." What the Israelites, therefore, carnally did, all true believers spiritually do. As they fed bodily upon the lamb, we feed spiritually upon the Lamb of God in our inner life, and the flesh is alimented, strengthened, and increased by believing participation in the Son of God, so that faith, hope, love, joy, patience, meekness, temperance, long-suffering, and charity are all foreshadowed by the crucified Saviour, and the beautiful figure pictured in the passover of the Jews is still more beautifully pictured in the Christian passover, for "as often" (as we have it in the lesson for the day) "as ye eat this bread, and drink this cup, ye do show the Lord's death till He come;" and in the beautiful language of our own scriptural communion service, "the body of our Lord Jesus Christ, which was given for thee, preserve thy body and soul unto everlasting life. Take and eat this in remembrance that Christ died for thee, and feed on Him in thy heart by faith with thanksgiving." Thus we have still our blessed passover.

Then never let us forget that it was not the eating of the lamb that saved the Israelites, it was the faith in the Lamb of God that was represented. It is neither the carnal eating of the bread, nor the drinking of the wine, in the paschal feast of the Christian Church, that saves, but the feeding on Christ in our hearts by faith with thanksgiving, and to have the blessed Lamb of God that taketh away our sins dwelling in us and we in Him, Him one with us and we with Him. This blessed and beautiful picture carries us from the letter to the spirit, from the shadow to the substance, from "the letter that killeth" to "the spirit that giveth life;" and we, in the Supper of the Lamb, have the beautiful figure carried out in the glorious efficacy of the blood applied, "When I see the blood I will pass over you," and in the manner in which the whole feast is to be partaken of, "not with the old leaven" of hypocrisy and malice "but with the unleavened bread of sincerity and truth," with our "loins girt," with our staffs in our hands, as pilgrims and strangers partaking of this spiritual and heavenly food, till we reach the land where we "hunger and thirst no more."

Now, dear brethren, pausing here, let each one of us ask

himself, Has the blood of Jesus ever been effectually applied to my conscience? has it given peace to my heart? has it washed away my guilt? have I indeed "the witness" within myself? and do I believe in the Son of God to the saving of my soul? Can I indeed look upon the Holy Lord God Almighty through the propitiation made for me, and look to Him as my Father, my reconciled Father, whom I trust, whom I love, and whom I serve? Oh, rest not till you have this blessed assurance, and rest not but in "Christ and Him crucified." Brethren, if we are not Christ's, we are not abiding in Christ—and we should not need to be told this so often—if we are not abiding in Christ, we are alienated from Him. Let us seek to be blessed in Him, and being in Him and with Him, we have nothing to fear, for "neither death, nor life, nor angels, nor principalities, nor powers, nor things present, nor things to come, shall be able to separate us from the love of God which is in Christ Jesus our Lord." What can harm us if we are found in Him, the only place of safety in the universe for poor sinners?

And then, dear brethren, surely we ought to love the opportunity whenever it arises of partaking of the Christian passover. You had in the lesson to-night very beautifully the revelation given to St. Paul, the confirmation of the divinity of the gospel, of the unity of the gospel, and of the exactitude of its unity; for when it was given it was not through man, but by direct revelation to St. Paul, and it corresponds in every point to the gospel of the evangelists, witnessing, as it were, to a fresh publication of the gospel by direct communication from heaven. He received on that occasion this revelation:—" In the same night that He was betrayed He took bread: and when He had given thanks, He brake it, and said, Take, eat: this is my body, which is broken for you: this do in remembrance of me. After the same manner He took the cup, when he had supped, saying, This cup is the new testament in my blood: this do ye, as oft as ye drink it, in remembrance of me. For as often as ye eat this bread, and drink this cup, ye do show the Lord's death till He come." Let not those who are tempted fear and stumble at the expression eating and drinking unworthily, for if they come to the heavenly feast with the deepest sense of their unworthiness, and with a penitent and humble spirit, hating sin and loving Jesus, yielding themselves to Him at their Saviour's invitation, and taking the robe of righteousness, even His most precious blood, they may be most unworthy, but the more fitting their state of mind if they come with a good conscience and a firm trust in God's mercy.

Once more, surely the whole of the blessed ordinance teaches us to yield ourselves to Him who redeemed us, and we may say in the beautiful language you have been singing to-night—

> " Were the whole realm of nature mine,
> That were an off'ring far too small;
> Love so amazing, so divine,
> Demands my soul, my life, my all."

VI.

THE PASSOVER: THE EFFICACY OF THE SACRIFICE.

"And when I see the blood, I will pass over you."—Exodus xii. part of 13.

THE event which we commemorate this day,* is the most stupendous the universe ever beheld, the most vital that the archives of eternity record. It is at once an event that brings most glory to God, and the most glory to the universe. It is the song of the angels, it is the theme of the rapture of the archangels, and it ought to engage the hearts and the thoughts of the whole Church militant, as it will engage the songs and the adoration of the Church triumphant. "Thou art the King of glory, O Christ," ought to be the theme of the Church here, and "the Lamb that was slain," and "hast redeemed us to God by his blood," and made them "kings and priests for ever," will assuredly be the everlasting subject of the songs that will never cease to surround the throne of glory. We do well to assemble ourselves together within the walls of the sanctuary, that we may look upon Him whom we have pierced, that whilst we mourn we may rejoice, sowing in tears and reaping in joy. For that great sight, though it be one of the saddest upon which we can look, yet at the same time it is one of

* Good Friday, 1862.

the most joyful we can behold, for where would be our hope, where would be our peace, where would be our refuge from "the wrath to come," were it not for the stupendous event we this day commemorate? for now He "liveth for ever," and having conquered through the blood of Jesus, we may draw near and "obtain mercy and find grace to help in time of need."

We wind up this morning a course of sermons on the most impressive and the most beautiful of types, and we come to dwell upon the mode in which the holy feast was to be kept, and upon the blessed efficacy of the sacrifice, expressed as it is in these beautiful and expressive words, "when I see the blood, I will pass over you." May the spirit of Jesus be amongst His professing people, that His blood may be upon us, and that we may be passed over in the day of God's just judgment, "being found in Him, not having our own righteousness, which is of the law, but that which is through the faith of Christ."

The mode in which the feast is to be kept. We have seen that the turning point for each individual sinner is his own personal and individual acceptance of the sacrifice of the Lamb of God, who became his substitute, and shed His precious blood, thus sealing the everlasting covenant of protection, and becoming our salvation; thus showing the necessity of the sinner receiving the atonement, in order to become a partaker of the heavenly kingdom. Now we see that the participation of the blessed offering was twofold; first, the application of the blood to be sprinkled by the bunch of hyssop—a beautiful emblem of faith; and next, a participation of the flesh of the victim which had been slain—the feast upon the sacrifice; the former,—the sprinkling of blood—a symbol of our pardon and forgiveness; the latter,—the eating of the flesh—a beautiful and impressive sign of being made partakers of Christ, eating His flesh and drinking His blood in a spiritual sort, and so having life in Him and through Him, and having life alimented and perfected by participation in "Jesus Christ, and Him crucified;" the whole beautifully reflecting the Christian passover of the holy supper of Jesus, which took the place of the Jewish passover, as a perpetual memorial amongst us of the body broken and of the blood shed to make our reconciliation to God, so that "as often as ye eat this bread, and drink this cup, ye do show the Lord's death till He come."

Now this feast of the passover was to be kept in a peculiar manner. Time permits us but to glance at the leading points only. It was to be eaten with unleavened bread. A most scrupulous exactness was to be exercised in purging the dwelling of the individual who partook of the feast, and we are told by Jewish writers that their exactness was so great, that they used a lighted candle to explore every corner in their dwellings, lest any leaven should remain. In like manner, as "Christ our Passover is sacrificed for us," must we keep the feast, "not with the old leaven, or with the leaven of malice and wickedness, but with the unleavened bread of sincerity and truth." No man who is not sincere can be a partaker of Christ, but he incurs the guilt of drinking to himself damnation. If we call, "Lord, Lord," with our lips, and take the symbols of the sacrifice, and yet our hearts are far from Him, we do not take Jesus in honesty and sincerity, we do not take up His cross and follow Him. Therefore, beloved brethren, as often as ye eat of that bread, and drink of that cup of the Lord, examine yourselves, and "judge yourselves, that ye be not judged of the Lord."

Then in the next place, it was to be eaten with bitter herbs. This, I conceive, to be beautifully descriptive of that penitential and contrite disposition that should accompany the Christian, as through the whole of his pilgrimage so especially in coming to the Saviour's table. We are to feel "the remembrance of our sins" to be "grievous unto us," and what would be "intolerable" were they not sustained by our Substitute and Shield the "very Paschal Lamb," "who by His death hath destroyed death." Bitter herbs,—that which was bitter to the taste imparted a sweetness to the lamb; and so, "Blessed are they that mourn, for they shall be comforted." Those who come most humbly to Christ will find Christ most precious, while the proud, and the self-satisfied, have no interest in Christ. They call Him "Lord, Lord," but have no yearning towards Him, they do not grasp Him with trembling, they do not cling to Him with a great desire. "We are not worthy so much as to gather up the crumbs under thy table," is the breathing of those who eat the passover as it ought to be eaten, with bitter herbs; sin the more bitter, Christ the more sweet; and so sadness and gladness are beautifully mingled in those who meekly partake of these holy mysteries.

Then the attitude in which the holy feast was to be enjoyed is a beautiful description,—"having their loins girt, and their staffs in their hands;" and so, brethren, "To-day harden not your hearts." "Behold, now is the accepted time; behold now is the day of salvation." "Whatsoever thy hand findeth to do, do it with thy might." "The night is far spent, the day is at hand." "The night cometh when no man can work." *Now* therefore, brethren, *to-day*—not to-morrow, not at a future time but *now!*

Further, we must confess ourselves "strangers and pilgrims," having our "conversation as in heaven," citizens of the New Jerusalem. "If ye then be risen with Christ, seek those things which are above, where Christ sitteth on the right hand of God." "Mortify, therefore, your members which are upon the earth." We are "strangers and sojourners" here, and this is not our resting-place. Blessed thing therefore, to be weaned from the world, and to have our affections and our desires upon a future and a better state, and not upon the things we may have to leave to-morrow, or to-night, or even at the next hour. Oh let us take the pilgrim's guise, let us lean on the pilgrim's staff, and "forgetting those things which are behind, and reaching forth unto those things which are before," let us "press toward the mark for the prize of the high calling of God in Christ Jesus." If we are Christ's, we have "crucified the flesh with the affections and lusts." "If any man will come after me," says Christ, "let him take up his cross and follow me," and "where I am, there shall also my servants be." Beloved, may you thus approach the holy table on Sunday in a mourning, a quickening, and an animated spirit; more weaned from earth, and with a more earnest desire for heaven.

Then the glorious and blessed efficacy of the ordinance comes before us. We can find no expression more emphatic, or more eloquent of its fulness and blessedness than the one before us:—"When I see the blood," says the mighty God, "I will pass over." The inmates of the houses that were not so marked with the sign of mercy fell victims to the destroying angel, and the shaft of death pierced to "the firstborn in every house, from the first-born of Pharaoh that sat on his throne unto the first-born of the captive that was in the dungeon." What a night it must have been to the Egyptians! In the thousands of dwellings that had not the saving mark there was a corpse, and that the first-born. What a cry must have broken the silence of midnight! what confusion! what terror! what lamentation must have prevailed throughout the whole land on that fatal night! And yet there was a privileged portion where no voice of mourning was heard, but only the voice of joy, and of gladness, and of perparation for liberty. The destroying angel looked at each dwelling, and there was the expressive sign of reconciliation and propitiation, eloquent of the blood of the Lamb, and as he glanced he refrained. The destroying angel, mindful of his errand, looked, and seeing a certain sign passed by the dwellings, and withheld the shaft of death. How beautiful a picture of how God separates the pardoned from the unpardoned, the just from the guilty, His people from His foes! He sees the blood still sprinkled by faith through the Spirit on the contrite heart, and the believing and awakened conscience, and the sense of guilt is removed, and the favour of God secured. "There is therefore now no condemnation to them which are in Christ Jesus, who walk not after the flesh, but after the Spirit." "Whoso eateth my flesh and drinketh my blood hath eternal life; and I will raise him up at the last day."

And, dear brethren, what is there in that precious blood that marks the believer's conscience and soul and makes it not only the symbol of victory, but the means of grace? It is because that precious blood was the blood of Christ, who is God as well as man, for He Himself was infinite while finite, He was God while He was man, He was divine while He was human, dying while living. Wondrous mystery! Oh, who can conceive the preciousness of that "blood that cleanseth from all sin?" No stain so dark it cannot expiate, no sin so great it cannot put away. "Come now, and let us reason together, saith the Lord: though your sins be as scarlet, they shall be as white as snow; though they be red like crimson, they shall be as wool."

And, brethren, judgment has begun. The Lord, the judge, is now looking upon you, and upon me, and upon every one to whom the word of salvation has come; and if the blood by effectual faith and true repentance is applied to our consciences and hearts, it purges us from guilt, and purifies us from corruption. If we are feeding on Christ, if we are "crucified with Christ," "the life which we now live in the flesh we live by the faith of the Son of God;" sin hath no power to destroy us; the angel of judgment cannot come nigh us; there is no condemnation for us. What a glorious reflection! No condemnation for you when you appear before the judgment-seat of Christ; when heaven and earth pass away you will stand accepted; the mark is upon your soul, the mark of reconciliation is clear upon your forehead; the Lord sees it and passes you over, and you go to His right hand, and the language you will hear is, "Come, ye blessed children of my Father, inherit the kingdom prepared for you from the foundation of the world." Blessed truth, "when I see the blood, I will pass over you."

Dear brethren, I beseech you do not look upon this season and upon this solemn day as just a mere matter of form. It is intended to stir up our hearts and minds by way of remembrance. We are apt to get cold and indifferent, and there are many to whom these things do not occur but just for a day like this, and when they see the table spread they turn their backs upon it. But, beloved, regard the day. I do not say we ought to judge those who do not regard it; but let us judge ourselves who do regard it, so that it may leave in our hearts a deeper love for Jesus, a deeper hatred for sin, and a more earnest desire to "glorify God in our bodies and in our spirits, which are God's."

And remember that the Israelites were to remain in their dwellings, that if any went abroad the guarantee of safety was gone; and Christ says, "if ye abide in me," "there is no condemnation to them which are in Christ Jesus." St. Paul counted all things but dung, that he might win Christ and be found in Him. Remember you must cleave close to Jesus. To you that believe He is precious, He must be precious to you. How precious is He? What would you give up for Him? What are you doing for Him? What sacrifice are you making for Him? Would you go to the dungeon for Him? Would you go to the stake, and the rack, and the block for His sake? Have you the spirit of the martyr in you? If you have none of that spirit you are none of His. Christ must be "all, and in all." If you eat that blessed feast with bitter herbs you will come to the communion on Sunday with a holy joy and gladness, and lift up your heads, for your salvation is come. So let us commemorate the Saviour's death, who "was dead," and is "alive for evermore," remembering that if we suffer with Him in His humiliation, we shall be exalted with Him in His glorification. Let us, then, lie low at the foot of the cross, and we shall lift up our heads when we behold Him; and lifting them up, we shall be "more than conquerors" through Him that loved us and died for us.

VII.

GOD INCARNATE.

"The Word was made flesh."—St. John i. part of 14.

There are three books in the Holy Scriptures that begin somewhat alike, and with a kindred grandeur and majesty. In the first book we have the key-note of the harp of revelation:—"In the beginning God created the heaven and the earth. And the earth was without form, and void; and darkness was upon the face of the deep: and the Spirit of God moved upon the face of the waters." Then in this, which may be styled the deepest and most mysterious portion of the evangelical narrative, we have the same remarkable key-note: "In the beginning was the Word, and the Word was with God, and the Word was God." And again when the same apostle writes his high and mysterious epistle, he begins:—"That which was from the beginning, which we have heard, which we have seen with our eyes, which we have looked upon, and our hands have handled, of the Word of life (for the life was manifested, and we have seen it, and bear witness and show unto you that eternal life, which was with the Father, and was manifested unto us); that which we have seen and heard, declare we unto you, that ye also may have fellowship with us: and truly our fellowship is with the Father, and with His Son Jesus Christ." Is not this that which the Church and the world, or rather, its ears and eyes, are open to behold, and to wait, and desire for, the coming of Him that was at last to be "the desire of all nations." It was as on this day,* that these words were fulfilled, and before their eyes, "the Word was made flesh."

The expression is very brief, but it is very full; and, as briefly as may be, we shall first endeavour to call your attention to *the Being that is thus designated, and then to the Incarnation of that Being.* "The Word was made flesh." May we treat with all reverence, and not with prying curiosity, this high subject and fathomless mystery.

"The Word." We can be at no loss to know who is so designated. The whole context shows that it was that which was in the fulness of time to come into the world, sent by the Father, "made of a woman, made under the law, to redeem them that were under the law, that we might receive the adoption of sons." The apostle St. John especially designates the everlasting Son as "the Word," and yet some sceptical men hold that "the Word" means the wisdom of God, the Divine prescience and omniscience; but this scarcely requires refutation, for how could the wisdom of God or His divine agent be at once God and yet with God, showing a dissociation in substance whilst a unity in essence?

We shall not, however, dwell upon this, but the word itself is worthy of our dwelling upon for a little time. We make too little of words. They are the medium of communication between men for the manifestation of our thoughts, and minds, and spirits. "What man knoweth the things of a man, save the spirit of man which is in him?" When a man has to communicate his thoughts, how can he do so effectually but by words? Signs, and symbols, and pictures, and emblems would be but a poor and imperfect method of communication; but words have something

* Christmas-day, 1864.

in them almost spiritual and ethereal; they approach nearer to the invisible and the impalpable than anything the outward man can imagine. Perhaps the power of intelligent speech is one of the most distinguishing and palpable characteristics of man. So far as we know, we do not find that any other animal whatever has anything like rational speech, or can communicate its thoughts, its feelings, and ideas by means of articulate language. If we realize this we shall perceive a peculiar beauty and force in the employment of this designation of the eternal Son of God, who from the beginning was God's medium of manifestation to His intelligent creatures. It appears to be so in heaven, we know it is so on earth, we know that He "brought life and immortality to light through the gospel." He made God known, so that as He says, "no man knoweth the Son, but the Father; neither knoweth any man the Father save the Son, and he to whomsoever the Son will reveal Him. He that hath seen me hath seen the Father; and how sayest thou then, Show us the Father? Believest thou not that I am in the Father, and the Father in me? the words that I speak unto you I speak not of myself: but the Father that dwelleth in me, He doeth the works. Believe me that I am in the Father, and the Father in me: or else believe me for the very works' sake." In this view, then, we take up the very beautiful language in the appropriate epistle of the morning, "Who being the brightness of His glory, and the express image of His person," a transcript of the invisible, the utterance and manifestation of Him "that dwelleth in the light that no man can approach to, and who is sublimely designated "the Word of God." All knowledge of God in truth and efficacy is through Christ Jesus. "This is life eternal, that they might know Thee the only true God, and Jesus Christ whom Thou hast sent." Now mark it, brethren, for it cannot be more clear than it is in the words before us.

If Jesus, the Son of God, was in existence before He became the Son of man, and came into the world, and the Word was made flesh, and therefore existed before, it is clear that He was antecedent, before all things. And in the next place, what is more clear than that He was not only pre-existent, but also divine? "In the beginning was the Word, and the Word was with God, and the Word was God." Could language be more explicit? And if creation is the inalienable prerogative and attribute of the Infinite, then "all things were made by Him; and without Him was not anything made that was made." As we had it in the epistle this morning, "Unto the Son he saith, Thy throne, O God, is for ever and ever: a sceptre of righteousness is the sceptre of thy kingdom." His name even when He came amongst us was called "Immanuel," God with us.

But we hasten to that which more immediately calls for our earnest and deep attention. On this happy day "the Word was made flesh." Now, it is very clear that He took something into His Deity which was not before united with Him. He did not become another Word, but He became "the Word" in another form; and, if I may venture so to speak, He combined a compound nature. He who was the same Word that was "in the beginning," and "was God," and "made all things," and "upholds all things by His power," He was "made flesh." And by flesh we are distinctly taught He was made man, He took upon Him human nature in all its feelings, body, soul, and spirit; and these co-existed and associated with the Everlasting Word, that He ceased not to be just as much the word as He was before He became engrafted; and He was not less the Almighty Son of God when He stooped to the Virgin's womb, and received humanity in Deity. This, indeed, is a great mystery! Could it be otherwise? Could little mysteries save us? Could little mysteries be worthy of all the counsel of heaven, and all the preparation of earth? Could a little mystery reconcile the attributes of Deity in the salvation of the sinner? Could a little mystery, as you are reminded in the language of one of the Psalms of the day, make "mercy and truth" to "meet together," "righteousness and peace" to "kiss each other," in welcoming and receiving every penitent transgressor who should believe on Jesus back to the favour and family of God, without tarnishing His glory, or compromising His attributes, or enfeebling His government? Could it be a little mystery? Instead of desiring to abate it, or to extenuate it, as some would have us do, or to explain it by our poor little minds, we should rather, with the apostle, exclaim: "Without controversy great is the mystery of godliness: God was manifest in the flesh." Yes, brethren, it is the greatness of the mystery that commands our deepest reverence, and challenges our fullest faith. It is all sufficient to know that it is all that the sinner needs, and all that a holy God demands. It encircles His throne with a rainbow of perfect beauty, and illumines the dark lot of man with the blessed "Sun of righteousness," that arises upon every one who fears God with "healing in His wings." "The Word was made flesh." "In all things it behoved Him to be made like unto His brethren, that He might be a merciful and faithful High Priest in things pertaining to God, to make reconciliation for the sins of the people." Had He not been the Eternal Word "that was God," what would have availed the interposition for us? If he had not become "the Word" "made flesh," how could he have been our Mediator and the Daysman between us and God? Had He not been God, what would His sacrifice and obedience have been more than that of the loftiest creature? And the law of the creature to the Creator is, when he has done all, he is "an unprofitable servant." Had He not therefore, been God as well as man, how could He, by His obedience and blood-shedding, have expiated the guilt of the world, and secured our return to reconciliation? Not, therefore, more essential was His Deity than His humanity, or His humanity than His Deity. "Perfect God and perfect man," as our creed declares, "of a reasonable soul and human flesh subsisting. Equal to the Father, as touching His Godhead; and inferior to the Father, as touching His manhood." As God, He could not suffer; but as man, He suffered unspeakable agony. As God, He could not obey; but as man He obeyed, and His obedience was the obedience of Him that redeemed us, the Son of God. Though He obeyed as man, His righteousness was "Jehovah our Righteousness." Had He been only God, how could He have been an "ensample?" How could He have been "touched with the feelings of our infirmities?" How could He have come down to our capacities, and made common cause with us in our troubles and necessities, in our sorrows and difficulties, in all the temptations and trials of our earthly pilgrimage? He became as truly man as He was God; and He took upon Him, not the nature of angels, but the seed of Abraham; not the flesh of the man He made in Paradise, when man was first placed there, when all was beauty and blessedness, when there was no thorn, no poisoned arrow, no sorrow, and no sickness; but He was made in "the likeness of sinful flesh," yet "without sin." In that likeness He appeared, He was tempted, He suffered, and He died. He was made "in the likeness of sinful flesh," a "Lamb without spot or blemish." "The Word was made flesh."

Dwell upon it. What a blessed thought! If He is God incarnate, where is He not sufficient? If He was made flesh, is He not patient? is He not pitiful? is He not merciful? Will He not feel for you? will He not hear you cry?

Will He shut the bowels of His compassion? will He not be with you on the bed of sickness? will He not be with you in your death? And in the day of judgment will He not stand beside you, when "heart and flesh fail" you? And when you stand over the grave of the flesh that was dearest to you, yet you will still look up from the dark grave in the full assurance that He who passed through the gate of the grave and of death, and rose again for our resurrection, will bring with Him also those that sleep, and not one shall be wanting of the seed that His Father has given Him. What a beautiful subject for the holy communion, which seems most seasonable and precious on two days; on the day when Jesus rose—for that feast is connected essentially with His resurrection—and on this, His natal day, when "the Word was made flesh." And surely, to those who come in faith and truth, "His flesh is meat indeed, and his blood is drink indeed."

Then, brethren, keep holy this season; be joyful in keeping it, but let your joy be a holy joy. "Is any merry among you, let him sing psalms." Remember that "the Son of man was manifested that he might destroy the works of the devil." Let not the works of the devil abound, when He came to destroy them. Keep away from the tavern and the theatre, and the scenes of giddy, thoughtless, and impure mirth and enjoyment, as people call it. Keep the season holy, and keep it happy. "Eat the fat and drink the sweet, and send portions unto them for whom nothing is prepared;" remembering that "the joy of the Lord is your strength," and the announcement of this morning to us: "Behold, I bring you good tidings of great joy, which shall be to all people."

VIII.

THE PROMISE OF THE HOLY SPIRIT.

"For the promise is unto you, and to your children."—
Acts ii. part of 39.

THE article, when thus prefixed to an expression, is designed to indicate the individuality and force of that expression. It is not here said *a* promise is unto you, and to your children; but it is said emphatically, "*The* promise is unto you, and to your children." The context shows us at once what that special promise was, the promise of the Holy Ghost, the Comforter, to be poured down from the throne and majesty on high by Him who, from the grave, had ascended to the throne to receive "gifts for men, yea, for the rebellious also, that the Lord God might dwell amongst them." It was of the fulfilment of this most precious promise, in a palpable and visible manner, that the people assembled together were reminded by the apostle Peter, and they were encouraged to repent and return to God, and seek for fruits meet for repentance on this ground—"For the promise is unto you, and to your children." Each dispensation has had its promise—that has been as the sun standing out from all around for its glory. In the first dispensation it was the seed of the woman that should bruise the serpent's head, "the desire of all nations," "the Lord" that should "come to His temple;" and the great promise, the sun of the Christian dispensation, is the promise of the Holy Ghost, associated as it is with the second coming of the Lord; not in deep humility and in lowly guise, but in glorious majesty, to reign. We are on the verge of that solemn season when we keep in remembrance the glorious fulfilment of the promise;* we are on the eve of an occasion when the offspring of very many of us will be brought together to receive the invocation of the gift of the Spirit, that they may be established and confirmed in their Christian covenant. Could I, then, select a brief promise more seasonable and suitable in every way than the words before me? " The promise is unto you, and to your children."

The promise:—the grandeur and greatness of the promise— "unto you, and to your children:"—*the grace and extent of the promise,* not only to us, but to our seed; for the Lord our God is a faithful God, "keeping the covenant, and mercy to them that love Him and keep His commandments." May that Spirit of whom we are to discourse open our hearts to receive the truth, and enable us to bring it home to you, for Christ's sake.

The promise. If the promise of a Saviour was a glorious promise under the old dispensation, to which the faithful from the beginning looked forward with expectant and eager eyes, the promise of the Spirit under the gospel economy is not a whit behind the former promise, and is not in the least degree to be less looked for, longed for, sought for, and enjoyed by all those that would attain eternal life. We can touch upon but a few of the points fitted to advance our estimation of that greatest of Christ's gifts—the gift of the Holy Ghost, the Comforter. Very few points may suffice to raise somewhat our narrow conceptions and enkindle our drooping desires; for the more we thirst for the Spirit, the more we shall receive the Spirit; and when we thirst not

* Sunday, May 28, 1865.

as we ought, it is because we are not alive as we should be to the intense importance and inconceivable preciousness of that gift of all gifts.

Could anything tend more to enhance our estimation of the gift than that it is not less than the gift of one of the persons of the glorious Godhead? Not more truly is the Son that was "the desire of all nations," "the mighty God," "the Everlasting Father," "Immanuel, God with us," inhabiting eternity, whilst coming down to sojourn with us, than is the coequal Spirit God with Christ, "very God of very God," "with the Father and the Son," "very and eternal God." We are not to conceive of the gift of Christ as if it were a mere influence shed upon us from afar, like the rays of the sun that bathe us with light, while the sun itself is far away in the heavens; but we are to conceive of the blessed Spirit of God as personally present; that where He dwells, there God dwells; where He works, there God works; where He manifests Himself there God manifests Himself. Could anything be more explicit than the language of the apostle Peter, when he said to Ananias— "Thou hast not lied unto men, but unto God?" therefore, he lied to God when he lied to the Holy Ghost. "What? know ye not that your body is the temple of the Holy Ghost, which is in you?" for, as it is written—"I will dwell in them and walk in them," saith the Lord God. Could the eternal Father bestow, could the eternal Son, through the mediation, intercession, and atonement, obtain for us any gift like this, sealed with His precious blood, any promise compared with this promise—"I will give you another Comforter, that He may abide with you for ever, even the Spirit of truth, whom the world cannot receive because it seeth Him not, neither knoweth Him: but ye know Him, for He dwelleth with you, and shall be in you?

But to enhance our estimation of this promise, and of all

promises, let us remember, in the next place, that it is only by having the Spirit that we can have the Son. "If any man have not the Spirit of Christ, he is none of His," and he that is none of Christ's has no salvation; he is dead while he lives; he is in the flesh, and they that are in the flesh shall die. "We know that we have passed from death unto life," "by the Spirit which He hath given us;" and Jesus himself told us that the Spirit should come to us, as it were, in His place, His representative, His spiritual and divine witness and testifier. The Spirit, He says, "shall glorify Me," "He shall take of mine, and shall shew it unto you," and "no man can say" in truth, in experimental faith that alone saves, "that Jesus is the Lord, but by the Holy Ghost," by the witness, the evidence, the demonstration of the Spirit of God. If, therefore, the gospel come with power and efficacy to any one of us, to our salvation, it comes not "in word only, but also in power, and in the Holy Ghost, and in much assurance." Surely, then, if we prize salvation, we must prize the promise of the Spirit.

But let us not forget that Jesus himself regarded this gift as more than a substitute for His bodily presence, and that we have more reason to bless God that Jesus was elevated from the world than if He had continued bodily in the world; because if He had continued in the world, we should have lacked that which far more than compensates for His absence from the flesh. His own words on this point are explicit—"It is expedient for you"—it is better for you—more advantageous for you—"that I go away; for if I go not away, the Comforter will not come unto you," in the fulness of His personal manifestation; "but if I depart, I will send Him unto you."

Let us think again of the worth of that gift of all gifts. We must remember that it is the Spirit of life that produces in the soul of man "a new birth unto righteousness." "Sanctify them by Thy truth : Thy Word is truth." The Word itself does not sanctify, but through the power of the Spirit, whose word it is. He it is that polished and pointed that two-edged sword. He alone can wield it effectually. He it is that descends, silently and secretly indeed, as dew in the hush of the night, fertilising, refreshing, and beautifying all it falls upon. "I will be as the dew unto Israel." And that heavenly dew is pre-eminently the Spirit of God, that descends upon any sinner, and softens his hard heart; convinces him of sin, brings him to humiliation and repentance; convinces him of righteousness, and brings him to justifying faith in Jesus; convinces him of judgment, and leads him to prepare to meet his Judge upon the throne.

What shall we say more? Are not the fruits of the Spirit "love, joy, peace, long-suffering, gentleness, goodness, faith, meekness, temperance?" Whence do all these come? Not from the soil of our corrupt nature, but from the quickening power of the Holy Spirit.

Once more, in all our duties and trials, in all we have to hope for, the Spirit is essential. We pray not unless we pray in the Spirit, we rejoice not unless we rejoice in the Spirit. "The kingdom of God is not meat and drink," not in outward observances and forms and ceremonies, "but righteousness, and peace, and joy in the Holy Ghost," and that blessed Spirit in the soul thus working in it a heavenly light is a pledge and proof that life everlasting is ours. "Now He that hath wrought us for the self-same thing is God, who also hath given unto us the earnest of the Spirit." The Spirit is "the earnest of our inheritance until the redemption of the purchased possession." He "beareth witness with our spirit, that we are the children of God," and He it is that "helpeth our infirmities; for we know not what we should pray for as we ought;" but He that worketh in His people "knoweth what is the mind of the Spirit, because

He maketh intercession for the saints according to the will of God."

We can but very briefly dwell upon the grace and fulness of the promise. "The promise is unto you, and to your children." We are far too apt to stagger at the promises; and our unbelief probably arises more from our want of giving God credit for the greatness of His grace, than from our dislike for the holiness that grace will always enforce and require. People who know not the struggle of the Christian life are ready to think it is easy and natural to stagger at the precepts, but the child of God knows how hard it is not to stagger at the promises. Certainly there is no promise so grand as this, and therefore none so likely to stagger a man if he has no faith. A man will not avow himself an infidel and say, "I do not believe it," but does he believe in its power? Does he embrace it, and hold it fast in all times of tribulation, and temptation, and trial? The promise, dear brethren, is to yourselves, even to every sinner that will repent and turn to God. A man must not say, "It is for me only." There are many who think so, though they may not say it. There may be some reason for thinking it, even from the Word of God. A man may think, "Oh, but that promise is only for the faithful and true, those that have faith; it is only for the called and chosen, and how do I know that I am one of them." It does appear to me that Jesus foresaw—as He must foresee everything—and forestalled this ground of doubt, and took it away in the most effectual manner, in the passage in the 7th of St. Matthew, in the sermon on the Mount, and again, in the 11th of St. Luke, where we have a reiteration of much that was delivered on the Mount, and where we have a more explicit and direct reference to this great gift, the promise of the Holy Ghost; for, while in Matthew, it is "give good things," in Luke, it is "give the Holy Spirit to them that ask." We have in each passage the same reiteration, as if to shut up a man from any excuse, as if to rescue from despair and the suggestions of the devil the man that would from any idea of God's greatness, or His purposes, or counsels, excuse himself from asking and seeking the Spirit. Christ not only puts the promise positively, "Ask, and it shall be given you; seek, and ye shall find; knock, and it shall be opened unto you;" but He gives us the promise in an individual, and special, and universal application. He does not say He will give it to the chosen alone, or to the man who knows the secret purposes of God; but He says *every man*, for mark the mode of expression: "I say unto you," "*every one* that asketh receiveth." If, then, a man ask in the sense in which it is here meant, if he seek in the way here intended, if he knock in the way in which it is here designed, as the Lord God liveth and is true, the promise shall not fail. You may be assured of it, no man ever proved God false, and no man will dare to say so when he comes to the bar of judgment and looks his God in the face.

But I must touch for a moment upon *the extent of the promise*. It goes beyond the parents to the children. The promise is "unto you, and to your children," and this does appear to be more especially to the children of believers, of professed believers at least. It is in the spirit that the Church requires that those brought to be baptized shall be brought by those who profess to be believers, and who undertake that the child shall be taught and reminded that it is under a promise and pledge to repent, and believe, and obey, keeping in its sight the covenant made. Now, then, the promise is "unto you, and to your children." We will only mention one form of promise made in Isaiah, where it is said, "I will pour my Spirit upon thy seed, and my blessing upon thine offspring. And they shall spring up as among the grass, as willows by the watercourses. One shall say, I am the Lord's; and another shall call himself by the name of Jacob; and another shall subscribe with his hand unto the Lord, and surname himself by the name of Israel." So that you see here is the effusion of the Spirit upon the young, here is the blessed springing forth of the grace of faith, here is the open profession that they are the Lord's, as it is beautifully expressed in that remarkable passage, "with the heart man believeth unto righteousness, and with the mouth confession is made unto salvation." Both are to be regarded; and so these young people who are coming together on Saturday next will be asked, Do they, in the presence of God and the congregation, renew and ratify the promise and engagement made by them? and each one will answer—I trust, with faith in their heart, and therefore, properly, with the confession of the mouth—"I do." That is, therefore, the faith founded upon this promise, " the promise is unto you, and to your children," and we ought not to doubt, but earnestly to believe, and the Lord will give His Spirit to them that ask, seek, and knock. We are not to limit God by our little, narrow, petty, halting, wavering faith, but we are to have strong faith in His promises. I would especially exhort you, my young friends—whom I should have rejoiced to see more of had my strength allowed me—I exhort you with all affection and earnestness to seek those promises. Be assured, Christ has not forgotten His promises, He has not failed, and well will it be for you if you have faith in those promises, and claim them as your own prerogative. "The promise is unto you," and it is also "to your children. Ask, seek, knock, and do not, I beseech you, be discouraged and disheartened; do not look at what you have to give up, but look at your own gain, strength, help, hope, joy, peace, happiness and safety.

And, dear brethren, pray for the young. "My little children," said St. Paul, "with whom I travail in birth again until Christ be formed in you," so ought Christian people to "travail," as it were, in holy fervency of faith and prayer, that God would graciously fulfil His promise. "Put me in mind," saith the Lord, "put me in remembrance." Should we not put Him in remembrance of that His gracious promise?

And let no man live without praying earnestly for the Spirit of God. What does a man expect? Let his breath stop, and where is he? If he does not breathe, as it were, the spiritual life, even the inspiration of God, he is dead while he lives, and what is to become of him, therefore, when he dies? Make it then your daily prayer, "O my God, for Christ's sake, give Thy Holy Spirit to me, fulfil Thy promise in my immortal history." And let those who have somewhat of the Spirit desire more, and remember that the first fruits are only to incite us to seek for the fulness of the harvest, and you are to seek it, according to the beautiful prayer that will be invoked upon your children, and desire to have the daily fulfilment in yourselves, that you may "daily increase in His Holy Spirit more and more, until you come unto His everlasting kingdom."

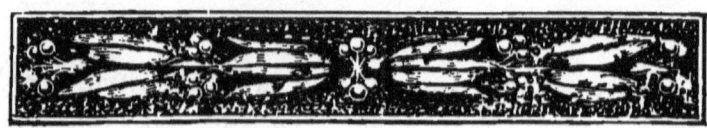

IX.

THE MARVELLOUS GRACE OF CHRIST.

"Behold, I stand at the door and knock: if any man hear my voice, and open the door, I will come in to him, and will sup with him, and he with me."—Rev. iii. 20.

It is impossible to conceive anything that could enhance and emphasise the force of this most impressive announcement that does not pertain to it. It comes direct from the Lord of the universe; it comes from Him who made us, who redeemed us, and who will judge us; it comes from Him, not as "a Man of sorrows and acquainted with grief," walking on this earth despised and derided, who "came to His own, and His own received Him not;" who was "in the world, and the world knew Him not;" but it comes from the glorious majesty of the throne of God; it comes from him who is seated at the right hand of the Creator of all things, who reigneth, and "must reign till He hath put all enemies under His feet." It is from Him, sent by His Spirit, through His inspired messenger, that this marvellous message comes. It comes not to those who love Him, but to those who live in neglect of Him; not to those who have been pardoned in Him, but to those who have backslidden from Him; not to those who rejoice in Him, but to those who turn a deaf ear to His expostulations. To them, in His long-suffering, and tender and pathetic persuasion, He addressed these words. I know not in the whole compass of God's Word an address more fitting to reach the ear, if not altogether sealed; to touch the heart, if not altogether petrified; to awaken the sinner, if not altogether obdurate, than this wonderful passage. "Behold," says the Lord of glory, "I stand at the door and knock: if any man hear my voice, and open the door, I will come in to him, and will sup with him, and he with me."

The marvellous grace of the Lord Jesus Christ: the consequent duty of every sinner:—*and the unspeakable promise and privilege held out to such:*—they believe and live. May the Spirit of Christ accompany the Word of Christ, so that it may reach, not the door only, but the inmost recess of every one that "hath an ear to hear."

The marvellous grace of Christ. "Behold, I stand at the door and knock." The door is clear—the door of the heart of man. Jesus knocks at that door—does He not?—again and again, with His tender finger, sometimes gently, and sometimes loudly and importunately, and sometimes unseen —unseen comparatively. Sometimes it is by His Word that the finger is knocked at the door of each one of us. How long He has knocked with some of us! "Behold, I stand and knock," with the finger of Providence, on the bed of sickness, in sorrow, in loss, in disappointment, in distress, in bereavement, in open graves, in the tolling bells, in the "mourners" going "about the streets." Has He not knocked thus, and does He not knock secretly with the hand of His Spirit? What stirrings we sometimes have! what misgivings! what resolutions! what earnest purposes! what good intentions, and prayers, and thoughts, that pass away "as a morning cloud, and as the early dew!" "Were not these the knockings of the Saviour's finger? "Behold, I stand at the door and knock." We do not keep a friend we love waiting long at the door. We can distinguish his ring or knock from the house, and it awakens immediately an echo in our breast, as servants that wait for their master with loving hearts, and spring forward to the door, and through it, and wait to welcome him home; or as the father in the parable looked out and saw his poor vagabond son from afar off returning, and he ran, and fell on his neck, and kissed him. One would imagine it would be thus with every sinner when he hears the knock of the Saviour. What! does He come as a thief in the night, to rob us and alarm us? Does He come to drag us to judgment, and to condemn us? Does He come into the world to condemn? Does He not come to save the world? Should we then cry out with fear as the apostles did, when they saw Him walking on the waters, and thought they saw a spirit? No, verily, for He comes to us as He came to them on the stormy deep. "It is I, be not afraid." We only need to fear that we may not have cause to fear, and to be aroused that we may not have cause to be overwhelmed with shame. If He *does* disturb us, He disturbs what is false in our peace to give us what is true, to convince us of our peril, to rescue us from ruin, to disclose to us our disease, because He is the "Physician" "in Gilead," and His "balm" can heal every disease. "Behold, I stand at the door, and knock;" and we keep Him standing! Yes, how many keep Him standing from infancy to youth, from youth to manhood, from manhood to hoary hairs, and still the Saviour waits. One would have imagined God would long since have cut these down as "cumberers of the ground;" that He would have broken in the door and dragged the culprit to a righteous judgment, but still "mercy rejoiceth against judgment." He still waits and says, "How shall I give thee up?" He still says to the fruitless tree, "Spare it another year." "Oh the depths of the riches both of the wisdom and knowledge of God; how unsearchable are His judgments!" It is we that ought to plead with Him, and He pleads with us; it is we that should wait on Him and He waits on us. He still strives with us, He still warns us. "O Jerusalem, Jerusalem, thou that killest the prophets, and stonest them which are sent unto thee, how often would I have gathered thy children together, even as a hen gathereth her chickens under her wings, and ye would not!" "Ye will not come to me, that ye might have life." "Behold, I stand at the door and knock." Ah brethren, are you not conscious of this? "Awake thou that sleepest, and arise from the dead, and Christ shall give thee light."

And surely the immediate, the urgent, and the vital duty of every man is to open the door immediately he hears the voice. Peter, when he came to know the voice, and distinguish it, said immediately, "It is the Lord." He knew the voice. The Magdalene, out of whom Christ cast seven devils, knew the voice, and when He turned she said "Rabboni; which is to say, Master." She knew the Master's voice, and a man must be alive to the voice of the Saviour or he will never come to his senses. The voice of the minister cannot do it, the voice of the parent cannot do it, the voice of a friend expostulating cannot do it, the voice of conscience within itself cannot do it,—it must be the voice that speaks and it is done, it must be the voice of Him that said to the wind and storm, "Peace, be still; and the wind ceased, and there was a great calm," that said to the legion of devils, "Come out," and they obeyed. There is no other voice that can speak peace to the soul of the sinner. The Lord God speaks by His Son, and the Son speaks by His Spirit through His Word, and therefore you must not simply hear the voice of the preacher, you must not simply hear and read God's word; that is simply the instrument; but you must seek Jesus personally, and He must effectually call you as He did His apostles, and they immediately "forsook all and followed Him" when they heard His voice. So man must hear the voice of Jesus. O brethren, how few comparatively hear it. Many come and hear and listen to the message; they receive the letter, but they never hearken to the Spirit; it never comes to them in the depths of their inmost heart to awaken them from their false and fatal stupor, but it leaves them like those of whom Jesus says, "Thou sayest, I am rich, and increased with goods, and have need of nothing; and knowest not that thou art wretched, and miserable, and poor, and blind, and naked. I counsel thee to buy of me gold tried in the fire, that thou mayest be rich; and white raiment, that thou mayest be clothed, and that the shame of thy nakedness do not appear; and anoint thine eyes with eye-salve, that thou mayest see." Oh! let Jesus put His finger into the ear of our hearts as He did into the ear of the deaf man of whom we heard this morning, and say, "Ephphatha," and it shall be opened. Yes, He opens the blind eyes, He unstops the deaf ears, and He works moral miracles still higher than those that made the deaf to hear, and the dumb to speak, and the lame to walk. If He did these things in the body, mightier works are still done by Him in the souls of men; and if He bless, then it may be said, "Blessed are your eyes, for they see: and your ears, for they hear." "If any man hear my voice." It must be with the ear of faith. Many hear, but they mix no faith with that hearing, and it is but sound to them, or something that interests their intellects, or moves their fancy, or stirs their natural emotions. To hear with faith is to hear with "power," and "with much assurance."

And then, brethren, the effect of hearing, the proof of hearing, the result of hearing—of effectual hearing—is this, we open the door. Christ does not deal with man as a mere passive subject, as a carpenter does with a plank, or a statuary does with a block of marble hewing it into shape. He works in us, "both to will and to do of His good pleasure," but as we can do nothing but as He moves us, so He will do nothing but as we are moved. He does not force men to be saved, He does not save them against their will, He does not force the door, He does not burst in the door —He must have the door opened. Ah, He is ready to put in His hand to help us unbar the bolts and hindrances that stop up the way. The very heart of man is naturally shut against the Creator and Redeemer; and that a man does not know who never had it opened, who comes at once, as he thinks, into the fellowship and faith and love of Christ, with no effort, no trouble, no labour, and no travail in birth. Save in some few instances that have been sanctified from their mother's womb, and never fallen from the covenant of grace,—and even that they are thus nigh is not of their own doing and striving, but it is all of grace that they are what they are—I say, with few exceptions there must be and will be a sense that the door was bolted, a deep humiliation and shame that Christ's desires to have the heart have been disregarded so often and rejected so often, that they have turned a deaf ear to Him, and have listened to the syren song of "the world, the flesh, and the devil," and have been charmed by fashion and folly and sin, when their Redeemer went to them with pardon, and peace, and righteousness. Ah, brethren, look back upon your own history and lives, and mark the heart; go back to the sick-bed, go back to the death-bed, go back to the grave, go back to the sermon, go back to the secret reading of God's Word and the weeping over it in your closets;—were not these beginnings to listen to the voice? And were you not then thinking of opening the door? But lo! when you found that the world remonstrated with you, and the devil tried to lure you back into sleep, and the flesh whispered difficulties and struggle and self-denial, and loss of friendship and renown, then you left the door barred. The knock was still there, but you ceased to hear it, you drowned it in clamour and din and turmoil, and left the Saviour to serve the devil. Ah, brethren, cannot many of you look back and say, "I would not open the door?" But it *must* be opened, and in order to it you must take away every bolt, you must undo every lock, you must deny yourselves and take up your cross and follow the Redeemer; you must turn out His enemies, and make room for himself; you must dethrone the usurper, and then enthrone the rightful king. "Brethren, we are debtors, not to the flesh, to live after the flesh. For if ye live after the flesh, ye shall die: but if ye through the Spirit do mortify the deeds of the body, ye shall live." You are traitors, you are disloyal, if you reject and shut out your Saviour for the sake of any of these His enemies, that like a serpent have wound their way into the heart and coiled themselves there, and are lulling you with their poison, which is eternal death. Then, brethren, the door *must* be opened.

And oh! how great and glorious *is the promise and privilege* if you will thus open and thus welcome. "I will come in to him, and will sup with him, and he with me." A Saviourless heart, how desolate and dreary a heart! No matter what it has, wealth, ambition, power, the enjoyment of all that is vain and earthly, has it Christ? The bark may sail a long way on a waveless sea in calmness and be undisturbed, but a time will come when the winds and the waves will beat into that little ship, and it will be ready to sink. Oh! if there is no Saviour in the hinder part of the vessel to arise and say, "Peace, be still," what a wretched wreck will that vessel be after all! It may cast all its wares and merchandise into the deep, and it may be too late, and the deep will swallow it up. Oh! to have

Christ in the heart is to have heaven in the heart, is to have happiness in the heart, is to have safety in the heart, is to have God in the heart. "I will enter in." What a beautiful and simple act of condescension! Christ does not simply say, as He says elsewhere, "I will abide with him," but "I will enter in." I will make his heart my palace, my throne on earth. "Thus saith the high and lofty One that inhabiteth eternity, whose name is holy: I dwell in the high and holy place, with him also that is of a contrite and humble spirit." Oh! the condescension; from the throne of glory down to the poor sinful contrite heart that was so unclean, and yet that He should enter in and cleanse it, and ennoble it, and exalt it, and purify it with holiness, and inhabit it to all eternity! "I will sup with him, and he with me." Do not let us stagger at the greatness of the promise. We judge after the flesh, and are creatures of sense and sight. Oh! there is reality here in comparison with which all that agitates us is as shining dust, or a light that comes and goes through darkness, and leaves it darker than before. Be assured of it, there is nothing so real as this:—"Christ in you, the hope of glory." Who shall separate us then from the love of Christ?

"I will come in and sup with him, and he with me." The supper in oriental countries is mainly the meal of the day, it is the evening meal, and they love it for its great social spirit and character; and there, as they partake of it, resting on couches, one leans on the breast of a friend, and they seem, as it were, conjoined in special fellowship and brotherhood. The Redeemer condescends to use this figure: "I will sup with him." The poor pardoned penitent, who has opened the door, He shall sup with him. What a beautiful idea of intimate and entire intercourse. "There is a friend that sticketh closer than a brother," and such a friend is Jesus. "I will sup with him, and he with me." That we should sup with Him is indeed, as it would seem, no great thing; that He should spread the board with the consolations of His Spirit, the promises of His Word, the heavenly hopes of His glory, the assurances of His tender regard and the blessed consolations of His Spirit; these, indeed, may well furnish such a spread as angels themselves can scarcely have, for they do not know the fulness that is in Christ as a Saviour, they have not need of His salvation as we have. These things, I say, are natural, and we should expect them from such a guest; but that He should sup with us is marvellous beyond conception! Yet He does, for He condescends to love the little things with which His friends can furnish the table; He takes delight in their expressions of faith and love, in their penitential humiliations and confessions, in their expressions of gratitude and thankfulness, in their alms-giving, in the cup of cold water, if only that cup of cold water be given for His sake. Whatever present, out of love, one condescends to accept for love, makes a little thing sweet. If your child presents you with a gift, however small, of affection, though a fragrant flower, and very small, it is sweet, and the parent, because it is a present from a young child, can find pleasure and delight in it. Such is the condescension and grace of the Lord Jesus Christ. He accepts the joys and praises and expressions of love and acts of kindness and services done for Him by His people, He accepts them with delight, and rejoices over them; and even rejoices over them " with singing," as it is marvellously expressed in the prophet.

Then, brethren, what a picture! Surely none will turn a blind eye or an indifferent and cold heart to His message:— " Behold, I stand at the door and knock; if any man hear my voice, and open the door, I will come in to him, and will sup with him, and he with me." Dear brethren, it is not much longer that He will stand and knock; the time will come when He will arise, and depart, and say to the ungrateful, unbelieving sinner, "Let him alone, let him alone." "Take heed, brethren, lest there be in any of you an evil heart of unbelief" in refusing to hear the Saviour's voice, or, after you have heard, turning your back upon Him. "Return, ye backsliding children, and I will heal your backslidings." "Return unto me, for I have redeemed thee." No man can stand before his Judge on the great day, and say, "Thou never didst knock at the door of my heart, I never heard, I never had the overture of mercy, I never had a single awakening of conscience." I believe none shall be able to plead it wherever the Word of God is proclaimed and circulated; none will be able to say, "Thou never gavest warning." No, brethren; does He not say in a thousand ways, "Turn ye, turn ye from your evil ways; for why will ye die?" "I have no pleasure in the death of him that dieth." And, brethren, oh! do not be satisfied with simply listening to the voice. That seems to be almost worse than if you turned a deaf ear and listened not. What! are you to presume on His patience? Are you to harden yourselves because He is so long-suffering? Are you to turn His patience into occasion for greater rebellion? Are you to "treasure up unto thyself wrath against the day of wrath and revelation of the righteous judgment of God," because He awaits so long to see if haply you will open, that He may enter in? If you do, will He not justly say, "Depart from me?" Will He not justly say, "I know ye not?" You come and knock at the door of Him who has knocked so long in vain at yours; and He will say "Depart from me, into outer darkness." Though you may go to the door, it may be shut, it may be then too late, the lamp may be gone out for ever. Dear brethren, oh! seek to have enduring, intimate—I might say, friendship, for the original sense of the word familiar bears that construction—intercourse with Jesus, so that you may rejoice in hope, rejoice in all that He has done, in all that He does, in all that He will do. He will give clusters which He brings from the heavenly land of promise; and if sweet here, how sweet and rich they will be in the glorious Eden itself; what will be "the land flowing with milk and honey," where we shall have "fulness of joy and pleasures for evermore," at His "right hand." Therefore, brethren, we ought not to be straitened in ourselves, we are not straitened in Him. "Open thy mouth wide, and I will fill it." Seek for fulness and enjoyment in Christ; then, indeed, the world will have little charm for you, and its fancies you will comparatively disrelish and distaste, but you shall be filled with such peace and joy in believing that its sorrows will sit lightly upon you, and its pleasures and fascinations will have no charm. Then, brethren, look forward for the blessed period of which the sweet singer in Israel said: "When I awake up after Thy likeness, I shall be satisfied with it."

X.

CHRIST OUR PRECIOUS EXAMPLE.

"Christ also suffered for us, leaving us an example, that ye should follow his steps."—1 PETER ii. 21.

WE are perpetually prone to run into extremes. This is particularly manifest in our views of divine truth. Most of our errors arise rather from a distortion of than rejection of the truth. We exaggerate on the one hand, and we extenuate on the other hand, and thus we dislocate the beautiful body of divine truth, and we represent it to ourselves as distorted and incoherent. However this may be the case in our views of God's truth, it is not so in the blessed original; there we have all in glorious symmetry and harmony. In the present day, when people are indulging largely in extreme views, on the one hand manifested in setting aside to a great extent, and in distorting and overlooking the atonement made by the Lord Jesus Christ, the key-stone of the arch of our salvation—for the great gulf were fixed for ever but for that blessed arch over which we may return to God through Christ—if, on the one hand, there are some who would deny this, or at least deny its relationship to God, and so deny its excellency, and its efficacy, and its glory; there are, on the other hand, those who magnify the atonement of Christ, so as to overlook or disparage the example of Christ, as though an extreme view on the one side led them to an extreme view on the other side. In the beautiful Collect we have just heard, we have the scriptural balance, that, as God has given, by His atoning blood, Christ, to make our reconciliation, He has also given Him as an ensample of a holy and godly life. On the one hand, we must "most thankfully receive His inestimable benefit," and on the other hand, we ought to "daily endeavour ourselves to follow the blessed steps of His most holy life." To do the latter is the best evidence that we have done the former; and except we do the former, we shall never effectually do the latter. So far from their being in contrast they are in beautiful combination, and the reception of Christ's sacrifice for our salvation is connected with our following His will, and becoming like the perfect model.

I bring before you, this morning, the precious example of Christ. The apostle brings it before the suffering saints in the general Church in his day, and unfolds it to them in a special and in a general manner; special, in that Christ suffered for us; and general, in that He has left us an example that we should follow in His steps.

We shall then limit ourselves—for it is impossible to embrace both—to the general view, *Christ as our example.* May His Spirit rest upon us while we contemplate His own glorious image.

Christ as our example. He became man, and He was so truly man that He did as man what He would not and could not have done simply as God. Simply as God, He could not have been our example, for the finite can have no resemblance to the Infinite. He dwelleth "in the light which no man can approach unto: which no man hath seen nor can see." It was only, therefore, when the "perfect God" became "perfect man, of a reasonable soul and human flesh subsisting," that He became a pattern for man. As a heathen once said, "the essence of worship is to resemble the object that we worship," so it is essential for the Christian to resemble the

Christ we worship. That is the essence of sincere worship, "Ye shall be holy: for I the Lord your God am holy."

Let us enter somewhat into the distinctive and general features of Christ our precious example.

The fundamental ground of all the rest is *Christ's advancement of His Father's glory.* As the needle cannot guide the vessel except it point truly to the pole, even so "if thine eye be single," thy aim will be single, but "if thine eye be evil" thy aim will be evil. The want of a single aim is the fatal blot in many characters who call themselves Christians. Not that they have no fear of God, not that they have no desire to please Him, but they are continually swallowed up in fears and desires about earthly things, instead of keeping them subordinate to the one supreme thing. The object and aim the blessed Redeemer has set before us as our perfect pattern is God's glory. He says Himself—and he proved it by His whole course—"I seek not mine own will, but the will of the Father which hath sent me," and so constantly was this His aim, that even when He faltered in His humanity at the approach of the dread hour of darkness, when His human nature trembled, when He held the cup of bitterness, and in the dread and deep perturbation of His spirit He uttered such language as this, "Now is my soul troubled; and what shall I say? Father, save me from this hour;" yet He added, "but for this cause came I unto this hour; Father, glorify thy name." There is the whole desire merged in the one desire that God might be glorified, and then He was satisfied. Whatever He had to endure was nothing to Him if His Father was magnified and exalted, and He could say, when He came to the end of His course, and the bitter cup was half drunk: "I have glorified Thee on the earth: I have finished the work which Thou gavest me to do." And so, when He taught His disciples to pray, He did not teach them first to begin with their own poor wants, and sins, and sorrows; but He taught them to begin—as His faithful people are ever to do—with the beginning: "Hallowed be thy name. Thy kingdom come." If God be glorified, His people are satisfied, they know that their salvation is bound up with His glory. The whole of our conduct must be, "whether therefore we eat or drink, or whatsoever we do," we must do it "to the glory of God," then will our religion become the trichord of holy obedience, and the minutest service, the most ordinary engagements, all our relative ties and our various occupations are elevated into the religion that is the creation of God.

But next to this blessed feature which crowns the character of Jesus, and renders Him so utterly unlike most of us, is what follows as a necessary consequence: *His conformity to His Father's will.* If God is to be glorified, God must be obeyed; and he that obeys Him honours Him best, therefore it follows in immediate connexion, "Thy will be done in earth, as it is in heaven." Oh what a wondrous thing is the will of God, His moral will; how it pervades the universe. As the atmosphere is interfused everywhere on every side of us, even so the will of God touches everything within and without man. The moral empire of God is surrounded by His will, and if all men were magnetised by it and in harmony with it, and all went into the universal mould, oh, what a universe it would be! And it is as far as that will is realised in this world. Look at the Redeemer's whole life; was it not a texture woven in the loom of the divine will? He comes into the world with this upon His infant lips, if we may so speak: "Lo, I come to do Thy will, O God;" and He could testify, "My meat is to do the will of Him that sent me." When His disciples thought He was starving Himself through rejecting meat, they said unto Him, "Master, eat." But He said unto them, I have meat to eat that ye know not of.

Therefore said the disciples one to another, Hath any one brought Him ought to eat? Jesus saith unto them, My meat is to do the will of Him that sent me, and to finish His work." What beautiful consistency, what inimitable truth of character thus was stamped upon the Redeemer! And when it was put to the test in the extremest hour of agony and anguish, and despondency; when He was so crushed in His inmost spirit that He could not but pray, " O my Father, if it be possible, let this cup pass from me;" still He added, "nevertheless, not as I will, but as thou wilt." There was complete submission in everything, and He could testify, " I have kept Thy commandments;" and when His last breath was yielded up it was in saying, " It is finished;" His Father's will was accomplished. And how did He teach us to know that will? By the Scriptures; that it might be accomplished which was spoken by the prophets, It is written that the Scriptures might be fulfiled. We have that very rule illustrated in His whole course and conversation till crowned in His death, and we have that rule in our hands. It is written, " I will be their God: and I will give them one heart, and one way, that they may fear me for ever."

Look at the next feature in beautiful harmony. " Thou shalt love the Lord thy God with all thy heart," and " thou shalt love thy neighbour as thyself." *Active delight in doing good.* By night and by day His heart was set upon doing good to the sinful and rebellious children of men. Though He " came to His own," " His own received Him not;" though He " was in the world," " the world knew Him not," but treated Him with scorn, and misconstruction, and contumely, and " contradiction of sinners;" still His love many waters could not quench, many unkindnesses could not mar, but He toiled on; and when John sent to Him two of his disciples to inquire of Him, He said, " Go and show John again those things which ye do hear and see.

The blind receive their sight, and the lame walk, the lepers are cleansed, and the deaf hear, the dead are raised up, and the poor have the gospel preached to them." An epitome and compendium of His whole life is given by him who had been His most intimate attendant, and is contained in one short sentence: "He went about doing good." Doing good! Oh, how beautiful His unweariness in doing good. Again and again He proved Himself. He took our sicknesses, and carried our sorrows. What a pattern for us, and how we should love to follow His example, so that "whether we live or die," we may be the Lord's. What is the Lord's will concerning our life? It is that we should "look not every one on his own things, but every man also on the things of others. Let this mind be in you which was also in Christ Jesus," who left the throne of glory for the manger, the cross, and the sepulchre, "for us men, and for our salvation;" who gave Himself for us, "the just for the unjust," the good for the bad, "that He might bring us to God."

Then, brethren, mark the next feature—*the tenderness, the sympathy, and the long-suffering of Jesus.* He did not temporise or compromise, as some will do, merely to get rid of trouble, but "the Son of man" came "to seek and to save that which was lost." With what patience, with what gentleness, and with what tenderness He did it! The "bruised reed" He did "not break," and "the smoking flax" He did "not quench." His voice was not heard in the streets. He never cried aloud, nor sought for human applause, but He always, secretly as well as openly, endeavoured to scatter the manifold gifts of His bounty to every recipient wherever opportunity offered. How beautiful the tenderness of Christ! How He showed it to the multitude when they were hungry. He did not cease to make provision for the wants of the body while administering to the wants of the mind, and therefore He multiplied the bread for the hungry multitude. In all the afflictions of His people "He was afflicted."

Look at another feature in this beautiful portrait—*the patience of the Lord Jesus Christ*. Oh, how wondrous was His patience! No provocation ever aroused Him to anger, for if He was angry, it was anger for the sin, and not for the sinner; and His anger was tempered with grief, and had more of love in it than it had of resentment. What patience He displayed when He was buffeted and spit upon, and mocked, and scourged! I know no instance in the earthly life of Jesus that had more of patience in it than that when one of the ruffian servants of the high priest smote Him with the palm of his hand, and said, "Answerest thou the high priest so? Jesus answered him, If I have spoken evil, bear witness of the evil; but if well, why smitest thou me?" Oh, what tenderness, when He could, with a glance of the lightning of His eye, or by a thunderbolt snatched from heaven, have stricken the miscreant, in a moment, to hell! Yet He says, "If I speak well, why smitest thou me?" And so "He was led as a lamb to the slaughter, and as a sheep before her shearers was He dumb." Surely, if to that little band, in the midst of their suffering and disappointment, and distress, one glance of the Lamb of God before His shearers led to the slaughter, one glance of Him in His agony in Gethsemane, and on the cross, sufficed, it should silence us, and we should say, "I became dumb, and opened not my mouth."

One of the last features to be noticed is that which gives transcendency to the whole. It is *the perfect harmony that belongs to the character of Jesus*, and places it alone in its perfection. In all human character there are sometimes shadows, disappointments, and incongruities; the human instrument is out of harmony, it is not in tune, it is not in the key-note, there are jarring chords, there is something unloose in the instrument; but not so in the divine harp of heaven, when heard amongst us. There all is exquisite, all is melody, all is symphony, there is not one note out of tune. How beautiful it is to see this in effect amongst Christ's people. We hear of men being distinguished for such and such virtues, which must mean that they have more of some and less of others in comparison; but what is spoken in praise of others in human affairs, to Jesus would be a disparagement, for Jesus has no prominency of virtue, but all His divine character is in admirable proportion and harmony; one feature never entrenches upon another. He was not more tender and humble than He was zealous and bold; He was not more full of divine love than He was full also of holy and just resentment against sin. We cannot say that He was in anything the more of the one than of the other, but each virtue was exquisitely balanced, and each one had its proper place and symmetry. Like the rainbow that encircles His throne in heaven, with all the colours in such exact proportion that we cannot say that the red is more distinct than the blue, or that the yellow is more distinct than the green, but each one is in exact proportion, forming one lovely and entire circle; so it is with the character of Jesus; no man can find any defect, no man can find one redundancy, and there is no one grace that takes the place of another. How beautiful the character of Jesus! He left us an example, that we should follow His steps.

But, brethren, remember, if you follow His steps, you must first receive His inestimable atonement. Until you are at peace with God, you will never have strength to hope and grace to follow the footsteps of the Saviour. This is the work of God. "He that believeth on the Son of God hath the witness in himself." "Believe on the Lord Jesus Christ, and thou shalt be saved." Thou shalt follow thy Saviour, and love Him, and why? "Because He first loved us." "We have known and believed the love that God hath for us." If so, then herein is the ground of all: —"The love of Christ constraineth us; because we thus judge, that if one died for all, then were all dead. And that he died for all, that they which live should not henceforth live unto themselves, but unto Him which died for them, and rose again." Well, then, it follows, if we are thus constrained by His love, we shall invariably walk in His steps. "Learn of me, for I am meek and lowly in heart, and ye shall find rest unto your souls." "I know my sheep, and am known of mine."

Then, brethren, do not rest in a hope in the atonement that is not authenticated by a gradual transformation to the likeness of Him, for if you have the atonement, hereby we, indeed, shall perceive and know that we are in Him if we become gradually like Him.

And, brethren, do not despond. Remember, Christ was human, though divine. Follow Him as human, not as divine, because many things Christ did and said as God, therefore they are not "ensamples" for us; but what He did in the ordinary course of His human life He did for our pattern, and you must set them before you as your pattern. "Wherefore . . . let us lay aside every weight, and the sin which doth so easily beset us, and let us run with patience the race that is set before us, looking unto Jesus, the author and finisher of our faith." Then, brethren, if we are thus faithful, we shall at last realise that blessed assurance of David, "I shall be satisfied, when I awake, with Thy likeness."

XI.

STUMBLING AT CHRIST.

"And blessed is he, whosoever shall not be offended in me."
ST. MATT. xi. 6.

THESE words of Christ give us the key to the state of mind which prompted the Baptist to send two of his disciples to his Master. Many have supposed that John sent them in order that their faith might be confirmed, but the words of Christ in His reply to the Baptist seem to me to decide the question, and to show that they were intended to meet the particular temptation and trial in the mind of Christ's harbinger. And if we realise his circumstances we can hardly marvel that such a state of mind should have befallen him. He had gone before the Lord, turning "the hearts of the fathers to the children, and the disobedient to the wisdom of the just; to make ready a people prepared for the Lord;" he had accomplished his work with zeal and diligence, and Christ Himself bore him witness that He was "a burning and a shining light." Not only had the Baptist done this, but he had shown a beautiful humility, and a lovely complacency in the lower office that he held of morning star to usher in and be lost in the effulgence of the rising sun. And now, for the testimony of the truth, he had long been a prisoner, it may have been in a damp and dismal dungeon, there he was deserted and uncared for, his friends had no access to him, and it was scarcely possible but that the circumstances that surrounded him would depress his spirits and act upon his mind.

When a man becomes a saint, he does not become a stone; because he has his heart submissive to the will of God, he does not, therefore, prove insensible to the struggles and the sufferings of his body. A Christian, while in the body, is more or less oppressed by the body. And then it must have seemed very strange and mysterious that the Lord whom he had heralded, and of whom he himself bore testimony, that he was "not worthy to stoop down to unloose His shoes," that He who "spake and it was done," who could have opened the prison doors had He wished, that *He* should seem to forget His poor messenger, and leave him unpitied, and without so much as a message of sympathy and kindness, without any interposition on his behalf, that He should leave him oppressed and loaded with chains, and should seem as if He had forgotten him altogether. It was scarcely to be marvelled at, though it may be mourned, that the messenger began to feel his spirit faint, and there arose in his mind doubts whether this was the very Messiah, whether the Messiah had come after all, whether he did not lack more evidence to satisfy him that he had not placed his confidence and exercised his faith in vain; therefore he sent two of his disciples to say, "Art thou He that should come, or do we look for another?" Jesus dealt with him tenderly, as He always did with His followers, when sincere though weak; He did not send him a sharp reproof or rebuke, but a gracious cordial and succour for his faith, to enable him more to vindicate and more to prove by comparison and prophecy, that He was "the mighty God, the everlasting Father, the Prince of Peace," who was foretold by the prophets and harbingered by John. At the time the disciples were sent to Him He was surrounded with resplendent monuments of His mighty power. Though He stood there as "a man of sorrows and acquainted with grief," and was "without form or comeliness," yet, all around Him, there were beautiful and loving tokens of His majesty and love. He said to the disciples, "Go and show John again these things which ye do hear and see: the blind receive their sight, and the lame walk, the lepers are cleansed, and the deaf hear, the dead are raised up, and the poor have the gospel preached to them." Then He adds the gentle reproof, which evidently was intended to come home to the Baptist to rebuke him for his wavering faith, and the doubts that distressed his mind. "Blessed is he, whosoever shall not be offended in me." The word "*offended*" we do not understand aright in its original meaning. As we use the word now, we say a man is offended when something has provoked his wrath or excited his indignation and resentment, but the original meaning of the word was "stumbling"—falling over a thing, and hence the word "stumbling-block," over which a man trips and falls, and therefore it became used in this sense—that which leads a man to draw back or turn aside when he wishes to become a Christian or follow Christ. Such is the meaning of the word, and such is the meaning of the passage. It is a passage that has its application and reference not the less to us whether we are wishing to become Christians or not, whether we are weak or strong Christians—for strong Christians meet with their hours of difficulty and doubt, and have their stumbling-blocks as well as wavering and weak ones.

The words set before us these two points:—*Many are very apt to stumble at Christ, and there is much in Christ to stumble them: he, therefore, is especially blessed who does not take offence at Christ.* May He send His Spirit to teach us to be willing to take up His cross, and deny ourselves and follow Him, for His own name's sake.

There is much in Christ to offend and stumble. There is much in Him—very much—to stumble the careless, and worldly, and unbelieving; and there is much to stumble—though not so much—the faithful, and believing, and obedient. There must be a great deal in Christ to stumble and stagger a man who is in his sins and in his natural condition and state of unbelief, and that for the very obvious reason that a man is so unlike Christ, and Christ is so unlike him. Christ is a pure, perfect and spotless model, and man is just the reverse; and so if you bring two things together which are antagonistic there is a natural repulsion. In this case, there is a repulsion indeed on one side; Jesus is not repulsed even by our sins, He feels still and yearns over us, and He longs to save us. The repulsion is in the sinful heart of man, that shrinks from Christ, and dislikes and doubts Christ.

There is much in Christ to lead to this, much in His *person* though we do not see him bodily now, yet if we saw Him what was there in Him, as far as the outward appearance went? Doubtful, sceptical men, judging according to their reason and sense, and comparing spiritual things with secular, looking at the outside and not taught of the Spirit, would see in Christ very much to stumble them. "He grew up as a root out of a dry ground, He had no form nor comeliness about Him" that the carnal eye should desire; " His visage was marred more than that of any of the sons of men;" He came in deep poverty, and "had not where to lay his head;" "He was a man of sorrows and acquainted with grief;" He " came to His own, and His own received Him not;" "He was in the world," and, though " the world was made by Him," " the world knew Him not," men " hid as it were their faces from Him;" "He was despised and rejected of men." What was there in all this to commend to reverence or to challenge to faith? Nothing; but, on the contrary, there was everything to repel. He was, therefore, "to the Jews a stumbling-block, and to the Greeks foolishness, and they said of Him, "is not this the carpenter's son—are not His sisters with us, and His brothers, are they not known to us?" How are we to believe in Him, to trust in Him, to adore Him as the incarnate God, and to commit our souls to Him for everlasting life? There is still the same feeling; and you have only to read—though you had better not if you have no occasion—the writings of scoffers, and scorners, and unbelievers, and those who deny the Deity of Christ, to see that they are offended at Him. They stumble at the idea of the Infinite being contained in the finite, they stagger at "the fulness of the Godhead bodily," they despise the great mystery of "God with us," they are offended at it.

And there is very much in Christ's holy person and *life* to stumble and stagger the ungodly; for Christ, in His life, shows them that they must be above the world, and they are after the world; He shows them that they must mortify the deeds of the flesh, and they indulge and follow the flesh; He tells them that they must take up the cross, and they want to take up the crown; He tells them to come after Him and follow Him, and they wish to follow the world, and to walk "according to the prince of the power of the air;" hence, the Redeemer's example repels them, and they do not relish it. They love pride, He would have humility; they love indulgence, He requires self-denial; they are for extolling themselves, He comes humbling Himself; they are for gratifying the lusts of the flesh with its affections, He teaches us that "if we suffer, we shall also reign with Him," that "if we deny Him, He also will deny us," and that if we acknowledge Him, He will acknowledge us; but this is not to the taste of the world, a man's heart is just the reverse of this, and therefore he is ready to say, "'I pray thee have me excused,' I cannot take such a master, I cannot follow such a leader."

Then, again, there is very much in Christ's *doctrine* to stumble a man. Men naturally rely on themselves, and expect to make their own peace with God; they set about weaving out a patchwork garment of their own righteousness in which to appear at the judgment-day, they do not like to be mendicants, they would like to be merchants, they would rather buy than beg for salvation, they would rather do something to make themselves, as they think, worthy of God, and fit for God. In their heart of hearts they fancy oftentimes that they are good enough, that they are so much better than others, and, therefore, that they must stand well before God; and so they delude themselves, and go with a lie in their right hand to the bar of judgment, and they find out their mistake when it is too late. But the Redeemer strips a man of all his righteousness, and brings it as filthy rags to the foot of the cross, He leads him to put off himself that he may put Christ in the place, he is brought low as the publican when he smote upon his breast and said, "God be merciful to me a sinner." Men do not like to be thus dependent entirely on grace, they do not like to admit that they can do no good thing without it is wrought in them and implanted in them, and so, like the proud Pharisee, they would rather thank God that they are not as other men, than thank Christ that He has made them to differ and give Him all the praise; hence, they are offended at this doctrine of free salvation and sovereign grace and righteousness by another, and dependence for all help and holiness upon divine succour.

Then, again, men are often stumbled at Christ's *purposes*. They receive the record of which we heard to-night, "that God hath given us eternal life, and this life is in His Son; he that hath the Son hath life, and he that hath not the

Son of God hath not life;" they have received this, they have received Christ Jesus the Lord, they profess to yield themselves fully to Him, but still " the flesh lusteth against the Spirit, and the Spirit against the flesh," and they oftentimes are sore straitened and staggered, God's ways are not as their ways, nor are His thoughts as their thoughts, no marvel then that our thoughts should misjudge His very often, and we should be ready to say, How can these things be? what does He mean? how does He deal with man? People get into difficulties and distresses, and they fancy themselves better judges than God, and they rise in rebellion against His appointments, and are ready to arraign His ways, forgetting that " clouds and darkness are round about Him," and that they cannot penetrate the thick pavilion that encompasses Him. And hence it follows, that often very Christian and good people are stumbled, and offended, and distressed, more especially in their early walk as Christians, when they are disposed to judge the Lord by " feeble sense," instead of trusting Him for His grace, and because they do not get the assurance, and joy, and comfort that they expected, and are left alone, as they think, to grope in darkness,—because God seems to make things turn out different from what He had promised, because His providence often seems to contradict His promises, therefore, because they cannot fathom and comprehend Him they are offended, and many draw back and cease to follow Him. Christ led us to expect this in that picture He gives us of the visible Church in the parable of the sower, a prophetic parable for all time. He teaches us there that there are those who listen and hear the word, and " receive it with gladness," but when affliction or persecution ariseth for the word's sake, and through obeying Christ, " immediately they are offended," and fall away. There are many such. The sea of the Christian Church is scattered with the wrecks of many who have dashed upon the rock of offence and have gone down, strewing the waves with the wreck. Alas! how many a man puts "his hand to the plough" and draws back. "Were there not ten cleansed, but where are the nine?"

We might enlarge, and show you that Christ is apt to give offence in other ways because His course of dealing with men is altogether above our comprehension. What then are we to do? Instead of meddling in matters too high for us and daring to arraign the Infinite, we should put one hand upon our mouths, and our mouths in the dust, and say, "'My soul is even as a weaned child.' 'Not as I will, but as Thou wilt;' it is right because Thou doest it. Who am I, and what am I, a poor worm of threescore years and ten at most, that I should dare to judge the Eternal? Thou seest not things as I see them, and Thou judgest not as I judge; it will be far better for me for my little child to call in question my doings than for me to dare to presume to say to the Infinite, What doest Thou? It is mine to 'be still, and know that Thou art God,' to become dumb and not open my mouth because Thou doest it."

Blessed, then, is he that is not offended. And why is he blessed? Because, if he has come to wisdom he has come to his senses. While the foolish prodigal vainly thought he could make himself happier than his father could, better than in his own country, better when revelling in licentiousness, he proved himself to be a fool, he was beside himself, he was out of his mind; but when he came to himself, and saw his father's house and his father, and was brought again to the door of the house, he said, "I will arise, and go to my father," I will stumble no more at the gentle restraint of a father's house. Then he sighed no more for the liberty that turns to licentiousness, and despair, and misery, and so he arose, and went to his father. A man is nothing better than a fool, though he have all the wisdom of the philosophers, and all the learning of the scholars, if he have not learned this—how blind, and short-sighted, and dependent he is in the presence of the Infinite, before whom the heavens are not clean, who charges His angels with folly, before whom the angels veil their faces. When a man comes to wisdom,—to the beginning of wisdom,—when he comes to be no longer offended at the ways of God or the works of Christ, then he is blessed, because flesh and blood would not have taught him it, because he is taught by the Spirit of God the Father in heaven. When a man comes to believe in Jesus in truth and simplicity, it is not by his own intelligence, or wit, or wisdom, or resolution, and therefore it is written, "No man can say that Jesus is the Lord but by the Holy Ghost." "Whosoever believeth that Jesus is the Christ, is born of God." That is the evidence, the invariable evidence, that a man has turned to God. When Jesus was confessed by Peter to be the Son of God and the Saviour of the world, Jesus said unto him, "Blessed art thou, Simon Barjona; for flesh and blood hath not revealed it unto thee, but my Father which is in heaven." That man is blessed who is so taught of God that he receives Christ Jesus the Lord, the truth as it is in Jesus, without staggering and without finding fault, but in simple faith. When he receives it as a little child, and so enters into the kingdom of heaven, he is blessed.

He is not offended at Christ, because Christ will not be offended at him. What does Christ require of a man but just to take Him at His word, and receive Him as he is? There is nothing whatever in Christ to contradict or outrage a man's reason. It is pride, prejudice, passion, worldliness, and "the evil heart of unbelief," that stumbles at Christ; it is not sound reason—for that is the echo of the voice of God. And yet some men foolishly talk of the self-verifying faculty, and say they will accept only what they can prove by their own reason. That is just to make God " such a one as themselves." If a man will not bow himself to the authority of God, he should own himself at once as an infidel or atheist; for he has no faith if he will not bow himself in submission to the unfathomable and illimitable God. Blessed is he that is brought low, and can say, with David, "Lord, I am not high-minded, I have no proud looks; I do not exercise myself in great matters, which are too high for me. But I refrain my soul, and keep it low, like as a child that is weaned from his mother: yea, my soul is even as a weaned child." Blessed is the man that is brought to that.

Then, again, he is blessed that does not take offence at Christ, because nothing shall offend him. The psalmist sweetly says: "Great is the peace that they have who love Thy law, and they are not offended at it." Not to be offended at the law, is not to be offended at the Lawgiver; not to be offended at Christ's word, is not to be offended at Christ Himself. When a man sees everything to be right that God does, the mind chimes in with it, the soul is in sympathy, so to speak, with the Infinite, and is, as it were, in beautiful response to the Saviour's voice. "Great praise have they that love Thy law;" then nothing disturbs them, come sorrow, come poverty, come bereavement, come sickness, come difficulties, come trials, come losses, come crosses, come shipwrecks, come bankruptcy, come persecution, come prison, come scourge, come the faggot, come the sword, come the block, come death, a man still says: My God allows it, He permits it, He overrules it for me. "The cup that my Father gives me, shall I not drink it?" "If it be possible, let it pass from me; nevertheless, not my will but Thine be done." Do you not see that, even in this world, men must have great peace that thus submit themselves, and do not contend and struggle against God's providence or dealings with them? It is not men's trials that make them miserable; it is their wrestling with them, and struggling and fighting with them. Man himself is tormented by his own susceptibilities and staggerings against God, and many a man is like a wild bull entangled in a net—the more he struggles the more he entangles himself, and the greater his difficulties become; whereas, if he lay calm, as clay in the hands of the potter, all struggle would cease.

Once more, blessed are they that are not offended, because Christ will own them in the great day. If we confess Him, He will confess us; but if we deny Him, He will deny us; and He Himself says, if we are ashamed of Him and of His words, He will be ashamed of us when He cometh in the glory of the Father with the holy angels. A man best confesses Christ by having no will but Christ's, and a man must stumble at Christ who sets up his own petty wisdom and will against the Lord's, that made him and will judge him; and therefore, at the last day, it will be the hinge on which a man's condemnation or acceptance will turn whether he believed in Christ and submitted to Him, or whether he rejected Him and would not have Him to reign over him. "These mine enemies, that would not have me to reign over them, bring them hither and slay them;" but the meek, and the lowly, and the humble, that own Him, and confess Him, and love Him, He will love them, and will say to them, "Come, ye blessed children of my Father, inherit the kingdom prepared for you from the foundation of the world."

Now, dear brethren, are not many of you offended at Christ? The offence of the cross has not yet ceased; but though it is true you cannot reject Him in His bodily appearance, you may reject Him, and do, if you do not put your trust in Him, and yield yourselves to Him, and follow Him; you reject Him as much as if He walked into this church, and said to each one of you, "Wilt thou have me to reign over you; wilt thou yield thyself to me; wilt thou be renewed, and sanctified, and saved?" How many would say, if they dare—and many do dare to say it, just as much as if He walked in the midst of us—"We will not have this man to reign over us?" Take your choice. Who must reign, Christ or Satan? Which shall be your inheritance, heaven or hell? Whether will be your eternal dwelling "in blackness of darkness for ever," or "where there is fulness of joy and pleasures for evermore?" Make your election. "No man can serve two masters." "Ye call me Lord, Lord, and ye do not the things that I say unto you." Do remember, what a folly, what an infatuation it is to be offended at Christ. Was there ever any being so beautiful, so benign, so kind, so generous, so loving, so just, so almighty, so spotless in holiness? Why, then, be offended? why let your poor, blind, wretched lusts and passions, your pride and worldliness, your doubts and murmurings, lead you to be offended at Him? Does He wish to make you miserable, or happy? Is it any advantage to Him? Does He require you to give up anything but sin, and what leads to sin; and is not that misery? Does He command anything but what is for your real interest for time and eternity? If He commands you to give up sin, is it not a viper that stings, and torments, and degrades you? If He commands you to cherish love, and obedience, and moderation, and honesty, and uprightness, and truth, are not these the very elements of happiness, and beauty, and morality, and the excellence of your nature? It was well said, in the lesson of this evening, "His commandments are not grievous;"—not in themselves, when a man is in his right mind; but when a man has no faith, when he does not have the Spirit of God, he grieves Him, he dislikes Him, he dislikes His words, He quarrels with His requirements. O brethren, you will never find happiness in rebellion against your God and Saviour.

And, then, brethren, once more : Let those who are trying to serve God not forget that they are very apt to be offended at Him, that they are ever ready to think, "Why is this? why am I thus tempted? why does God deal thus with me? He lets me pine away in distress, and does not seem to think of me." Thus the Baptist must have thought of the Saviour; but oh! we should not thus think; for, "look how high the heaven is above the earth, so high are God's ways above our ways." We should remember that it is the perfection of our nature to have our wills so absorbed in His, that we have no will besides; then all is right, because all is according to His will. Oh, let us pray and seek for that divine key-note, that our affections, our desires, our thoughts, our conduct, our words, our ways, may be attuned to that key-note—may be in harmony with His will; then shall we be strung and attuned for the concert of perfect harmony of the will of God throughout everlasting ages!

XII.

CHRIST SERVING HIS PEOPLE.

"I am among you as he that serveth you."—St. Luke xxii. part of 27th verse.

Perhaps the darkest evidences of the plague of our fallen nature are not to be found in the distorted scenes of profligacy and debauchery and cruelty that deface and defile this ruined world, but they are to be found rather in holy scenes, in holy circumstances, when the deep evil of the human heart comes forth, on occasions and amid surrounding solemnities from which you would imagine it must be wholly driven away. In the sick-room, at the death-bed side, in the house of prayer, at the table of communion, evil tempers will stir, and bad thoughts will intrude; and what does this all prove but that even in the regenerate there is still a taint of their nature, and that they need each to pray not only in the midst of what they deem to be sin and temptation, but on the most sacred and on the most solemn occasions. The words you have heard were spoken in connexion with such a sad manifestation of such evil amid even the servants of God. It was at the last supper, at a season the commemoration of which we are now approaching, that Jesus, in the upper chamber, surrounded by His chosen band of followers, kept the last passover on earth, and superseded, or rather substituted for it, that Christian paschal feast to which you are now invited to draw near. He had warned His apostles that one of the twelve that dipped his hand in the dish with him should betray Him. He had told them that He was about to leave them; and leaving them a holy memorial of His departure, He bid them keep the holy feast in memory of it. It was at such a season, on such an occasion, amid solemnities the most impressive, and in circumstances that you would have supposed would have banished every thought from their minds but the thought of their own sinfulness, their Saviour's love, and His approaching suffering for them—and yet it was not strange, but natural; it was true, alas! to the evil heart of unbelief, that begins even in the children of God—it was then, under such circumstances, and at such a juncture, that we read, "there was a strife amongst them who should be the greatest." Such was their intense love of position and authority, such the desire for what men vainly call advancement—if it were as it ought to be, advancement in holiness, that were right and well—but it was intense desire for advancement amongst poor worms of the dust, whose praise is but the breath in their nostrils, and whose honour will soon be withering in the grave. It was said that there should be such a strife. How it must have pained the blessed Master, and how He must have felt wounded in His lowly spirit as He traced their strife. How foolish they were, anticipating the worldly kingdom, that they vainly looked forward to, striving who should stand highest in that kingdom, when He was undergoing already the anguish of the travail of His soul, stooping down to the dust, that He might elevate them for ever. It was under these circumstances that He thus touchingly, and by an appeal to His own example—and there is no eloquence like that of example—said, "The kings of the Gentiles exercise lordship over them; and they that exercise authority upon them are called benefactors. But ye shall not be so: but he that is greatest among you, let him be as the younger; and he that is chief, as he that doth serve." And then He says, in contrast with the mere worldly, who have their portion in this world, who seek for no higher wealth and honour than this perishing scene can afford, "I am among you as one that serveth." What a remarkable force and pathetic power there is in such a statement from the lips of Jesus! How His whole life was beautifully exemplified in this divine statement! Just at this crisis, when we are entering upon the period in which we commemorate "His agony and bloody sweat," "His cross and passion," "His death and burial," "His glorious resurrection and ascension;" for us how beautifully seasonable and suitable is this portion of divine doctrine; how it seems to condense into one sentence all that He was doing for us: "I am among you as he that serveth." Let us, then, brethren, illustrate the expression, and show *how Christ serves;* and let us then show *the efficacy and blessedness of His service;* and seek to be won by His example to tread in His steps, to "put on the Lord Jesus Christ," and to "learn of Him to be meek and lowly of heart."

We would illustrate the service of Christ. The word "service" is, in the original, the same as the word "minister." To serve is to help another, to aid another, to do a kindness, to do what is needful and advantageous to another; and he that ministers is much the same in its import. It is to supply something that is desirable and good for another, and to be as under service, under authority, under obedience to another for his good. "The Son of Man," Christ said, "came not into the world to be ministered unto, but to minister." He did not come to receive homage, or to receive aught that we could give Him; for, alas! we have nothing that is worthy of His reception, but it is all of His free grace and mercy. He expects nothing of us, He came to supply us and to bless us, and to benefit us by serving us. If we look into the history of Jesus from the beginning, as far as we have it revealed to us in His Word, what does it show? under what aspect does it reveal Him? Under the aspect or attitude of one that ministers, who is therefore made known to us because He has ministered to us.

In the first place, we see that, "Lo, I come to do Thy will," was His motto and His watchword. He came to do that will. Though He was Son of the everlasting Father, and of coequal dignity, yet He learned obedience by the things which he suffered, and became the servant of the Father, though the Son of the Father; coequal, yet under the yoke, for man's sake. And from the beginning we are told that His delights were with the children of men; and in Paradise, when the first promise broke upon the ears of the trembling, guilty pair, He ministered hope to the hopeless, life amidst the darkness. He ministered the prospect of victory under the darkest discomfiture and defeat, and ever afterwards, wherever the angel of the Lord, emphatically the Messenger of Peace, is brought into view, He is brought into view ministering. He ministered to the patriarchs and prophets, He ministered to Abraham, Isaac, and Jacob; and the promises of all revelation, the merciful interpositions and the wondrous deliverances that He has vouchsafed to His faithful, what were they but the ministrations of His grace, the manifestations of His love and power? And then, brethren, when He came into the world, what did He come to do? To minister. "Who, being in the form of God, thought it not robbery to be equal with God; but made Himself of no reputation, and took upon Him the form of a servant, and was made in the likeness of men." His whole sojourn here below was one of lowliness and submission and meekness; He showed no pride, no ambition, no lust of power, no desire of homage; and those who would have Him to be their servant and had God to minister to them for their salvation, these were they that He deemed to honour Him. His yearning desire was to help the helpless, to cleanse the impure, to give sight to the spiritually blind, to give ears to the spiritually deaf, to cleanse the spiritual leper, to give life to the spiritually dead; and when this was accomplished, then the heart's desire and purpose of the blessed Lord of all was accomplished. He was most in His element, if we might so speak, when He was most ministering. "I am among you as he that serveth."

How beautiful, above all, was this display, as He approached the depth of His humiliation for us; for when they sat around the last Supper, Jesus knowing all things, and that He came from God, and would return to God in all the fulness and consciousness of His Godhead, arose from the table, laid aside his upper garments, and took a towel and girded Himself, and poured water into a basin and began to wash the disciples' feet, and to wipe them with the towel wherewith He was girded; and then, when He sat down and resumed His garments, he said, "Know ye what I have done to you? Ye call me Master and Lord: and ye say well, for so I am. If I then, your Lord and Master, have washed your feet, ye also ought to wash one another's feet;" so ought ye to minister to the humblest and lowliest of my followers, out of love to me. "For I have given you an example, that ye should do as I have done to you. Verily, verily, I say unto you, The servant is not greater than his lord; neither is he that is sent greater than he that sent him. If ye know these things, happy are ye if ye do them." What a wondrous sight! What must angels and archangels have thought, what the powers and

7—2

principalities of the unseen world, looking down and seeing Him who had made them all, and whom they had adored and worshipped since they were in being,—what must they have thought as they looked down at this wondrous sight! They would contemplate it, and would behold no vain ambition or strife or envy or vain pride of perishing mortals. What grandeur and simplicity! what inaccessible and incomprehensible majesty was there! And then, brethren, in His betrayal, in His mockery, in the derision that He underwent, in the contradiction of sinners against Himself that He endured, in His agony, when His sweat was as great drops of blood, in His nailing on the cross, and in His languishing there—

"Lingering, bleeding, fainting, dying;"

in His stooping down to the sepulchre, in His rising triumphant from the grave, in His afterwards appearing to His beloved and chosen ones, and giving them such evidences that it was He that had died for them and that was raised again as He gave the unbelieving Thomas, till he was constrained to exclaim, "My Lord and my God;" in all this, what was He doing but ministering to us, the servant of all, the servant of sinners? "Ye know the grace of our Lord Jesus Christ, that, though He was rich, yet for your sakes He became poor, that ye through His poverty might be rich." Then, brethren, how in His ascension into glory, and His entrance into heaven itself, He still entreats for us and ministers to us. For what is He doing now at the right hand of God the Father? There He stands daily before the throne and pleads for those that come to God by Him, and He still is our propitiation and mediator. What, therefore, is He doing but ministering to those for whom He lived, and for whom He died, carrying out His glorious work till He consummates it in bringing in many sons and daughters to glory. And even then, the Scriptures teach us His ministry shall not be done; He shall still appear when the Judge of the universe in the attitude of him that serveth, for He says, if a man do His will He will make him to sit down with Him, and He will come forth to minister to him, He will come forth to serve him, subservient to the blessedness of His faithful people. It will be His delight to minister to them where there is fulness of joy, and pleasures for evermore at the right hand of God. He contributes to their good on earth; and to contribute to their ecstacy, and transport, and blessedness in heaven, will be the delight of that heart of which we read, that He sees of the travail of His soul in the salvation of sinners and is satisfied,—satisfied in serving, satisfied in the restoration, and exaltation, and perfection, and bliss of His reconciled and chosen people. "I am among you as he that serveth."

Brethren, oh, how glorious the result of that service! We can but glance at it. How He has served his people in order that they might be a forgiven people, restored to the favour and peace of God. His service has been effectual, for He has served them so that He has saved them; as the Substitute for them, He has accomplished what was needful in order that they might be accepted of God in harmony with and in glorification of all His perfections, His moral government, His immutable law. What a marvellous service! "In burnt-offerings and sacrifices for sin Thou hast had no pleasure." How could they make a sinner's peace with God? Wherefore, when He cometh into the world, He saith, Sacrifice and offerings thou wouldst not, but a body hast Thou prepared me to be the true, the one, the infinite sacrifice. Then He saith, Lo, I come to do Thy will, O God. He taketh away the first, that he may establish the second; He taketh away the shadow, that He may supply the substance; He taketh away the poor, earthly ritual, that could not avail, and gives the sinner peace. He is a just God in the vindication and manifestation of His holiness, that He may bring in the glorious economy of the gospel in which God is just in justifying, and man is saved, and sees sin to be most hateful, God to be most glorious, and Christ to be most precious. Then, again, He serves His people, and ministers to them in renewing them after His own image, He brings the same mind that was in Himself into them, He ministers in spirit to them, He ministers the beauty and glory of His own precious example to them, and teaches them, whilst they most thankfully receive that, His inestimable gift, they should daily endeavour that they may be changed into the same image, from glory unto glory, as by the Spirit of the Lord; He ministers to them effectually in keeping them through this evil world, comforting them in their sorrows, coming to them in the chamber of affliction, standing by them when they are sore beset with temptation and trouble, upholding them when they are ready to fall, rescuing them when they are almost overcome, teaching their hands to war, and their fingers to fight, their present help in time of trouble; He ministers to them on the bed of sickness, and when every earthly consolation fails them He draws near and says, "It is I, be not afraid;" He ministers to them in the dark valley, when human help is vain, and the dearest friends cannot help us any longer; when all must stay behind, and leave the pilgrim to go alone through the darkest stage of his existence,—even then Jesus is the friend, the servant, and the companion of His people, His rod and His staff they comfort them, and they are enabled to say, "Thanks be to God, that giveth us the victory, through our Lord Jesus Christ." Could there be a more touching, humbling picture of Jesus than He himself thus sketches for us? In one simple stroke it stands out in full and glorious manifestation: "I am among you as he that serveth." What a marvellous thought it is! We are ready to stumble and stagger at it, it seems incredible to us, but what was His whole life, His whole work, as developed in His Word, but a fulfilment, and illustration, and exemplification of this simple picture, "I am among you as he that serveth!" How it ought to humble us to think that we, amongst others, are rebelling against the yoke, kicking against the pricks. A man wants to grasp after some vain object that he thinks will give him more power, and position, and honour. What a mistake it is! That is never the way to be happy. We must submit, sooner or later. Can a worm of the dust refuse at last to submit to his omnipotent Creator? By our yielding we gain, by submitting we are elevated. "He that humbleth himself shall be exalted." "Be clothed with humility, for God resisteth the proud, but giveth grace to the humble." We should seek to follow the beautiful pattern of Jesus, and minister in our day and generation to others. "It is more blessed to give than to receive;" it is more blessed to help than to be helped; it is more blessed to wipe the tear of sorrow away, than to have it wiped away from our eyes; and if it is our privilege and advantage that we can minister, how we should enjoy it and delight in it. We shall never be happy while grasping and winning all for ourselves, but we shall be happy in making others happy, in diffusing happiness, and in abating misery, in being fellow-labourers with God, sympathising with His dear Son. Be assured of it, if you have no happiness and peace, it is because you do not love Jesus. The man who is continually serving, who feels "the yoke is easy and the burden is light," the man who has conquered himself, who has broken down his own proud spirit and serves Jesus, who is "meek and lowly of heart," to him the promise is fulfilled, and he finds rest to his soul, the only abiding, perpetual rest that cannot be taken from him.

Dear brethren, let us in drawing near the table of Christ seek to learn that lesson at this season, to have the mind in us that was in Christ Jesus, and learn to be willing to serve Him, to serve God, and serve our generation according to the will of God, serve any poor being to whom we can do good, for Christ's sake. Above all, let us see that Christ serves us. We can only serve Him as He serves us in forgiving us, in renewing us, in making all things work together for our good, leading them that would suffer in patience and peace in this afflicted world, to commit their souls to Jesus in well-doing, as unto a faithful Creator and most merciful Saviour, assured that He will be found a faithful servant as well as a faithful master to His people. This is alike the secret of their joy, the secret of their victory, the secret of their exaltation, that they can say with the great apostle, whose I am, and whom I serve."

XIII.

PARTAKING OF THE SUFFERINGS OF CHRIST.

"Rejoice, inasmuch as ye are partakers of Christ's sufferings."—
1 Peter iv. part of 13.

There is nothing that brings persons more intimately together than suffering together. To meet in the house of feasting may produce a superficial companionship; but to meet and mingle sorrows in the house of mourning tends to weld and knit together the affections of those who are brought into intimate sympathy, in a way that the mere sunshine of prosperous times never accomplishes. How often we find it in the family that, when the household is clothed in mourning, when they meet solemnly and silently around the sick-bed and the bed of death, when they have been brought to feel the depth of their common ties and common affections, they are wondrously strengthened in their mutual regard, or at least that regard is called into an activity and energy that it did not exhibit before. How common it is to find persons, who have been placed in circumstances of trouble and peril together, retain their intimacy through after life. Thus, I remember one saying to me that the men who suffered together in the siege of Lucknow, where they were in great peril of their lives, and were reduced to circumstances of the greatest extremity and want and distress, became almost as one family, and they were woven together in mutual affection and sympathy in a way that would have appeared inconceivable had they not passed through that bitter experience. And you find where a wrecked vessel has had its little crew embarked in the perils of a voyage on the deep, where they have been tossed upon the waves, and have gone through sore troubles together, they have ever afterwards had that passage of trouble and difficulty stereotyped upon their memories, and they have felt for each other as they never could have felt in any other way. It would seem that this principle is recognised in the higher and holier communion and fellowship that God's children are brought into, in that intimate endearment with their Saviour from partaking of His tribulations; it would seem that the way to appreciate Christ's sufferings and realise His intense love for us, and to have brought home to us His "bowels of compassion" and His yearning tenderness, is in the house of mourning, and that it is done there in a way that we have nowhere besides,—so much so, that I have known persons wake up to a sense of Christ's long-suffering on their own bed of anguish, and to feel it as they have never felt it before. This furnishes us with a key to what the apostle seems to have had in his mind when, having warned his suffering fellow-saints not to count it " a strange thing," as if something not to be looked for had happened, if they had trial, and persecution, and distress, and perplexity, but it would be strange rather if the Master drank the bitter cup and they drank the sweet one; it would be strange if they only passed along the smooth and easy path, when His path was marked with His footsteps of blood. They were not to count it "strange," therefore, but rather "rejoice" that they were "partakers of Christ's sufferings."

At this season of the Christian year,* on the verge of the season of Christ's special sufferings, the time we commemorate

* Lent, 1865.

and call them to mind is peculiarly appropriate to the passage before us, as it contains very much that is deep in experience, and much that is somewhat difficult and delicate in comprehension. We call your attention to it as alike seasonable to very many, and suitable for the few of God's children who are partakers in Christ's cup of suffering. May God bless the contemplation of the subject to our guidance and consolation.

The sufferings of Christ:—*that we should rejoice if we are partakers of these sufferings:*—these are the two great thoughts that present themselves on the very face of the passage.

The sufferings of Christ. We must take care that we do not take to ourselves a share in those sufferings, unless our sufferings are indeed akin to His own. It is not the mere suffering that is the ground of rejoicing, but it is the suffering the sufferings of Christ. The sufferings of Christ are very different from the sufferings of the great mass of mankind. It is true the Saviour suffered for sin, and St. Peter says so in the chapter before us, but then to suffer *for* sin and to suffer *from* sin are two very different things indeed. He did not suffer *from sin*, for he knew no sin, but was "holy, harmless, undefiled, separate from sinners;" but He suffered *for sin*, on account of sin, sin imputed, sin assumed for us by Him as our substitute. It is most important, then, that we should distinguish between the sufferings of Christ *for the sin* and the sufferings of Christ *from the sin*. He did not suffer *from sin*, for He had no consciousness or sense of sin; *personal* sin He could not have. It is true that our sins were so imputed to Him, that He underwent their penalty as though they had been His own; but in His own divine mind there could have been no sense of personal guilt, and it is a sense of personal guilt that sinks deepest into the heart of most who suffer, of most who sorrow. They sorrow most because they are overwhelmed with the presence of their own folly, and baseness, and rebellion against God, and the madness of their career. Were there no intermixture of personal remorse, the sorrow would lose half of its intensity. It derives its intensity largely from a sense of personal guilt. If we would suffer the sufferings of Christ we must beware we do not occasion our sufferings by our own wickedness, or backsliding, or rebellion; if we do, we largely shut ourselves out from all sympathy with our blessed Redeemer. It never must be forgotten that the blessed Redeemer had no sense immediately in His mind of the divine displeasure. If He had a sense of what was the debt of sin, and a mysterious concealment of the Father's face from Him in a way we cannot comprehend, no doubt He never lost the sweet sense of a Father's love. However, the Father might say, "Awake, O sword, against my shepherd," still in the deepest hour of Christ's darkness He clung to His Father, and His prayer was, "Father, into Thy hands I commend my spirit." When in the garden His soul was so overwhelmed, still He prayed, "O my Father, if it be possible, let this cup pass from me: nevertheless, not as I will, but as Thou wilt;" and when in His last hour, in the fearful struggle of His death, He cried, "My God, my God, why hast Thou forsaken me?" still it is "*My* God, *my* God." He never, therefore, felt that despair and sense of divine displeasure that drives to utter desperation; there was nothing of despair in His sorrow, and if we are to suffer as Christ did, we must seek to so love and serve God, that we may not have that fearful dark despair in our souls, in our sorrows, and in our struggles, which Christ cannot sympathise in, because He never had.

Then there is another distinction. The Redeemer did not look forward to any terror or fear beyond the grave; death to Him, though an hour of fearful conflict and struggle, was yet the passage to His Father's presence, and therefore

He said, "If ye loved me ye would rejoice, because I said, I go unto the Father." He was going to "His Father and our Father, to His God and our God," and therefore there was not that terror that is beyond the grave, which fills many often with apprehension on the bed of sickness and in the hour of death. There is nothing in death itself to make it so terrible. What is there in the mere pang of dying? There is often more pain in living than in dying, than in the disentanglement from the tenement of clay of the immortal inhabitant. That which constitutes the pain is the dark shadow that comes from beyond. The blessed Redeemer could not know this. Death to Him was the gate of life; He knew that He was passing from the cross to the crown.

Let us just look into the sufferings that were specially Christ's, and of which, when we suffer on His account, we may be said to know the fellowship of His sufferings and to be in communion with Him. And, first of all, the Redeemer's sufferings were largely from breathing a tainted atmosphere, and from walking amidst a corrupt world. The more pure a man's mind, the more he is distressed at the wickedness around him, distressed in heart to think how God is dishonoured and iniquity abounds, how God's good gifts and endowments are turned into instruments of misery and sin. He cannot help feeling this, and the more pure a man's mind is, the more is he full of tenderness and compassion to men, and ready to say with David, "Rivers of water run down mine eyes, because they keep not Thy law;" or as Jeremiah said, "Oh that my head were waters, and mine eyes a fountain of tears, that I might weep day and night for the daughter of my people!" "I am horribly afraid," says David, "because of the ungodly that keep not Thy laws." Wicked and foolish people laugh at sin, and make light at the dark crimes that abound around them, but a man with anything of the mind of Christ will feel sad, and be ready to mourn over the things others make light of.

Then we must recollect what was the intensity of the purity of the mind of Jesus, how He not merely saw the wickedness around Him, and heard the sounds of words of blasphemy, but He could see into the heart, and hear the unuttered thought within. Oh! to His pure mind what a constant source of distress and anguish to come in contact with such a world as this, and to have intercourse with those who were dishonouring his Father, who can tell? We know that sometimes He could not help uttering His feelings, as when He looked around upon the thoughtless and wicked men who surrounded Him; and when some who were His own disciples showed their want of faith, He said, "O faithless and perverse generation, how long shall I be with you?—how long shall I suffer you?" And when He came near and beheld the city, the inhabitants of which were about to bathe their hands in His blood, He wept over it and said, "If thou hadst known, even thou, at least in this thy day, the things which belong to thy peace! but now they are hid from thine eyes." And again, when He beheld and bemoaned their obstinacy and dark doom, "O Jerusalem, Jerusalem, thou that killest the prophets, and stonest them which are sent unto thee, how often would I have gathered thy children together, even as a hen gathereth her chickens under her wings, and ye would not! Behold, your house is left unto you desolate." We must not forget if evil, and sin, and misery, and folly, distress a man in the world at large; they distress him still more the nearer they come home. If they enter his own household, if they wound him through the side of those he most loves, and if he finds those he cherished and fondly set his heart upon have plunged into evil, and folly, and ruin, how it comes home to him and agonises his heart, and he feels as though the evil had come upon himself, he feels grieved to think how God is offended, and how those he himself has cherished have been accessory to it. And was it not so with the blessed Redeemer? He consented to become our brother, " bone of our bone, and flesh of our flesh," and He was " not ashamed to call us brethren." Marvellous that it should be so! Yet so it was. And when He " came to His own, His own received Him not;" " He was in the world, and the world was made by Him, and the world knew Him not;" and instead of meeting with a tender reception, He met with scorn and almost universal rejection, and insult, and mockery, and contumely. Oh! how great was His distress, that one that dipped his hand with Him in the dish lifted up his heel against Him, that another denied Him with oaths and curses, that another—though He foresaw His perfidy—should betray Him with a kiss. All this wounded the Redeemer; and when we, brethren, feel somewhat the same resentment for sin, somewhat of the same grief when God is grieved, somewhat of the same righteous indignation when God is dishonoured, we know something of the sufferings of Christ. Then how much of sorrow and suffering the blessed Redeemer knew, because of that wondrous way in which the world around Him was suffering for its own sin and its own guilt! What misery He saw and redressed! what deaf ears He unstopped! what lame feet He made to leap! what wondrous sorrow He saw as He went about in the streets working signs and miracles! how He sorrowed that they " would not come to Him that they might have life!" He came to bless them, and they treated Him as though He came to curse them; they met Him with presumption, and rejection, and reproach, and injury; His very sorrows were made subjects of congratulation, and His agonies were matters for insult and outrage!

Oh! if we suffer for His name's sake, we partake of His sufferings. It is not for our own misconduct, but because we are Christ's. The world hates us because it hates Him. Ought we not to drink of His bitter cup? Ought we not to share His cross? and then shall we not have cause to rejoice because we share it? It ought not to be a matter of shame and sorrow, but of humble thankfulness that we are counted worthy to share in any measure the cross He bore, to pledge Him in the cup He drained for us. We ought to rejoice that we partake of the sufferings of Christ. This seems a hard saying, and yet if God gives us grace to do it, we shall rejoice; and therefore St. Paul says, "and not only so, but we glory in our tribulation also; knowing that tribulation worketh patience, and patience experience, and experience hope; and hope maketh not ashamed." And so you "rejoice, inasmuch as ye are partakers of Christ's sufferings;" you rejoice that you have the honour put upon you of being considered the companion of your Master, as having fellowship with Him in His humiliation. Surely it is a matter of greater honour for a man to be suffering with an eminent and righteous man, than to rejoice and exult with a wicked and depraved man. Are there not circumstances in which friendship and love tell so powerfully that they will lead a man to be happy in suffering with those he loves and reveres, leading him to feel that he would rather go to the house of mourning than to the house of feasting? He finds that honour dwells with humility, and is oftentimes draped in sorrow, and, therefore, he can be reconciled to a state of suffering because it is suffering with those he loves. And so if we suffer with Christ, ought it not to be counted by us a privilege?

Let us not forget that "if we suffer with Christ, we shall rejoice with Him." No cross, no crown; no share in the mortification and crucifixion of the flesh, no share in the glorification of the body. The path of sorrow alone leads to the world where there is no sorrow. You find it even in things natural, a man must have the qualifications for the enjoyment of that which is to give him happiness. The musical ear that keenly feels the dissonance that disturbs it is more capable of appreciating the melody that ravishes it; and the eye most alive to what causes a feeling of repulsion has the steadiest appreciation of that which is refining and exquisite in taste. It is so in spiritual things; the man who has the keenest sense of sin has the greatest enjoyment in being freed from it for ever. And then, too, the Saviour has told us in His Word again and again, "If we suffer with Him, we shall also reign with Him." "If so be that we suffer with Him, that we may be also glorified together."

Who would not, therefore, count it a matter of rejoicing to suffer for Christ's sake? Thus it is said of the servants of God in heaven :—"These are they which came out of great tribulation, and have washed their robes, and made them white in the blood of the Lamb;" and, therefore, they are before the throne, nearest to Him to whom they were nearest on earth; nearest to Him in the hour of glory, as they were nearest to Him in His hour of sorrow.

. Then have we not reason to rejoice, because that blessed Redeemer in making us partakers of His sufferings, is making us partakers of His holiness. Affliction oftentimes makes a man worse. The house of trouble is not always the house of repentance and humiliation; it is sometimes the house of repining, and fears, and wrath, and sad rebellion; but where it is sanctified affliction—and participation in Christ's affliction will always be sanctified—then, indeed, He brings us through His own sufferings, that He may conform us to His own image, and stamp His coin with the image and superscription of the King, whose it is. Therefore, may we not rejoice in tears, and weep in joy, knowing that if we bear a part in Christ's kingdom here, we shall at last be made to enter that blessed kingdom, where the Redeemer, who has suffered with us and for us, tells us He will come forth and wait upon His people, and they shall sup with Him, and He with them?

You see, therefore, what is the character of the suffering we may rejoice in; and you see that we have abundant reason to rejoice in that suffering, if it be ours, because it is the suffering of Christ, who has called His people to share His sufferings. He tells them at the very vestibule, that they must deny themselves, and take up their cross, and follow Him. If there is no willingness to bear the cross and follow Christ, we have yet to learn the first lessons in the school of Christ—the hatefulness of sin, the preciousness of Christ, and the joy of sanctified sorrow. How sad a thing it is, then, to have sorrow and to have no sympathy with Christ, to have no share in the hope that our sorrows shall end in everlasting joy; how sad to go mourning through the world, and to go down in despair to the world to come, because we do not look up to Christ, and follow Him, and because we have nothing in common with Him! Do not pray so much that you may not suffer, as that you may suffer in fellowship with Christ, that you may bear His cross clearly stamped upon your breast, that you may be willing to take the cup the Father gives you, and to drink it without repining, and without murmuring. If you do not reap comfort and consolation from your trials, it is because you have not Christ in your trials. He must sanctify and alleviate them, and turn them into occasions of thanksgiving and gladness.

Let me remind you of one important point. If you suffer with Christ, you may well anticipate how soon your sufferings will be over. What are threescore years and ten of suffering? Oh, what a folly it is to make so much of this poor passing hour, and so little of that illimitable immortality to which we are going! Let us remember that "our light affliction, which is but for a moment, worketh for us" —for those who suffer with Christ—"a far more exceeding and eternal weight of glory." Let us remember, if it is indeed distressing and troublous to us to bear the bondage of corruption, what will be our joy when we emerge from it into the glorious liberty of the sons of God! What will heaven be when there will be nothing to distress or disturb us, when our joy will be the joy of the Saviour! as our sorrows were the sorrows of the Saviour; for He Himself has prayed for it, and it cannot but be fulfilled: "Father, I will that they also whom thou hast given me be with me where I am, that they may behold my glory, which thou hast given me."

XIV.

THE SUPREME AFFECTION.

"Set your affection on things above, not on things on the earth."—
Col. iii. 2.

WHAT the anchor is to the bark, that the affection is to the soul. Where the affection is set, there the soul tends; or, as Christ himself expresses it, "Where your treasure is, there will your heart be also." The affection signifies the bias of the soul in the pursuit of certain objects. The soul is *set*— a strong word—either on things on earth or on things in heaven. "No man can serve two masters;" and in like manner, no man can have two supreme affections. The very expression implies the necessity that there should be no rival to that affection which is enthroned in the heart. It is very difficult sometimes to ascertain where the supreme affection is fixed. There can be no doubt that it is fixed above when the heart is renewed by the Spirit of God; yet that heart may itself be unable to ascertain and determine at the time what is the ascendant sentiment of the soul, more especially when objects of deep interest and attraction in the present world surround us. Affection for these things need not be wrong, but it becomes wrong when it occupies an undue proportion of our interest and attention. It is peculiarly profitable, therefore, for the minister of Christ; indeed, it becomes incumbent upon him to direct attention to the transcendency of the things of God over the little, petty, passing, shadowy things of this sinful world, as showing to us that we may "rejoice as though we rejoiced not," that we may love as though we loved not, and that we may sorrow as though we sorrowed not. The meditation of such a subject becomes a servant of God, under all circumstances, and it is peculiarly seasonable at the present very interesting period in the history of our own vicinity,* following the very affecting and impressive scene many of us witnessed so recently—the display of human skill—showing what human ingenuity can accomplish, and the accompanying circumstances of show and display of ostentation and grandeur which inevitably attend such a scene. I need not suggest to you that it is too often the case that such scenes absorb the mind and affections beyond a due proportion, and lead away from the great thing, always pre-eminently great, important and interesting. Therefore, in beautiful harmony with the Collect of this morning, teaching us that it is God alone who can order our " unruly wills " and " affections," and can surely fix our hearts " where true joys are to be found," I take up the words of the apostle, " Set your affection on things above, not on things on the earth," and make them the subject for our instruction and meditation.

We shall endeavour to illustrate to you *the necessity of the admonition*, and *the nature of the admonition*. May God, who alone can quicken our souls, accompany His word with His own power, that we may be so aroused as to seek to have our treasure where our heart is—in heaven.

The nature and state of man in this present world is very peculiar. In order that we may form a just conception of it, we must recollect that, as man is of a twofold nature, physical and spiritual, so man has relation to a twofold economy—earthly and heavenly, present and future, temporal and eternal; that he has to do with certain passing scenes and

* The closing of the Art Treasures Exhibition, 1857.

things. He has to serve his generation according to the will of God; he has to give an account of his stewardship; and at the same time he has to do with the great realities which revelation unfold. He has to do with his Creator; he has to do with his Preserver; he has to do with his Judge; he has to do with his Ruler and Lawgiver; he has to do with his Redeemer; he has to do with that unseen world where to the wicked it is everlasting woe, and to the righteous it is everlasting blessedness; he has to do with angels, and with "the spirits of the just made perfect;" he has to do with the things of the present scene, where all is sublunary; and he has to do with the things of another world, where all is real, where all is final, where all is unmixed, and where all is eternal. Man has to do with the things of eternity, and he has to do also with the things of time; he has to do with the relationships of life—social, civil, and religious; and he has to do with the pursuits of life. Each man must do his duty in the state of life to which it has pleased God to call him. It cannot be otherwise; and God never intended that it should be otherwise. These things give a man pain or pleasure; they minister to his wishes or to his disquietude; and he is not insensible to all this. He is not to become a stoic, and crucify his natural feelings; nor is he to become a recluse, and withdraw from the world. He is not to abandon his duties; that is not the will of God, and that is not the duty of man. It is clear that God has made us susceptible of pain from certain things, and of pleasure from certain things; and he does not require us to undergo that pain, or to forego that pleasure, except as it is necessary for our duty to Him, and our preparation for our everlasting and distant home. Man is allowed to shun what is baneful, and to enjoy what is pleasing. Only let it be done in subordination and subservience to the will of God, and to his own all-important interests, then man is allowed to rejoice, and to weep, and to indulge his taste, and his imagination, and his affections. It is not annihilation of these, but it is subordination of these that duty requires. I need scarcely remind you that our danger lies not in the direction of giving an exaggerated importance to the things unseen, but in giving an exaggerated importance to things visible. Every man's consciousness and reflection will assent to the proposition that man is more in danger of setting too much value on things that surround him, than of setting too much value upon things that are above him. No; it may be doubtful whether man can duly estimate the things that are to come, and it is clear that nothing is more easy than to estimate the things that are perishable.

Let me show you by one or two considerations how imminent is our danger of setting our affections on things below.

It arises, first and chiefly, from this cause: that the things on earth are ever in contact with us. They are things that appeal to our natural senses, they force themselves on us, and require no effort on our part, for what is beautiful at once reflects itself on the mind, and we quickly take up with what is easy, and indulgent, and pleasing to the taste and touch. All that man has to do is to come in contact with these things; yea, he can hardly avoid them; the forms picture themselves on his eye, and force themselves on his ear, and enter into his soul almost whether he will or not. But it is not so with the things above, and with the objects of eternity. Hell must be realised and looked upon in order that we may be afraid of its terrors; heaven must be marked on the soul by faith, and must be grasped by that faith which is "the substance of things hoped for," in order to produce any impression upon the soul. So that you see things seen and temporal urge themselves upon us, and force themselves upon the affections, while things unseen and eternal must be solicited, must be sought, must be run after, must be seen in the mirror of faith, in order that they may reflect themselves upon the soul.

Nothing, then, is more clear than that things unseen and eternal stand at great disadvantage when compared with things seen and temporal, and unless man maintains a mighty struggle with a power and a strength more than his own, he cannot but be carried away by the things that "perish in the using;" and it is no marvel that he is carried along as by a whirlpool, without reflecting whither he is going or what is his destiny, until he plunges into a dread eternity, and wakes up with a knowledge of its true nature. It is not to be wondered at when we consider what man is, and what earth is, that nothing but the mighty power of God can bring the soul from under the dominion of things temporal, to realise the power of things eternal.

There is another fear, brethren, that still strengthens this view of the case, and it is this, that man in his constitution and in his moral state is not what he was when God made man; and therefore he labours under a fearful disadvantage in setting his affections on things above. No doubt, when man was in Paradise in purity and peace, when the image of God was implanted in his soul, the two relationships of man's nature—his relation to heaven and his relation to earth—were in beautiful harmony; then he gave to things present their proper affection, and to things eternal their transcendent affection, and all was harmony because all was holiness. But it is not so now. Man has come under the dark dominion of the world, has allowed the flesh to usurp the place in the soul, and has been led into temptation by "the lust of the flesh, the lust of the eye, and the pride of life," so that man is keenly alive to everything which appeals to his senses. He is spiritually dead, and, instead of being an unbiassed judge, he is warped by fearful idolatry, and he is fearfully unbelieving and indifferent to the future condition of man; therefore, the things of the present press upon him in such a way that he is prepared to receive every impression, and to yield himself up to the fascination of every hour, and he lets them lead him captive at their pleasure. Man, for the most part, walks "according to the course of this world, according to the prince of the power of the air;" he goes down the stream unresisting, and though conscience makes a temporary struggle to resist the downward flood it still rushes on, and at last he is utterly involved in it, and, in hopeless despair, he gives himself up to its power.

I think you will at once perceive, then, that there is need to exert ourselves, to set our affections on things above, and not on things on the earth. You will see that we gravitate earthward. When the king of Israel prayed, "My soul cleaveth unto the dust:" "quicken Thou me according as Thou art wont," he uttered the consciousness of trying to rise to heaven, and finding that he gravitated downwards, he exclaimed, "My soul cleaveth unto the dust." We doubt not that harm has been done, and many good men and ministers have done disservice to the cause of God's truth, by enforcing the entire renunciation of all earthly enjoyment and all earthly pursuits, which God does not require from us, and which would be contrary to our state and to His purpose. I am far from thinking it is wrong that we should exercise the faculties and cultivate the capacities God has endowed us with; I am far from thinking that it is wrong for the painter to use his pencil on canvas, and the statuary to make use of marble; I am far from thinking a man is not to cultivate his own self in all his parts and properties of body and soul, for God. The man who would not delight in what is ornamental and beautiful, who would not exert himself in endeavouring to maintain the life and vigour of his body, does not study to keep himself and make himself what God had made him, and intended him to become. The law of man is to advance, and it is sin that has hindered man from progressing. But then, whilst we doubt not this, we still less doubt that all this must be done to the glory of God, that we must act as feeling our responsibility as immortal beings in contact with the unseen world, and in our relationship with Him " in whom we live, and move, and have our being," ever seeking to please Him as the Lord of the creation, and to escape displeasing him as the one only evil in the universe. Man is not to set no affection upon his health, upon his family, upon its comfort, upon its greatness and its glory; he is not required to yield no impulse in the performances of art, and the achievements of human skill, and the discoveries of science; he is not to hold himself aloof from the commonwealth and family of which he is a member; he is to have his affections more or less engaged in these things, but then he is to keep the supreme supreme, the great point is to keep the ascendant ascendant; to see that the affection for the things below is as nothing to the affection for the things above. We must "count all things but dung," in comparison, that we may "win Christ." We are not to regard all things in the present world as if they were sinful in themselves; they are not so, but it is our corrupt heart that perverts them. In themselves, all things that God has made are "very good" and beautiful. Music is good and sweet; lights and shades, everything is good; therefore it is not in the thing itself that there is evil, but it is the abuse of the thing that renders it sinful. We may use God's good things in moderation and sobriety if the affection is centred upon heaven, in our occupations, in our pursuits, in our pleasures, in our enjoyments. If we live the life of faith, we walk with God whilst we mix with mankind; and whilst we pursue our ordinary calling, we convert it into a life of faith and obedience to God.

"*Set* your affections on things above, not on things on the earth." Oh! this, beloved, is the great point; *set* it, do not let it be an occasional yearning after a better state of mind; do not let your good purposes and desires be as "a morning cloud, and as the early dew," but let your anchor be "sure and steadfast;" let it be fast within, let it keep your little bark in dangerous currents and cross winds, until you steer true towards the haven where is your everlasting home. "Seek first the kingdom of God and His righteousness," and all other things shall be added thereto, and will follow in their proper order. "One thing is needful," that one thing therefore do. It would not be difficult, by arguments which none of you would be able to answer, to show you that this is man's true dignity and his true happiness, that this is his true interest and his true glory.

I pray you, therefore, beloved, bear with the word of exhortation. You have had, many of you, much to excite, much to please, much to gratify you; I beseech you, do not let these things usurp in your souls an undue place; do not let the spell of these enjoyments incapacitate you for communion with God, for spiritual work, for the day of holy rest, for the higher and better things that will be the things you will care for when you come to a death-bed, and the day of judgment. Do not be led away by the fascinations of the present hour, for, after all, what are they? In the late scene many of you witnessed there was much that was beautiful, much that was attractive, much that was pleasing, but what is it now? So it will be with everything you set your affections on, fleeing away, passing like a shadow. The fashion of this world is passing away. What does the sight you have lately seen signify now? All that is left of it is but the moral trace on you for evil or good; this alone will survive, all the rest will pass away, and be lost and forgotten. I beseech you seek to study, to know, and ascertain that your affection is supremely set "on things above."

You love your parents, if you have them still spared to you; you will love them in another world; you love your relatives and friends, and what is sweet to the taste, and pleasant to the ear, and beautiful to the eye; you naturally love these things, and I do not say you are wrong, but take care that all your love is not centred here. Is not your heavenly Father more to be loved, is not your Redeemer more to be loved, is not heaven more to be loved, is not the inheritance prepared for the saints in the life everlasting more to be loved than friends, family, fortune, rank, distinction, riches, position, and place? What are they all? and what will they be? Things are now what they will be then. Measure them aright, put them in the balance, and let eternity weigh as it ought to do, and the things of this life as they ought to do. "Set your affections on things above."

How is this to be done? Not by voluntary lacerations, not by fastings or by retiring to the cloister; it is to be done by the mighty magnet of the Saviour's love, by the mighty power of His Holy Spirit. We admit these eternal things; why do they not produce their effect upon us? It is through a want of faith! Oh for the strength of faith to come up to the power of God's word, then we should love the "things unseen and eternal," as we now do the "things seen and temporal." Let us pray God that He will realise to us this blessed faith; let us keep before the thoughts of our hearts the grand and beautiful rule of the apostle; knowing that "the time is short," let us "weep as though we wept not," and let us "rejoice as though we rejoiced not," and let us "use this world as not abusing it; for the fashion of this world passeth away."

XV.

SEEKING THE LORD THE GRAND DUTY OF MAN.

"And he did evil, because he prepared not his heart to seek the Lord."
—2 Chron. xii. 14.

There are few points on which men are more apt to run into extremes than that of where Infinite aid touches upon and intervenes with the responsibility of finite man. You find, on the one hand, some attaching so much importance to human effort, that they seem to overlook the necessity of divine succour, without which there is no effectual effort whatever; yet, on the other hand, there are those who, dreading this extreme, and perceiving its evil, rush into the opposite extreme, and make the grace of God a pillar of presumption instead of a starting-point of strength and vigour, and energy, and diligence. It is difficult to say which extreme is the worst. The one turns the grace of God into lasciviousness, the other turns the effort of man into self-salvation and self-righteousness. The truth is that they are both in beautiful harmony, if we did not make them discordant; that they are both combined, if we did not separate what God has joined together. It is not necessary to be able to trace the boundary line, we may be assured there is such a line, and that that line demands as much human effort as it requires divine grace. There is no true effort without divine grace, and there is no true divine grace without human effort as a consequence and result. The passage before us is very apt to this point. It brings before us very plainly, on the one hand, how God may be sought; and yet, on the other hand, why is it that men seek Him not, or if they do seek Him at all, they do not seek Him aright, and therefore they never find Him. It is of Rehoboam, the godless son of the godly Solomon, the foolish son of the wisest of men;—but grace is not hereditary; it is " not of the blood, nor of the will of man, but of God;" —it is of him, it is said thus briefly, but still giving us the key to his sad life, his idolatrous presumption, which led to the rending of the twelve tribes, leaving to the house of David only two tribes; it is said of him as the key to his whole character and conduct;—and mark it well, for you have here the ground and secret of the whole:—" He did evil, because he prepared not his heart to seek the Lord." A brief and sad picture of his course: " Because he prepared not his heart." That was the elucidation of the whole mystery and maze of his life.

The words, then, place before us three points very plainly: *The grand duty of man*, to " seek the Lord :"—*The way in which the Lord is to be sought;* we must " prepare our hearts" to seek Him :—*The fatal consequence of neglecting so to seek the Lord, and to find Him;* " He did that which was evil in the sight of the Lord." God grant that His Spirit may accompany His word, that we may be led, each one that has neglected to prepare his heart to seek the Lord, and that those who have sought Him may still persevere in seeking Him; for we must never cease to seek till we find Him in the fulness and light of His presence.

The grand work of man is to seek the Lord. All our faculties of mind, all our moral qualities, all our opportunities of life, all the discipline we pass through, all the chequered scenes through which we are led—the joys, the sorrows, the griefs, the pains, the sicknesses, the bereavements, the losses, the crosses we have to pass through, why are they sent but for this one end, to bring man to seek his God? We should not have had to seek Him if we had been born in a sense of His presence and the enjoyment of His favour; and so we should have been born if man had retained the image of God, if he had continued in His likeness. Then all our thoughts would have been truth; then all our emotions would have been holiness; then all our course would have been righteousness; then all our tendencies and all our desires would have been heavenward and Godward; we should have walked in the light of His countenance, we should have borne His perfect image, we should have done that which is right as instinctively as we now do that which is wrong, and we should have known that which is true and right as much as we are now in perplexity and darkness. Alas! for it; how fearful the fall, and how fatal, were it irreparable, and were there no return to God! But the glorious truth revealed to us in the gospel of Christ is, that God may be sought again. In one sense we cannot seek Him, and in another sense we need not seek Him. It may seem strange, but both are true, though it seem a paradox. We cannot seek in one sense: "Canst thou by searching find out God?" Alas! alas! what groping in darkness has been all moral philosophy, all the vain mythology of poor fallen man, the wisest we have ever had! You have only to read the works of Aristotle, and Plato, and Cicero, and Seneca, in order to find out that, after all, their best emotions, their loftiest thoughts, were but uncertain knowledge; and the greatest knowledge that has ever been found by human intellect unaided, by human science and philosophy uninspired, was never better than mere conjecture and uncertainty, mere day-dreams—often the most debased, and always the most uncertain. In the other sense, though it is useless to seek God by our own knowledge in the pages of science, as one said when he had read them all, "I have searched them all, and am more astray and more at sea now than I was when I began;" so the man seeking to know God by himself, by human wisdom alone, sets out on a bootless task, and bootless and fruitless will be his search. In another sense it is needless to seek to know Him by human wisdom alone. And it is not only needless, but it is presumptuous, it is blind infatuation. It is as if a man with the bright light of the sun were to kindle a candle at noon day, and turn his eyes down to the little flickering lamp he had formed instead of upward; it would be wiser in a man to do *so* than to reject the simplicity of the gospel, and to turn to the paltry glow-worms of human philosophy and science, and to pretend that he is seeking God, when, as the apostle says, He is not far off from any one of us. He that was beyond the reach and range of our loftiest conceptions, has come down to us in the person of His Son; so that, as Jesus says, "No man knoweth the Father but the Son." And again He says, "Believest thou not that I am in the Father, and the Father in me? He that hath seen me hath seen my Father." Yes, brethren, God in Christ is God nigh to us, God brought level to our capacities, God brought home to our hearts. A little child may know more of the true God by means of the gospel of Christ and the teaching of the Spirit, than Socrates, or Cicero, or Plato ever imagined or conceived. The noblest conceptions of earthly and uninspired men are nothing to the conceptions of the simplest peasant, of a poor widow woman, or of a little child, when taught of God. We may well exclaim, with the Saviour, "I thank thee, O Father, Lord of heaven and earth, because thou hast hid these things from the wise and prudent, and hast revealed them unto babes."

But now, brethren, though it is impossible and useless to seek a knowledge of God independently of God's teaching; though it is needless and useless for a man to seek it because he has got it in his heart, so that it may be beautifully said, as the apostle Paul says, "Say not in thine heart, Who shall ascend into heaven? (that is, to bring Christ down from above); or, Who shall descend into the deep? (that is, to bring up Christ again from the dead). But what saith it? The word is nigh thee, even in thy mouth, and in thy heart: that is, the word of faith which we preach; that if thou shalt confess with thy mouth the Lord Jesus, and shalt believe in thine heart that God hath raised Him from the dead, thou shalt be saved." So that a man needs not, as it were, to go to seek by human wisdom or wit; and, on the other hand, if he sought thus, the search would only lead to confusion and disappointment. All he has to do is to come as a little child, and receive the revelation of God in Christ, and then He "who commanded the light to shine out of darkness" will shine gradually into his mind, and "give the light of the knowledge of the glory of God in the face of Jesus Christ." "This is life eternal," to know "the only true God, and Jesus Christ, whom He hath sent." Nevertheless, brethren, a man will not find except he seeks the Lord, and the Lord will seek him first. He seeks him, to teach him to seek; He as it were turns him round, that he may find his way. The first impulse is divine, but it is our effort that follows. It is not less of man than it is of God. God works "*in* man to will and to do." He does not work *on* him, but *in* him; and so there is a beautiful harmony between the inworking of God and the outworking or onworking of man. It is not the mere intelligent conception of divine truth, it is not a mere speculation about Christ, or of what Christianity is, that is true Christianity: it is a personal, practical, experimental knowledge of Christ in a man's heart and spirit and whole course of life; it is becoming personally acquainted with Christ; it is the difference between merely reading about a man and coming into intimate contact and communion with him, interchanging soul with soul. There must be a "fellowship with the Father, and with His Son Jesus Christ;" and all short of this is but a mere creed—a mere theory. It is important in its place, but only as it leads to experimental religion. When it is experimental, then a man knows God and is known of Him; and if a man has not learned to love God in Christ, he has learned nothing yet as he ought to learn, he has not sought and found God.

This leads us to the next point, *a man must seek God as the grand end of his life.* He is here for the purpose, and if he accomplishes it he answers life's end; if he fails in it he fails in life's end. If a man is shipwrecked in this all is wrecked; but if he gains this all is gained. "What shall it profit a man, if he shall gain the whole world, and lose his own soul?" Far off from God, he perishes; near to God, and in communion with Him, he is saved for ever. Without that, life is a wretched bankruptcy, a miserable abortion; but when a man gains a true knowledge that Christ loved him, that he is accepted in Him, that he shall stand before Him in the great day as one that is uncondemned, as one to be welcomed into his Father's house, he has gained the grand purpose of life; and this is the grand purpose of life, whether we make it so or not.

Then we are led to think, how is this to be set about? how is it to be attained? Rehoboam found it not, because "he prepared not his heart to seek the Lord." Here, again, we are driven back upon human responsibility very distinctly. We have nothing to do with the secret purposes of God, but with our own duty and the responsibilities that rest upon us. It is not said he did that which is evil because God rejected him, or he was reprobate and outcast because God did not give him grace, or show him His favour; nor is it said that he did evil because Solomon showed him a bad example, and though he repented afterwards, yet left a sad blot upon his name; but it is said, "He did evil, because he prepared not his heart to seek the Lord." Had he sought the Lord and found Him, he never would have done the evil, he would never have had that fearful wail that accompanies his name continually, that he had rent Israel asunder, that he had broken up, as it were, God's commonwealth through his own wanton wickedness and folly. This we have brought home most clearly and distinctly to every man that is living without the love and obedience of God. And why is it? Is the door of mercy shut against a man? has there some sad calamity or fatality happened? has he not the same opportunities that others have? has God told him he is not to be saved? has he made trial of Him in honest truth and sincerity, with all his heart, perseveringly and determinedly, fully resolved not to turn back, not to draw back, not to be disappointed? has he felt that he dare not and could not come short of salvation? has a man been thus roused to exert himself to work, "to take," as it were, "the kingdom of heaven by violence," agonising to enter in at the strait gate, and to lay hold of eternal life? If he has done so, he has prepared his heart, he has made up his mind, his heart has been united to fear God's name. When a man is brought to that determination, he will be ready to cut off the right hand, or to pluck out the right eye, rather than to fail of finding God. He has turned his back upon Sodom's pleasures and indulgences, and turned his face towards Zoar, the city of safety; he has felt that it is not in the plain that there is safety, but on the mountain-side; and though he may have to encounter rocks, and precipices, and difficulties, and trials, and dangers, he presses onward, if only he may reach the city of refuge; he flees for refuge, "to lay hold of the hope set before him." Ah! it is the great thing to "prepare the heart to seek the Lord." Some never make the effort. The great object of life is to seek; it is our great work; we are to go about seeking until we find the pearl of great price. Yet, alas! there are many who say they cannot be saved, that they cannot find God, that all is difficulty, that all is doubt, that all is darkness. No; you have not " prepared your heart," you have not set about it in good earnest, you have not been led to leave all, to part with everything to find God. God has not been first, and you know He *must* be and ought to be. This is the first commandment with promise: " Thou shalt love the Lord thy God with all thy heart, and with all thy soul, and with all thy strength." If God is not first, He is nowhere; He will not be subordinate, He will not be second, His place is supreme, He must be enthroned over all, and you must be willing and should be ready to welcome Him and subordinate all your interests in life to that one great object, to please, to love, to serve, to glorify, and to enjoy your God. Oh, how few there are that thus prepare their hearts to seek the Lord! Ah! a divided heart has turned many aside. They were half-hearted, they halted between two opinions, they were like Agrippa, "almost persuaded." This is not to " prepare " a man's heart "to seek the Lord." A man must have his heart made up, he must have counted the cost, he must have been willing to part with everything that comes in his way, willing to set about whatever God requires. Rehoboam did not do this, though the son of a godly father. Doubtless he often had good convictions and good desires, but they passed away like " a morning cloud " and " the early dew." He never felt to want to know the Lord, and therefore he never knew Him in full assurance and enjoyment. His goodness had been like the morning cloud; though the Lord was prepared to meet him, he was not prepared to meet the Lord; though grace and salvation were within his view and his reach, yet he had not prepared his heart to receive them. Many a man who prays to be saved does not wish to be; many a man wishes to be saved, if he may retain some idol, if he may keep back some part of the price; but there must be no reserve, God will never accept a divided heart. The Israelites were forbidden to intermingle the linen and the woollen, there was to be no linsey-woolsey worn by them. Many say, Was not this a mere capricious, unmeaning institute? No; it taught them the great lesson that there must be but one warp in the garment of salvation, that a man must put on the *whole* armour of God, that he must be dressed in *all* the raiment of heaven, that he must not think to choose parts or portions, that he must not expect to wear this, and reject that. No, Jesus says, "If any man will come after me, let him deny himself, and take up his cross, and follow me." If any man come not to hate, in comparison with Me, even father and mother, he cannot be My disciple. We are to prepare ourselves, and whatever may be the conditions, or the requirements, or the struggles, or the difficulties to overcome, we must overcome them all in the strength of the Lord. "The kingdom of heaven," I again repeat, as Jesus says, "suffereth violence, and the violent take it by force."

Then, brethren, *how sad and fatal the consequences of neglecting thus to prepare our hearts to seek the Lord.* Rehoboam "did evil, because he prepared not his heart." There is a weight and a force sometimes in a simple expression of Scripture, which no exaggerated language or accumulated hyperbole can reach. How much there is in that one simple expression, "He did that which was evil!" His whole life was one course of rebellion and idolatry and obstinacy; such was his life, and such, we have reason to think, was his death; he lived in evil, and he died in madness. What a sad picture as we trace it up to its starting-point, "He prepared not his heart to seek the Lord!" How many young persons, well taught in Christian truth, well disposed and earnest at times, never come in after life to salvation. They live all their lives in evil, because they have never fully realised the necessity for decision; they have never felt the wish of the prodigal for his Father's house, or, if they have felt a wish, there has been no rising up and going home; whatever the shame and the sorrow for their past conduct might be, they have not gone towards home, never stopping till they reached their Father's table, and nestled on a Father's heart. Nothing short of coming home will do; but a man never will come home unless he has made up his mind to do so, unless he prepares his heart to come back. Do not let it be supposed that there is a kind of negative or neuter character. I have heard people say, I am not good enough to go to heaven, but I am not bad enough to go to hell; for if I look back on the course of my life, I have not been a thief, neither have I been an idolater, nor a murderer, nor a blasphemer, nor an infidel; surely I am not so far wrong. Ah! but God looks at the heart. The outward appearance may be very fair, but what is the inward appearance before the heart-searching God? Does He not ask for the heart, and will He be satisfied with anything short of it? Has He not promised to give you a heart of flesh instead of a heart of stone? Has he not promised to put His laws in your minds, and write them upon your hearts? Has that been done? Have you prepared your hearts for the divine engraving? Have you in your inward parts the laws of God drawn out in living characters? None but Christ, and nothing but Christ, can satisfy the soul, can give peace to the conscience, can enable you to bear the burden and the battle of life, and to face without dread the last enemy and the dark dread valley, can usher you into the awful realities of the unseen world, and enable you to stand undismayed before the judgment-seat of Christ. Have you felt this? have you realised this? have you made up your minds? You say you intend to do it hereafter, by and by, on the sick-bed, in old age, when you are weary of life, when you have done with present pleasures and pursuits; you are not yet prepared, you have some secret idol, you have some stumbling-block in the way. Ah! but you must make up your minds, you must not delay, for "the night cometh when no man can work;" and if you delay, the night may come upon you, and the man who has been purposing and resolving all his life dies, and the work is not done. And what a wreck and ruin it is! What an awful thing to awaken in the last hour, and find you are too late!

May you, who are invited to renew your covenant and to decide your choice, and whom I hope soon to meet again, and to urge and induce you to choose the Lord for your God, Jesus for your guard and guide—may you lay this passage to heart! It is a very weighty and a very practical one. Do you prepare your hearts to seek the Lord, and do it not in your own efforts, yet make your efforts in dependence on that grace that alone can make the effort effectual. Ask, that you may receive; receive, that you may use; and use, that you may receive more of the interchange between the spirit and the Father of spirits; then you may say, in the language of the psalmist, "My soul followeth hard after Thee; Thy right hand upholdeth me." And do not forget that if you have never prepared your hearts, you have reason to fear that you are doing evil, though man's eyes may not see it. Recollect that while man looketh at the outward appearance, God looketh at the heart. He wants to know whether the heart that was afar off has been brought nigh to Him, where there is safety; whether the dark mind has been illumined and renewed, the estranged mind brought into reconciliation and friendship. If it be so, if ye that were sometime afar off are now brought near, then to serve God is no longer a task, and a trouble, and a weariness, but joy, and delight, and perfect freedom. Lay this to heart, and consider it. A man must sooner or later prepare his heart to seek the Lord. He does not surely intend never to seek Him; surely he does not desire to be cast out from His presence for ever and ever! Distance from God is hell, nearness to God is heaven. Surely no man would choose to be far off; he must desire to be near. But he must not desire only, he must prepare his heart to follow his desire, he must give all diligence in the great work.

And, finally, my dear brethren, oh that those who have sought and found Him may not be content simply with having found Him, but may abide in nearness to Him. "He that dwelleth in the secret place of the Most High shall abide under the shadow of the Almighty." " He shall not be afraid for the terror by night; nor for the arrow that flieth by day; nor for the pestilence that walketh in darkness; nor for the destruction that wasteth at noonday." He shall feel calmness, and assurance, and security, whatever betide, because the great point is settled, the grand secret is found, the abiding and everlasting dwelling-place of immortality is secured; therefore he abides in God, and he rests in peace, come what may, and befall him what may.

XVI.

DIVINE TOKENS FOR GOOD.

"Show me a token for good."—Psalm lxxxvi. part of 17.

We are told again and again in God's Word that we are not to walk by sight, but by faith. To walk by sight is a comprehensive term, and includes walking by feeling rather than by faith. We are very strongly disposed to do so. We want something tangible and palpable, something sensible to our nature. The Jews required a sign, and professing Christians often want a sign; but the more simple our faith, reposing on the unchanging Word of God, the more pure and spiritual and elevated is that faith. Nevertheless, there is a desire for God's immediate and direct communication with the soul, there is a desire to feel the drawings of godly emotion, there is a desire to be assured that we are in the right way, and that our faith is of a genuine and divine kind, and that we are not deceiving ourselves, or are under any uncertainty with regard to our immortal state. It is allowable and right that this should be, because a man cannot be in earnest unless he wishes to be assured that he is right, and he is not on the wrong tack in his voyage heavenward. In seasons of doubt and darkness, and of depression, when our spiritual foes seem triumphing over us, and treating us as if we were at their mercy, as Satan sometimes will; in seasons when our minds are darkened, when we are thrown into timidity, and seem to be able to realise nothing of the Lord, when we seem to have loosed our moorings and to be tossing up and down upon the waves of the sea, there is at such seasons, especially, and naturally, such a desire as prompted the psalmist to pray the brief but beautiful prayer you have listened to. In a time of distress, when he was insulted by his enemies, and was getting but little strength to resist them, at such a time he prayed—and who is there that is earnestly anxious to feel accepted and safe in Christ, but will feel the same desire cross his mind?—" Shew me a token for good," give me some sign to assure me, and gladden me, and sustain me, and animate me in my struggle and conflict. This brief prayer, as many of you will feel, awakens an echo in our hearts, and if we proceed to dwell upon it for a little time, it will, if God bless it, be for our profit.

What prompted this prayer from the heart of the psalmist, "Shew me a token for good?" It is very clear that such a prayer will not be prompted from the heart when there is no desire after God, when there is no earnestness in seeking salvation, when there is no wish to be right. In such a man the prayer, if it go forth at all, will be in the direction of life, of prosperity, of deliverance from danger, of restoration from sickness, of escape from worldly calamity or disappointment. The natural mind, if it pray at all, will take no higher flight than the narrow horizon of the present state of things. To ask of God spiritual good, spiritual tokens of fatherly regard, implies that a man has been at least awake to a sense of knowing God and loving God, of being blessed of God, of having security and support in the law of his Creator and Preserver. A man must be in earnest who desires God to assure him and to establish his faith, and therefore the prayer was prompted, no doubt, in the psalmist by earnestness to know the Lord, to seek peace with God, to sustain his Christian conflict, to overcome "the world, the flesh, and the devil" in earnest, to obtain his full stature and measure. If he had been presumptuous and self-righteous; if he had believed in mere voice and vision, in vain impressions and vague imaginations, to give him assurance again, he would not have thus earnestly cried, "Shew me a token for good."

We conceive the prayer was prompted by another feeling —a feeling of earnest hope that his labour should not be in vain in the Lord, that He would not fail or flee him, that He would not leave him without succour in the hour of need, without strength in the hour of weakness, without light in the hour of darkness. Where there is no hope, there is no true prayer. When a man purposes and does not hope, he will not be encouraged to act upon his faith. If there be a trembling and following up, it must attract a man's heart to the place from which his hope comes, to the quarter from which he draws his hope; therefore I cannot conceive that, though the psalmist was in darkness and distress, he was not without hope. He believed that if he waited upon God, God would not ultimately deny a faithful soul; he hoped in his heart, therefore, and he prayed, "Shew me a token for good." And we need it, because I have no doubt the prayer was prompted by the psalmist feeling his hope deferred, and "hope deferred," we know, "maketh the heart sick." It does make a man's knees more feeble if he waits and sees no light, if he draws and finds no strength. If he endeavours and trusts, and his faith seems not to be regarded by his God, then a man is apt to think, Surely I am wrong, or God would not thus keep me waiting, and let "the clouds return after the rain;" surely He would not thus let the day seem to go backward, and the morning thicken with clouds again, and darken my horizon; surely there must be something wrong. Hope deferred, therefore, leads the soul to pray, "Shew me a token for good," let me have some evidence and assurance that I am right, though Thou regard me not; give me some assurance that though I walk in darkness it is not because Thou hast deserted me; let me feel that thou art shining though still behind a cloud, and that at last Thou wilt assuredly come, and wilt not tarry. "Shew me a token for good."

Then we may just consider what the prayer implies, what the psalmist meant. I do not conceive he meant, as some men mean, Give me some visible sign, some tangible, sensible token, a whisper even from Thee, to tell me I am accepted. These impulses of enthusiasm have been common in all ages. There seldom has been a time but the superstitious have been wanting some tangible sign of this kind; but I do not think anything in the Word of God warrants this, for the evidence is complete: "If they hear not Moses and the prophets, neither will they be persuaded though one rose from the dead." You generally find the man who is wanting some visible and sensible sign is wanting not to believe at all, but rather to have his unbelief confirmed than his belief strengthened. His "heart is not right with God," he will not believe, and he wants to justify his unbelief by challenging God, and tempting the Most High in asking of Him a sign, when He has given him abundant promises that cannot fail. I do not conceive that the psalmist desired any miraculous interposition, that his enemies should be destroyed suddenly, or that the lightning, or thunder, or a messenger from above should tell him that his name was written in the Lamb's book of life. Assurances of this kind are not vouchsafed to us, and it would not be well for us if they were; therefore the psalmist did not desire such a token as this. The token he desired was that sweet sense of God's favour and love towards him which he longed for, and for which he prayed so earnestly in the 51st Psalm, "Restore to me the joy of Thy salvation," where he pleads, "Uphold me with Thy free Spirit;" give me a blessed perception of Thy favour towards me; apply Thy promises to me in such power and conviction, that I shall doubt Thee no more; give me that inward power and strength, that I may be rooted and grounded in Thy truth, for which I so much long and desire. Therefore our desire should be that God would indeed give us, I will not say a sensible and perceptible token of His favour, but so put forth joy in the soul that we should feel glad; so put forth His power that we should feel enriched in running the way of His commandments, and no longer halt in the way, "faint, yet pursuing;" not cast down and disheartened, but be enabled to rise above the waves and winds, pursuing one pathway, and never swerving to the right or to the left. "Shew me a token for good" in my secret soul, in my emotions with the Holy Spirit, give me much assurance, and holy confidence, and heavenly calmness, and peaceful serenity, that I may "run the way of Thy commandments," that my spiritual and temporal foes may be put to shame, because they see the Lord is on my side, and may know that if they fight against me they will fight against God, and I shall be "more than conqueror," as is beautifully said. "Shew me some token for good; that they which hate me may see it, and be ashamed: because thou, Lord, hast holpen me, and comforted me." Give to me "beauty for ashes, the oil of joy for mourning, the garment of praise for the spirit of heaviness;" then my spiritual foes, my enemies, will say, This is the Lord's finger, this is His mighty deliverance: He has bound up the broken-hearted, and has set him free to run the way of God's commandments. "Shew me some token for good; that they which hate me may see it, and be ashamed."

Now let us just notice how an answer is very often vouchsafed to such a prayer, how God can give us most easily and evidently such a token for good. He does it in His own time and in his own way. We must not be impatient if God seems to make as if He heard us not. We know that Jesus made as though He heard not the poor suppliant who said, "Lord, help me;" for He turned aside, and seemed to turn a deaf ear; and when He did answer, it seemed rather in the way of injury than of blessing; for he said, "It is not meet to take the children's bread, and to cast it to dogs;" but the poor woman would take no denial, and borrowed a fresh plea from the very denial of Jesus, and turned it into a prayer, "Truth, Lord: yet the dogs eat of the crumbs which fall from their master's table." She could not and would not be denied, therefore He gave her the token she desired, "O woman, great is thy faith: be it unto thee even as thou wilt. And her daughter was made whole from that very hour." So we must not be impatient. We know how David himself, though he said, "Shew me some token for good," had to wait for that token. He said, "My soul waiteth for the Lord, more than they that watch for the morning." His soul, therefore, had to wait, and still he says, "In thy word do I hope;" I am sure the Lord will, must, and does answer, and though I cannot perceive it yet, I shall by and by, when the night will become clearer: then I shall know it is day, when the clouds will break, and the sun shall shine upon me again.

Yes, God *can* and *does* give tokens for good. Let us look at what may be. Suppose a man gets into perplexity and distress of mind,—it may be about his family, or in whatever way it pleases God,—he learns to see his way through these difficulties, he learns to see a blessing, and to make his path plain, he no longer allows it to be hedged about with difficulties. Cannot God immediately give him a token for good, by shedding such light in his pathway that all is clear? And even if he has to go in the dark, and feel his way step by step, he is willing to be led on the way without being able to see the end, or even a step before him. And how God can give him a token for good by giving him perfect acquiescence in the state he is placed in, and enabling him to feel that he can walk in the dark as well as in the light! How easily God can make a difficult way plain! How easily He can say, "This is the way, walk thou in it," and when His troubled servant would turn to the right hand or to the left, He will keep him straight on in the right path; he grasps the hope set before him, and knows it is the Saviour who has said, "Thy sins be forgiven thee." He wants at the same time the joy that flows from such assurance. If the voice of Jesus said, "Thy sins be forgiven thee," what liberty would flow! Could I have that assurance, I would gladly bear all the world, the flesh, and the devil can heap upon me; let me get a smile from God, and I care not who frowns. Surely God is able by His power to give some such divine demonstration as shall completely take away all doubt and despair and distress; so that the soul shall spring, as it were, from the dust, and rise with triumph to the skies. "They that wait for the Lord shall mount as do the eagles; they shall run, and shall not be weary; they shall walk, and shall not be faint." Therefore God can most easily fulfil the prayer, by giving at once light instead of darkness, by giving joy instead of heaviness. How remarkably it is illustrated and represented in that lovely picture of Bunyan's, where we are shown Christian on his way to the Interpreter's house. When the burden that he has long borne, and of which he is weary, causes him to walk with tottering footsteps, at once, when he comes in sight of the cross, and sees the open sepulchre at the foot of the cross,—to indicate how Christ was raised for our justification, having died to pardon our guilt, which no longer rests upon us,—immediately, as we are told in that wonderful parable, the burden, that had so long been clinging to him with a deathly embrace, was loosed from his shoulders, and, falling to the ground, rolled and rolled, and never stopped till it was plunged into the open sepulchre, and so he felt it no more. What a striking picture of how God can by a single glance at once change a burden into liberty, and give a man holy emotions and delight in God's service he never enjoyed before. "The joy of the Lord is your strength." When we joy in Him, all nature seems glad; everything is illuminated in a moment by the light of His face.

Again, you can conceive the Christian man long struggling hard to get rid of bad thoughts, and evil desires, and sinful tempers, and the sudden assaults of the wicked one, and the fiery darts that so much trouble him. He sometimes seems so entangled and embarrassed that he sees no way of escape. But how easily God can put the enemy to flight. He can speak the word, and he must depart to his own place. It is not without God that Satan is permitted to tempt us. It is perhaps to lead us to a more earnest desire for the light of God's countenance that Satan is allowed to assault us, and in order that his defeat may be the more signal, that the enemy may "be ashamed." We often find that long doubt and difficulty will flee away immediately, and there is a remarkable departure of the enemy from the tempted person through the simple application of a single passage of the Word of God, as when in the case of a tempted and tried servant of God, who had almost given up in despair, at last there came home to him with irresistible force the beautiful language of the prophet, "Rejoice not against me, O mine enemy: when I fall, I shall arise; when I sit in darkness, the Lord shall be a light unto me." And so it was; the enemy did depart from him, the light of God shone upon him, all his outward troubles and trials seemed as nothing to him; even "when I sit in darkness, the Lord shall be a light unto me." And so we might pursue the various phases and vicissitudes of Christian feeling, we might show you the soldier of the cross in adversity and dismay and difficulty, we might show you how immediately the Lord has power to give him deliverance. He speaks the word, and he is made whole; He brings him to His truth, and it at once sets him free; for one touch of divine truth can at once allay the temptation. We know how sometimes God gives it in a different way to what we expect. We want deliverance, and he gives support; we want light, and He continues darkness, as with the apostle Paul, who was buffeted and tried, who prayed thrice to the Lord that He would deliver him; but the answer was not deliverance, but more than deliverance, it was a sustaining power: "My strength is made perfect in weakness;" and therefore he says, "I would glory in my infirmities." Thus can God give an answer—not a sensible, tangible one, by removing the difficulty—but by making it light to bear, and enabling a man to go on his way, as one that is "sorrowful, yet always rejoicing."

You see, therefore, that this short prayer is a very full one, and a very beautiful one, and we have oftentimes occasion to offer it up to God, though we must not go on walking by sensible feelings, and if we have no joy and assurance, therefore draw back, having "put our hands to the plough." We must not think that it is in vain to wait upon God. To do so is a sad mistake, and would be requiring a sign when we ought to be satisfied with the promises and assurances of God. It is allowable, and natural, and right that a man should desire much of holy comfort, and joy, and liberty, and peace; not simply for his own comfort—that might be selfish—but for God's glory; not simply to be happy in religion, but more successful in his conflict against the world, the flesh, and the devil, for "the joy of the Lord is your strength," when a man is strong to overcome temptation and sin; therefore, I do not think the prayer is wrong, or that it is anything but a most natural one, and we cannot help but oftentimes find occasion for it.

If then you have never desired any token for good, you are not in earnest, because, though we are not to walk by sense, but by faith, at the same time, what is true religion but experimental religion, the religion of the heart? It is not a mere thing of notions and theories and creeds. A man may have his intellect enlightened, and not have his heart influenced and impressed; he may have no desire for God, no sorrow for sin, no joy in Christ, no comfort and hope, no fellowship and love, no "bowels of mercy," because his heart is not right with God, because there is no dedication of his heart to the Lord. God says, "My Son, give me thine heart." Light is necessary, but it is not enough. To have the intellect illumined is necessary, but it is not enough, unless it leads to moral feelings and impressions, unless there is a fellowship with the Father and with the Son and with the Spirit. Where there is the inward trial, the inward sorrow, the inward conflict; there is the inward joy, the inward emancipation, the inward going continually and running in the way of God's commandments; and hence the joy and love and liberty to enrich a man's soul. Therefore do not make light of experimental godliness—sigh after it, pray for it, seek it, and though you may be long before you enjoy it, still hold on and hold out. Though it tarry, wait for it, and at last "it shall come, it shall not tarry." "Now the just shall live by faith; but if any man draw back, my soul shall have no pleasure in him.'

Then I would say to those who are in perplexity and darkness, Do not be impatient, "wait upon the Lord—wait, I say, upon the Lord." Again and again the Psalmist says, "Wait upon the Lord, wait all your appointed time." Perhaps it seems to you that it is put off when you are in a troubled and disturbed state, and that it would be far better if you had a smooth and steady light; but "judge not the Lord by feeble sense."

You know not what is best for you. You have undertaken to be in God's hands as a little child in the hands of its father; and if you have given your hand to God, you must not begin all at once to think, my God and my Lord has forgotten me. You know the people of God murmured of old, as is expressed in Isaiah, and what does God say in reply to them? "What sayest thou, O Jacob, and speakest, O Israel, My way is hid from the Lord, and my judgment is passed over from my God? Hast thou not known? hast thou not heard that the everlasting God, the Lord, the Creator of the ends of the earth, fainteth not, neither is weary?" How beautifully that comes in. Is the mighty God then unable to help thee? What is Satan's enmity to thee if God can hold thee up in a moment, and make thee conqueror over all that opposeth thee? Though the waves pass over you, He can at once say, "Peace, be still." Can He not do it? Then why does He not do it? why does He act mysteriously? why are clouds and darkness round about Him? Can we search His understanding? Who art thou, O man, that thou shouldest reply against God? As the heavens are higher than the earth, so are God's ways higher than our ways, and His thoughts are higher than our thoughts. Then, if it be so, He is not more omnipotent in power than He is omnipotent in wisdom. "Tarry thou the Lord's leisure;" this is the way to come off more than conqueror, and "in due time we shall reap if we faint not;"

joy shall arise in darkness; and though we see it not amidst the tares, joy is already in the furrow; it is there bursting and fructifying, and is only waiting the time of God to break forth in a harvest of gladness and victory. Plead the prayer, and leave the result to God, leave it entirely in His own discretion, and remember that there is no searching of His understanding; then, at last, when joy and peace come, how they will be sweetened by the bitterness through which you have passed, how they will be increased by the very fasting you have undergone!

Finally, remember that these tokens for good are only to cheer us through the cloud and conflict till we enter the blessed world where we shall need no more medium of communication, no tangible or visible representation of joy, because all will be light, all will be joy, and all will be praise.

XVII.

ACQUAINTANCE WITH GOD.

"Acquaint now thyself with Him, and be at peace: thereby good shall come unto thee."—Job xxii. 21.

"Some," says St. Paul, in the 15th chapter of the 1st Corinthians, "have not the knowledge of God: I speak this to your shame." And what can be more shameful than for the creature not to know his Creator, for a man who lives and moves, and thus has being in that Creator, not to be acquainted with Him to whom he owes everything, who can curse him for ever, or bless him for ever, whose smile is the light of heaven, and whose frown is the darkness of hell? Yet how very sad it is to find that there are multitudes, even of those called by the Christian name, who have no right knowledge whatever of the God with whom they have to do. They have certain notions of His name, but they have no acquaintance with Him. The solemn advice given to Job by one of his friends may well be given to every one of us,—"Acquaint now thyself with Him,"—that is, with God,—"and be at peace: thereby good shall come unto thee."

You see that *we are to become acquainted with God:* and you see what was *the unspeakable blessing that flowed from that source.* May His Spirit teach us in His Word, "that we may know Him the true God, and Jesus Christ whom He hath sent," and "whom to know is life eternal."

If it were merely "*know* God," it would not carry with it the intimacy of connexion which the expression employed does carry. Many men *do* form a certain knowledge of God as far as nature can teach them, and reason can guide them. "The heavens declare the glory of God; and the firmament showeth His handiwork;" they have a voiceless music that tells of the hand that made them. And no doubt there are many who form somewhat of a grand and general conception of God in nature; they hear His voice in the thunder, they hear His whisper in the breeze, they see His beauty in the blue sky, and His magnificence in the ocean and the landscape. There are men who can think and write some grand things about God and nature, about His attributes, about His omniscience, about eternity, about immutability, and the other conceptions and attributes of God, such as truth, justice, faithfulness, and equity; but then they are not "acquainted" with God. If you want to think and know about a man, and be acquainted with him, that implies personal communion and intercourse, personal knowledge. It is a far more expressive term than merely to say you know a man, or know about him. To be "acquainted" is to know as a friend one whose communion you have cultivated, one with whom you have formed a more intimate personal conception than can be formed by any hearsay or general representation. The "acquaintance" a man wants with God is the acquaintance a child has with its father, as one in whom all hopes rest, in whom all happiness centres, and which is no mere distant, vague, general, undefined, uninfluential speculation or theory, but is a realizing, personal, practical, living, loving union and intercourse. To be "acquainted" thus with God is beyond the power of nature to inform us, it is beyond the page of Providence to disclose to us. All that these tell us of God might do if man was unfallen and innocent, might do for man in Paradise, with "the candle of the Lord" undimmed within him, and the image of God unblotted in his soul. In that happy state it might suffice, if we were with God, and walking with God, having entrance amidst the fair things that surround Him, partaking of the sweet scenes around, hearkening to the music within and the music without, and having purity abroad and purity at home. But it is not so; and man naturally and instinctively dreads God, and shrinks from Him; he likes not the thought of the Almighty, and if he dares to speak out from his ungodly heart, he is disposed to adopt the language of the psalmist: "no God for me,"—for that is the Hebrew of "the fool hath said in his heart there is no God,"—no God for me, let me not be disturbed. Is not that "the carnal mind" that "is enmity against God?" Is not that "the natural man" that "receiveth not the things of the Spirit of God, for they are foolishness unto him, neither can he know them, because they are spiritually discerned?" "Depart from us," they say to the Almighty, "we desire not the knowledge of Thee." There cannot ever be "acquaintance," there cannot ever be communion, there cannot ever be anything like intimate intercourse between a being thus debased and depraved, and the holy, holy, holy, Lord God Almighty, who is "of purer eyes than to behold evil, and canst not look on iniquity," who charges His angels with foolishness. How can man be clean or accepted of God? It is very clear, then, brethren, if there were no other manifestation than such as nature, and providence, and philosophy can disclose, and define, and elicit, and ascertain, there is naturally no real "acquaintance" with the great God.

But He condescended to come nigh to us, that we might draw nigh to Him;—He condescended to approach us through and by that wondrous plan of intercession and propitiation by His beloved Son, and He hath brought those nigh who were afar off, He hath "broken down the middle wall of partition." He hath made peace by the blood of the cross, bridging over the pass by His own precious blood. It is, therefore, only in Jesus that God can become our Father, that we can become "acquainted" with Him, that we can confide in Him, that we can have communion with Him; it is in Jesus only that God is known and seen in His moral perfections and in His new aspect. As John the Baptist said, "No man hath seen God at any time; the only-begotten Son, which is in the bosom of the Father, He hath declared Him;" and Jesus himself says, "No man knoweth . . . . . the Father, save the Son, and he to whomsoever the Son will reveal Him;" and when He was speaking to His disciples, and they could not fully understand Him, He said, "No man cometh unto the Father, but by me." "Philip saith unto Him, Lord, show us the Father, and it sufficeth us. Jesus saith unto him, Have I been so long time with you, and yet hast thou not known me, Philip? he that hath seen me hath seen the Father; and how sayest thou then, Show us the Father? Believest thou not that I am in the Father, and the Father in Me?" "In the beginning was the Word, and the Word was with God, and the Word was God." "The Word was made flesh, and dwelt amongst us (and we beheld His glory, the glory as of the only begotten of the Father), full of grace and truth." He is "the brightness of His Father's glory, and the express image of His person." A little child that has faith, and is taught by the Spirit of God to know God in Christ, in His word and gospel, knows more of what is beautiful, and grand, and true, and lovely, and great, and good, than Cicero with all his learning, or Socrates with all his philosophy. Men that prate about gods many, and boast and write upon their altars as they of Athens did—"To the unknown God,"—they know not God; but you know Him if you believe in Him. Where the Spirit is, there is God. 'What! know ye not that your body is the temple of the Holy Ghost, which is in you, which ye have of God, and ye are not your own?" Therefore it is only through Christ, by studying His Word, by knowing God as revealed in the economy, and work, and mediation of His dear Son, that any Christian becomes "acquainted" with God. Oh, then it is entire submission and intimate "acquaintance" with Him as He is; not as man is with man, but with one most "just and true," with one who is "of purer eyes than to behold evil," who "will by no means clear the guilty," and will assuredly punish the sinner; for, "heaven and earth shall pass away, but not one jot or tittle of His law shall pass till all be fulfilled." But, at the same time, He is a Saviour; while He is just, He is infinite in grace; while fathomless in truth and justice, mercy and truth are combined, peace and righteousness embrace in the work of Jesus; so we know that "through Him we both have access by one Spirit unto the Father," we have entrance and access to the holiest of all, and now, in Christ Jesus, God is known, He is with them as a Father and Friend, and they can look up to Him and say, "Whom have I in heaven but Thee, and there is none upon earth that I desire beside Thee;" they can say, "Thou, O God, art the thing that I long for;" "My soul, wait thou only upon God; for my expectation is from Him." Blessed acquaintance with God! And as it is through the Word that the Father is revealed, so it is by the Spirit that He is revealed to the heart and soul. "God, who commanded the light to shine out of darkness, has shined in our hearts, to give the light of the knowledge of the glory of God, in the face of Jesus Christ." He shines into the hearts of those who come to Him by Christ, and they all "with open face beholding as in a glass the glory of the Lord, are changed into the same image, from glory to glory, even as by the Spirit of the Lord." "For no man can say that Jesus is the Lord but by the Holy Ghost." It is the Spirit, therefore, that brings the soul into acquaintance with the Father, through the Son. His beloved disciple says—"That which we have seen and heard declare we unto you, that ye also may have fellowship with us: and truly our fellowship is with the Father, and with His Son Jesus Christ;" and Jesus Himself says,—"This is life eternal, that they might know Thee the only true God, and Jesus Christ, whom Thou hast sent."

Then, brethren, how unspeakable are the blessings which flow from this high and holy "acquaintance" with God. Thus, it is said, "Acquaint *now* thyself with Him, and be at peace: thereby good shall come unto thee." These are two short expressions, and no man can comprehend them fully, or exhaust them. First, to be at peace does not mean what so many are chasing and following; it does not mean the shadow, but the substance; it means abiding peace. "The wicked are like the troubled sea, when it cannot rest, whose waters cast up mire and dirt. There is no peace, saith my God, to the wicked." There may be insensibility, but callousness is not peace; there may be delusion and self-ignorance, but that is not solid serenity—it is not abiding safety. A man might as well deem his house safe if built on a quagmire, as to build his peace on ignorance. A man may have a kind of peace in forgetfulness; he may forget what he is, he may forget why he is, he may forget death, he may forget judgment, he may forget hell, he may forget God, he may forget eternity; he may cast all these out of his mind, as multitudes do. Men often succeed in brutalizing themselves, in sensualizing themselves, in carnalizing themselves. Alas! that men should reduce themselves to brutes, and then call it peace. Peace! alas, what peace! while you are at war with Omnipotence? what peace! with guilt behind you and hell before you? what peace! when a man has no certainty for an hour, nor for a moment, for the breath that is in him? what peace! when he has no certainty where he is to spend his eternity? Can a man be at peace in spite of God? Can a man defy the Almighty and come off conqueror? Therefore, there *can* be no peace worthy of the name until a man is at peace with God. "Being justified by faith, we have peace with God through our Lord Jesus Christ. "There is therefore now no condemnation to them which are in Christ Jesus, who walk not after the flesh, but after the Spirit." And Jesus himself hath said, "Peace I leave with you, My peace I give unto you; not as the world giveth, give I unto you." O brethren, what a blessing is this—what a seal of pardon is this, "That they might have peace!" Where is there one who does not wish to be at peace? where is there a man who has not a secret lurking desire for it? Men will not go the right way to obtain it. They will have peace with the world and the devil, and expect peace with God as well. That will never do. A man must cast down his arms, and capitulate unconditionally with God, and have his heart bound with cords; he must have his iniquity blotted out as a cloud, and then may he look up with full and solemn peace and say, "It is God that justifieth, who is he that condemneth? It is Christ that died, yea, rather, that is risen again, who is even at the right hand of God, who also maketh intercession for us." "I am persuaded, that neither death, nor life, nor angels, nor principalities, nor powers, nor things present, nor things to come, nor height, nor depth, nor any other creature, shall be able to separate us from the love of God, which is in Christ Jesus our Lord." Is not this peace? "Acquaint now thyself with Him, and be at peace?" You will never get peace until you thus seek it, and thus find it.

Then, brethren, it follows—can it be otherwise?—"Thereby good shall come unto thee." It does not say what particular good, but it leaves it open and wide; just like that glorious promise, "We know that all things work together for good to them that love God;" and that beautiful passage in Isaiah, "How beautiful upon the mountains are the feet of Him that bringeth good tidings, that publishes peace; that bringeth good tidings of good, that publishes salvation." All in one, for when we have that good, we have all in that good. "He that spared not His own Son, but delivered Him up for us all, how shall He not with Him also freely give us all things?" If you have that one great pearl, the peace of God, then "all things are yours; whether Paul, or Apollos, or Cephas, or the world, or life, or death, or things present, or things to come; all are yours, and ye are Christ's, and Christ is God's." Oh, brethren, the portion of him who is "acquainted" with God! He can indeed say, Depart what may, befall what may, strip me as you will, bring me ever so low, make me ever so poor, "Thou wilt keep him in perfect peace whose mind is stayed on Thee, because he trusteth in Thee. Trust in the Lord for ever, for in the Lord Jehovah is everlasting strength." Then, brethren, good must come to him who has God on his side. Acquaintance with God is acquaintance with pardon, acquaintance with purity, acquaintance with strength, acquaintance with consolation in every trial, acquaintance with light in every darkness, acquaintance with hope in every disappointment, acquaintance with riches in poverty, acquaintance with health in sickness, acquaintance with life in death, acquaintance with glory in eternity, where there is "fulness of joy," and where there are "pleasures for evermore." "Eye hath not seen, nor ear heard, neither have entered into the heart of man, the things which God hath prepared for them that love Him." O brethren, is not this good past all conception? is not this good such as becomes an infinite God to give to poor, needy, ruined creatures? and is He not able to "supply all your need according to His riches in glory by Christ Jesus?" What is there that God will withhold from you, when He did not withhold His own Son?

How beautiful the exhortation then, and how large the promise: "Acquaint now thyself with God, and be at peace: thereby good shall come unto thee." Are there not many who are sensible in their inward minds that they are not "acquainted" with God? Is God supreme in your hearts? is He indeed enshrined over all in your souls? is everything subordinated to Him? do you count all things but dung in comparison with His favour and life-givingness? "Prove yourselves," "examine yourselves." "Know ye not your own selves?" And, brethren, are there any that do wish to be acquainted with God? Do not seek Him mainly or merely in the pages of philosophy, or in the book of natural religion, in natural philosophy, or in the natural evidences. They are all very well in their places, but a man does not want tapers when the Sun is abroad. Let him go out, and let "the Sun of Righteousness arise" upon him "with healing in His wings;" then, indeed, and not until then, will the shadows be chased away, and the light shall shine into his soul.

Brethren, see to it that you may look in the light of God's countenance as far as you may. Beautiful are the words of the psalmist in the evening service, Blessed is the people, O Lord,—the Bible translation is: "Blessed is the people that know the joyful sound; they shall walk, O Lord, in the light of thy countenance: in thy name shall they rejoice all the day: and in thy righteousness shall they be exalted." Seek so to rejoice, so to walk, so to be happy. In all things that disquiet you, and distract you, and try you, and distress you, look up to Him with simple childlike love, through the light above to the light beyond. The want of this makes so many go mourning all their days. True, God does at times hide the full enjoyment of His favour from His people, and they are led to say as Job did, "Oh that I knew where I might find Him! that I might come even to His seat!" But still remember He knows our wants, and when He has tried us, we shall come forth as gold purified. Remember that beautiful assurance and promise if you still cling to Him, and turn not back from Him; if you count nothing to be satisfying to you till He satisfies you—"Who is among you that feareth the Lord, that obeyeth the voice of His servant, that walketh in darkness, and hath no light? let him trust in the name of the Lord, and stay upon his God."

XVIII.

THE NOTES AND MARKS OF TRUE REGENERATION.

"Hereby know we that we dwell in Him, and He in us, because He hath given us of His Spirit."—1 JOHN iv. 13.

IT was a noble definition of true friendship, which is said to have been given by a classical writer of distinction. He says, "Friendship is one soul in two bodies"—natural inhabitation, as it were; so that though the persons are twain, the sentiments, the spirit, the affections, the general tone of thought are one. This is the truest unity. Mere carnal union is a shadow, but spiritual union is the essence. In the Word of God it is revealed to us that there is a union infinitely more grand, and unspeakably more full, than aught that earth alone can furnish. The whole body of Christ's faithful people are again and again represented as manifold in members, but one in person. This union arises out of their having one spirit actuating and animating them. The union of the many faculties and members in the natural body does not lie so much in the mere fact that they are cemented and banded together by joints and muscles, as that they are pervaded by one actuating spirit: if it leaves the body, the body ceases to live; but whilst it is in the body, it controls and animates it, and the body lives in virtue of that soul that is in it. What the soul is to the body, that the Holy Ghost is to the soul. A man dies when the spirit leaves the body, and he begins to live when the spirit enters into it anew. All life of a holy kind that the people of God enjoy, whether inhabitant on earth or triumphant in heaven, is due to the blessed Third Person in the Divine nature, which, as on this day,[*] in the fulness of His revelation and the plenitude of His gifts was poured out and descended upon the waiting Church. It is meet and right that we should seek to keep in special memory that most excellent gift, the best of gifts that the Son hath bestowed, the promise on which He fastened the hopes and hearts of His people, the promise of the presence that was not like His own bodily presence, to be soon withdrawn, but a presence of which He said, "He shall abide with you for ever." The world, indeed, cannot receive Him, because it seeth Him not, neither knoweth Him, for it lacks the spiritual sense by which it can discern and know Him; but we know that if we dwell in Him, He dwelleth in us. He dwelleth with the Church from the beginning; and now, in a spiritual sort he dwelleth in the Church, or rather in every individual living member of the Church; He is in the soul, He is the soul of the soul, and from Him "all holy desires, all good counsels, and all just works do proceed." Those young persons who yesterday came up so solemnly and so simply to vouch and set to their seal to stand to their Christian covenant, had this prayer and blessing offered for them, that they might "daily increase in God's Holy Spirit more and more." It is this prayer, beloved, that we would indeed echo for them, for ourselves, for you all. If you have not the Spirit, you are none of Christ's; but if you have the Spirit, you know with humble confidence that He is in you. It is the special gift of God; and after God's people trust in Jesus, they are sealed with "that Holy Spirit of promise, which is the earnest of our inheritance until the redemption of the purchased possession."

[*] Whitsunday morning, 1865.

It is, indeed, a question of thrilling interest to every one of us, Are we received into union with God? They that are far off from Him shall perish, for distance from Him is hell; and they shall find it so, sooner or later, if they are not brought nigh through the blood of Christ; and nearness to Him is thorough union with Him in Christ Jesus. "Our fellowship is with the Father and His Son Jesus Christ."

The apostle whom Jesus loved, in his beautiful epistle, most clearly and remarkably sets forth the notes and marks of true regeneration, of a person who is indeed born of God, and adopted into His family, and brought into communion with Him. Amongst these marks, none are more prominent or unequivocal than the one in the passage you have heard: "Hereby know we that we dwell in Him, and He in us, because He hath given us of His Spirit."

We shall dwell very briefly on *the glorious fact:* He dwells in His people, and His people dwell in Him. Then we shall dwell on *the satisfying evidence of the glorious fact:* "Hereby know we," "because He hath given us of His Spirit." May that Spirit be given to us in the ministry of His Word, that so we may have it proved that He dwells in us, that it may not be to us "the savour of death unto death," but "the savour of life unto life."

This beautiful and blessed expression is by many toned down into something very tame and inanimate; but we have no right to take the Word of God at a lower standard than the Word of God itself interprets it. "Hereby know we that we dwell in Him, and He in us." As I have said, mutual inhabitation and fellowship does not lie so much in mere visible and tangible contact as in community of mind, spirit, and affection. Man, when God made him, was the very image of God, and God was in man. We read that "God breathed into his nostrils the breath of life." What was that life and soul but the inspiration of God? and, as a consequence, what was the condition of that soul? Man was made "in the image of God, after His likeness;" and while he retained that image, he remained in that likeness; there was an immediate connexion and union and communion between him and God, he having God dwelling in him, and having his dwelling with God. Was there not a blessed compact between his little finite spirit and the Infinite Spirit that had called him into being, and stamped him with His own glorious image? And how was it that that blessed union ceased? Our iniquities separated us from God. This is the vital nerve; the union was separated by the transgression of the first Adam, and can only be renewed through "the second Adam, the Lord from heaven." As it is beautifully said, "The first man was made a living soul"—could die; "the second Adam was made a quickening spirit;" that Jesus gives us. Then we come again to live in God, and God in us; then we come again to be united to Him, as He himself represents it, as the branch is united to the vine; or, as it is elsewhere represented, as the stone is cemented and tied into the building; or, as is again so beautifully said, as a member that is one in the body. And this is the point in the similitude that is more especially to be noticed, for in vain the body without the life-giving principle that supplies life to the whole. In the body every member, from the least finger to the eye, the ear, and the most important member, is actuated, and kept in life, and controlled, and influenced by the same living principle inhabiting the whole body, knitting it into one. This represents the union of Christ's genuine living people. They abide in Him by a trusting faith, while He abides in them by supplying them with the Spirit of life, and enabling them to live in Him, and walk in Him; and they have their spiritual being with Him. And this is nothing strange or mysterious; it is what God led us to expect. His promise is to this effect: "I will dwell in them, and walk in them." How beautifully full! how gloriously exalted! To think of poor worms of the dust, that had made themselves lower than the beasts that perish, being elevated into intimate, indissoluble, everlasting union with the great God!

But how shall we know this? what *evidence* of it shall we have? Shall we seek for it in dreams, or notions, or impressions, as some would have, of presumptuous assurance; or, as others would have, of confidence in our election and predestination? Far from it. The evidence is present, personal, clear, and conclusive. We may, indeed, for a time doubt, but we have not to say, "Who shall ascend into heaven? (that is, to bring down Christ from above;) or, Who shall descend into the deep?" who shall develop the dark secrets from the depths below? but, as it is said, "The word is nigh thee, even in thy mouth, and in thy heart." The evidence of our regeneration, and adoption, and acceptance, and communion with God, is in our own hearts, the evidence is in our own lives. "Hereby know we that we dwell in Him, and He in us, because He hath given us of His Spirit." The glorious persons of the Godhead in the work of our salvation each discharge a separate function, though all are alike combined, and all alike co-operate; for, as we had it in that scriptural creed, the Athanasian, "there is one person of the Father, and another of the Son, and another of the Holy Ghost;" and though these three Persons are so one that we are never to presume to speak of three Gods or three Lords, yet they are so distinct in their special functions in man's salvation, that whilst we regard the Father in the gift of the Son in the glorious scheme of redemption, and ascribe to the Son the glorious fulfilment of the propitiation and atonement in virtue of which we have access to God, and re-admission into fellowship with Him, we are to ascribe to the Holy Ghost, the heavenly Teacher and divine Sanctifier, the bringing of us into that blessed life divine which springs from and flows from union with Him; so that, as the sap is to the tree, as the living soul is to the body, so is the Spirit of God, the gift of the Father, through the mediation, satisfaction, and atonement of the Son. He comes to God's people, and abides with them. Where the Spirit is, there the Father is, there the Son is, and there is life. And that life is self-evidencing. Does not a man know that he lives? has he not the functions of life? Can a man's soul truly live, and he have no consciousness or sense of it? Life, it is true, may be alternating, as a man may be weak or strong. He may sometimes feel faint and prostrate, but still there is evidence of life, and there is always an illimitable distance between a living and a dead man. There is *that* distance between a dead and a living soul. Are we then to look for that blessed evidence of the Spirit in us by raptures and impressions, as some would do? or are we to look for it from confidence and assurance, as some boast, while they live in wilful and willing sin? God forbid. After all, the evidences of the Spirit's indwelling are to be sought for in the effects of the Spirit on the mind and temper, and life, and conversation. "Whereas I was blind," said the man who had been restored to sight, "now I see." And so may he that has the Spirit say, "I was blind to the things that belong to my peace, I was blind to my own moral state of mind and heart before God, I thought myself good, and safe, and relied upon myself; but now I have seen things in a different light, my God sought me by His Spirit, He has convinced me and reproved me, and I have seen my guilt as I never saw it before. When the Spirit taught me, then indeed I saw how the candle of the Lord searcheth the deep things of the heart; then I discovered the depth of my corruptions and imperfections in all I did and ever have done, and it has humbled me in the dust; and then the blessed Spirit lifted me out of my despair, discovered my sin, and led me to see my Saviour; then it enabled me to rejoice, and I find a joy I never had before, a peace to which I was hitherto a stranger, I feel strengthened also with might in the inner man, I have submitted in all things to the will of God, I have loved Him because He first loved me, and I have walked with Him in holy communion and fellowship. Could I be deceived in that? Far from it. The reality of the change I have humble consciousness of; I find now that I can restrain my restless tempers, subdue my selfishness, learn to love as I was beloved, I can crucify the world, with the affections and lusts, old things have passed away, and all things have become new, and though I still find the flesh lusting against the Spirit, and the Spirit against the flesh, and that I cannot do the things that I would, still I am not what I was, I am certainly changed, and it is not a mere matter of notion, influence, or sentiment, but it is a spiritual change." "He that believeth in the Son of God hath the witness in himself," and "His Spirit witnesseth with our spirit that we are the sons of God," "and if sons, then heirs, heirs of God, and joint-heirs with Christ."

You see, beloved, it is not a far-fetched, uncertain, unreal presumption or emotion; or a fantastical enthusiasm, when the humble Christian tries to do the will of God, and to be taught of His Spirit, and to enjoy it in His heart. "Hereby know we that we dwell in Him, and He in us, because He hath given us of His Spirit."

How much more might be added. You yourselves, brethren, may follow it out in your own secret reflections, and you will find all that is in you that is indeed divine and fit for you, bringing you into sweet communion and reconciliation with God in Christ, is evidence of the Spirit dwelling in you, and that Spirit dwelling in you is evidence that you dwell in God, and that God dwells in you. That blessed communion to which you are invited does most beautifully express the same sentiment; it tells you that if you receive it with a trusting, obedient heart, then you spiritually eat the flesh and drink the blood of Christ, "we dwell in Him, and He in us." Many of my younger hearers have this morning enjoyed, for the first time, the precious privilege, and many more, I trust, anticipate it in a little while. May you come in this blessed simplicity and in faith that He who has promised His Spirit will fulfill His promise to you. May you come to that holy communion because you are led by the Spirit, and in a deep sense of your own unworthiness, but in confidence in Him who has invited you to come and feed upon His own atoning sacrifice. May you be stablished, strengthened, settled in the good part; and may you indeed look continually to the Holy Spirit of God to guide you in every perplexity, to guard you in every danger, to cheer you in every distress, to solace you in every sorrow, to direct you in every step of life, to sanctify and bless all you do and enjoy, and finally, to receive you into the heavenly kingdom.

Finally, my brethren, may you, all of you, more and more remember it is "the spirit that giveth life," and "the letter that killeth." Mere form, and ceremony, and external outside godliness profiteth not, it is the spirit alone that profiteth. Let us then look to that spirit in everything—in our services, in our enjoyments, in our duties, and let us be guided by that spirit. "They that are after the Spirit do mind the things of the Spirit. For to be carnally minded is death; but to be spiritually minded is life and peace." If ye walk after the flesh ye shall die: but if ye through the Spirit do mortify the deeds of the body, ye shall live," true, imperishable, eternal life.

XIX.

THE INSPIRATION OF THE BIBLE.

"For whatsoever things were written aforetime were written for our learning, that we through patience and comfort of the Scriptures might have hope."—Rom. xv. 4.

THE whole Word of God is so woven together, that you must ravel the whole texture if you attempt to draw out any of the golden wefts. You must take it altogether, or reject it altogether. Its fundamental truths are so beautifully interwoven and inter-dependent, that if you reject one, you will impair—nay, to a certain extent, you will destroy—the whole structure. One of the subtlest tendencies of the present sceptical, while on the other hand superstitious, age is the tendency to disparage, not to say to set aside, the Old Testament Scriptures, as though they belonged to a former age, and had no immediate concern with the present; as though the New Testament were sufficient, and therefore they would supersede it; as though, because we have the top-stone of revelation, therefore they would set aside the foundation-stone; as though, because the temple is completed, we needed not the basis on which it stands. It is obvious, therefore, that those who would be found faithful will give special attention to the Old Testament Scriptures, and more especially as the things in the New are reflected clearly in the Old, and are calculated to stablish, strengthen, and settle our faith in the entire structure. The epistle of this morning* brings before us the testimony of the Old Testament Scriptures in a most striking manner. I therefore gladly avail myself of the text the epistle suggests, to call your attention to the great truth it sets before us. The apostle had been quoting from the Old Testament,—as the Spirit of God often led His witnesses in the New to quote from the Old, Jesus himself setting a clear and full example of thus honouring the whole revelation of God ;—the apostle had been thus quoting from the Old Testament Scriptures, in order to enforce unity, showing that, in order to unity, they must practise self-denial, that they must sacrifice their own inclinations and prejudices, in order to gain " unity of the Spirit in the bond of peace." The words which he had quoted were in the first instance spoken by David of himself, and secondly—as is frequently the case in the Old Testament—he seems to pass from himself to his Son and Lord ; so that it is especially of Christ he said, " The reproaches of them that reproached Thee fell on me." The apostle applies the words exclusively to Christ as the star fades when the sun shines ; and he at once follows up this quotation by reminding his hearers that he was not quoting from David and applying it to Christ, but that he was quoting from Christ himself, for the " testimony of Jesus is the spirit of prophecy ;" and therefore he lays down this fundamental axiom :—" Whatsoever things were written aforetime were written for our learning, that we through patience and comfort of the Scriptures might have hope."

The words clearly set before us :—*The Old Testament Scriptures and their general purpose: the special efficacy of the Old Testament Scriptures: and the blessed effects of the Old Testament Scriptures when rightly received and applied.* May God, who gave us His Word, give us His Spirit, that we may understand and believe, and follow His Word, for Christ's sake.

* Second Sunday in Advent, 1864.

The Old Testament Scriptures and their general purpose: "Whatsoever things were written aforetime." Aforetime is before the writer's time, before Christ came. He did not come till the fulness of time predicted, though not always understood; then "God sent forth his Son, made of a woman, made under the law, to redeem them that were under the law, that we might receive the adoption of sons." After that period, all that was predicted was future. God was pleased that the light of life should arise upon this dark world as the light of day: first the faint streak of dawn, then the gradual flush of dawn, then the brightening of dawn, till at last the sun appears and the day has come. It was even thus in the progress of "the day-spring from on high" visiting us, and all hope of Christ's coming was in what was "written aforetime." But as the first flash is as essential to the sun as its full blaze, so the whole of revelation was from Jesus, till He himself became manifest in the flesh. All that was written, then, "aforetime," was written with a view to Christ, and from the Spirit of Christ. How much reason have we to bless God for the written Word! If it had been—as some would have had it, and as some still wish to have it—a mere tradition from man, handed down from generation to generation—if God had committed His glorious truth to the mere fragments, the mere planks, of a floating tradition—how it would have been shipwrecked, how it would have been misrepresented and distorted, and handed down with everything of uncertainty and imperfection! We know that such is the case in human traditions, and that there is nothing more uncertain and unsafe. Tradition is proverbially a mere floating wreck. But it pleased God, from an early period, to commit His will and wisdom and truth to the ark of a written record. What was spoken He afterwards caused to be written, and it was written according to His own plan and purpose. Not such things, then, as were *spoken*, but whatsoever things were *written*. Mark the width and fulness of that. It does not say certain things, such as the commandments, which were traced with the finger of Deity on the tables on Mount Sinai; nor does it say such things as were spoken by God, or by the mouths of His prophets; but God sets upon the entire old Testament Scriptures His endorsement; and what God has stamped with His mark, let not man despise and disparage. Is not God the best judge of His own mind and will? and He says "*whatsoever*"—whether of precepts or of prophecies, whether of statements or of ordinances, whether addressed to saints or to sinners, whether for warning or for threatening, whether of hope or exhortation, whether for admonition or for instruction in righteousness—"*whatsoever* things were written." I pray you, brethren, do not narrow what God has made so wide; do not select where God has endorsed; do not separate, as if there were dross with the gold, where God has declared all to be gold. Wait to see before you dare to judge anything superfluous or unnecessary. There are, no doubt, degrees of importance in the Word of God, as in everything else: but while there are degrees, all is important; and we have no right to say of the least, any more than we have of the greatest, this is unimportant. And yet men dare to say so! Whatsoever was written was endorsed by God; the whole of the Scriptures are the oracles of God, and are binding upon men. "Whatsoever things were written aforetime were written for our learning." Here is the purpose, the drift, the design of the whole. We need to learn, for we know nothing as we ought to know of the things of God, and about ourselves—our destiny, our immortality, our ruin, our redemption, our hope, our life. Oh, what a miserable chaos! oh, what dark conjectures! oh, what wretched day-dreams! oh, what empty notions! are those of mere human writers, even the wisest and most learned and intelligent of them—Cicero, Socrates, Plato, and Seneca. Read their writings, and you will come to the conclusion that "the world by wisdom knew not God," knew not itself, knew not its salvation, knew not its hope, knew not its destiny. Where are they now? Therefore, brethren, let it not be forgotten that we need to be taught and instructed; and if God had not condescended to instruct us, the thick darkness never would have been broken. There might have been little rays of light, there might have been glow-worms in the night, meteors glancing through the air, but fixed light and certainty none.

"Written for our learning." It is ours as little children to learn from God; it ought to be ours to receive his instruction with meekness and pure affection, and to submit our understandings and hearts to the divine teaching. We *may* learn, and what learning is like it? What are all the teachings of philosophy and science, what are all the discoveries, the vain knowledge, and the boasted intellect of men, in comparison to the wisdom that is vouchsafed to a little child, a little humble Sunday scholar, an aged man, a simple peasant, when taught by the Word of God to know himself, his Maker, his ruin, his salvation, his hope of immortality, how to live, how to die, and how to attain life everlasting? "The fear of the Lord, that is wisdom, and to depart from evil is understanding." "Where is the wise? Where is the scribe? Where is the disputer of this world? Hath not God made foolish the wisdom of this world?" Hath he not "chosen the foolish things of the world to confound the wise; and "the weak things of the world to confound the things which are mighty?" "I thank thee, O Father, Lord of heaven and earth, because thou hast hid these things from the wise and prudent, and hast revealed them unto babes." "For our learning." We might dwell upon this beautiful point, but our time forbids. Think upon it, and remember, when you take up your Bibles, that you are going to learn. Do not come to judge or to teach, but make up your minds that it is the Word of God; and having made up your minds, do not come to tread the holy enclosure with a careless, or a cynical, or a critical, or a frivolous step, lest you be struck blind for your presumption; but "take off your shoes from your feet," and listen to God in the Bible, and hearken to Him as to one who will judge you.

"Whatsoever things were written aforetime were written for *our* learning." I must dwell for a moment upon that expression. Not for the learned simply, not for the Jews only, or for Moses, or for the prophets. If so, we might regard the Scriptures, as some presumptuously do, as past, and as having done their work. Such objectors say, "Oh, we live in modern, and advanced, and intellectual times; we live in the meridian of the world; we do not want to go back to the dim shades, to the alphabet and spelling-book of revelation. But it was not simply for their learning in days past, it is for *our* learning; and if God has given His word not merely for those to whom it was first addressed, but for all in every age; then let us not dare to set aside what God has thus endorsed. "Whatsoever things were written aforetime were written for *our* learning." Here then, brethren, is the general purpose of the Old Testament Scriptures.

Now we have *the special efficacy of the entire Scriptures:* "That we through patience and comfort of the Scriptures." Here is their efficacy. They are fitted to supply us, and strengthen us, and cherish us, and nourish us in patience, and in patience by comfort, and thus by patience and comfort they bring us to a high and holy state. We need patience in this dreary world; and if we have not patience, we never shall learn wisdom, for "tribulation worketh patience, and patience experience, and experience hope, that maketh not ashamed." If there be no patience there will be no experience. If a man is ever restless, and continually rising against the hand of God, if he is peevish, and self-willed, and presumptuous, he will never learn. You cannot teach a child that is impatient; and if patient application is essential to human learning, much more essential is it to divine learning. We need this. The apostle says, "We have need of patience;" and, again, Christ himself said, "In your patience possess ye your souls;" and a man cannot be learning experience unless he possess his soul, and he cannot unless he possess it in patience. Patience is the crowning grace; it finishes a man's course when he is patient to the end; therefore we have need of patience, and the Scriptures—the Old as well as the New—are fitted to nourish and cherish patience. Is it not so? Just read through the Old Testament, and see what beautiful language there is in the Psalms of David, see what precious language there is in the Book of Job. "Ye have heard of the patience of Job, and have seen the end of the Lord; that the Lord is very pitiful, and of tender mercy." And what beautiful representations there are of the blessed Redeemer as the Lamb of God in the Old Testament, teaching us that if He was so patient, shame upon us if we cannot bear a little! What beautiful patterns of patience we have in Daniel, in Shadrach, Meshech, and Abednego, and in the prophets. Ye have heard, brethren, of these examples, which were left for our learning. And then the punishments and judgments, as well as the blessings and promises, of God teach us patience. "These things happened unto them for ensamples: and they are written for our admonition, upon whom the ends of the world are come." Therefore the Old Testament Scriptures, as well as the New, are fitted to cherish patience. I can appeal to many of you if, when you have been cast down and racked with pain, or bereaved of those whom you have beloved, if, when you have been tempted to repine, you have not found the best resource to be in opening the Word of God. Hear what the Lord says:—"Be still, and know that I am God." Here is divine teaching, here is heavenly unction, to calm the troubled waters of your souls, and to refresh them, as with the dews of heaven. God comes down upon us as we read His Word and wait upon Him, and He is according to His promise: "I will be as the dew unto Israel: he shall grow as the lily, and cast forth his roots as Lebanon. They that dwell under his shadow shall return: they shall revive as the corn, and grow as the vine; the scent thereof shall be as the wine of Lebanon."

Then these blessed Scriptures are not only fitted to enlarge our patience, but they do so by increasing our comfort. What words of consolation there are in God's blessed Word! Take a few. "When thou passest through the waters, I will be with thee; and through the rivers, they shall not overflow thee: when thou walkest through the fire, thou shalt not be burned; neither shall the flame kindle upon thee. For I am the Lord thy God, the Holy One of Israel, thy Saviour." "Fear thou not; for I am with thee: Be not dismayed; for I am thy God: I will strengthen thee; yea, I will help thee; yea, I will uphold thee with the right hand of my righteousness." "Can a woman forget her sucking child, that she should not have compassion on the son of her womb? Yea, they may forget, yet will I not forget thee." And again, "For the mountains shall depart, and the hills be removed; but my kindness shall not depart from thee, neither shall the covenant of my peace be removed, saith the Lord that hath mercy on thee." I well remember hearing these words from the lips of my dear father, in a night of deep agony, and sleeplessness, and anguish, when the whole heart was torn with the deepest sorrow; and I recollect the comfort they ministered to him when the earth had, as he said, not one ray of light. Dear brethren, you may depend, we only need to cherish these precious grapes to find that they will yield wine that maketh glad the heart of man, making us "as sorrowful, yet always rejoicing." This is the efficacy of God's blessed Word, when it is applied effectually by His Spirit to the heart in its deepest conflicts, in its sorest anguish, in its darkest desolation.

Then we have the blessed result of this divine efficacy: "That we through patience and comfort of the Scriptures might have hope." What a dark world this would be if there were no hope! How the tides of the ocean would stagnate, and all the lights that glimmer over the wilderness would be quenched! But hope still remains with many, as our poet says:—

"Hope the charmer lingers still behind."

Yes, but earthly hope often lingers to deceive. It is a lie, it passes away, it goes like meteor after meteor, and then is lost; and if there is no firmer light left, darkness comes upon a man in his old age; or, if not in lifetime, he discovers it in eternity. What a comfort and joy it is to have the hope of heaven! not the meteors of the marsh, which expire at the coming of the sun, but the hope that is "the anchor of the soul, sure and steadfast." We cannot have too much hope, if it is a right hope, authenticated by a "love of God shed abroad in our hearts," evidenced by what God says is the evidence of that love. "He that believeth on the Son of God hath the witness in himself." Oh, how a vessel clings to the sheet anchor when all the auxiliary anchors are driven! and so, when all earthly anchors are driven, and the poor little bark of immortality is trembling beneath the blast and billows of a stormy sea, what a mercy it is to have a sure anchor by which to hold, and to feel this cannot be driven—this can never fail! Ah, we need, in order to this precious comfort, the whole of the Scriptures of God, to inspire, and sustain, and strengthen our hope. What examples we have of it. Listen to the aged psalmist himself, when his family was not as he could wish it to be; when he was wrung with domestic affliction, and he wept with the deepest sorrow, and his heart and flesh failed him; when all his earthly anchors had drifted: "Although my house be not so with God; yet he hath made with me an everlasting covenant, ordered in all things, and sure: for this is all my salvation, and all my desire, although he make it not to grow." Is not *there* a blessed confirmation of faith and hope? Do you not see that there is for the righteous a sure rock in the covenant of grace, through the righteousness of Christ, that never can be broken down, and therefore the anchor that is riveted on it can never give way? How much there is in the old Testament Scriptures to assure us that God will not fail His people, showing us that all those who walked by faith, and were taught in faith, though they "received not the promise," they "all died in faith;" they did not deplore their disappointed hope, their hope did not make them ashamed; even as Jacob said, "I have waited for thy salvation, O Lord," and so departed in peace.

I pray you, ponder on this passage in its bearing on the Old Testament in your own experience. "Whatsoever things were written aforetime were written for our learning, that we through patience and comfort of the Scriptures might have hope."

Surely we are taught the lesson, that we ought to prize more and more the revelation of God. If all this is true of the Old Testament Scriptures, it is still more so of the New. We are not to disparage the one; God forbid: and we are not to neglect the other. What were the Old Testament to us, if the New did not follow? What were the day-dawn, if the noon did not crown it? What were the promise of day, if the sun did not follow the promise? There is no disparagement of the sun, therefore, in magnifying the morning; but we magnify it only in order to the noon-day.

And surely we should learn further, as our collect for the day so beautifully says—and I think it is one of the loveliest of our collects; and that the collects, epistles, and gospels for Advent, are surpassingly beautiful for the bearing and connexion they have with each other,—to read, mark, learn, and inwardly digest" the Holy Scriptures, "that by patience and comfort of Thy Holy Word, we may embrace and ever hold fast the blessed hope of everlasting life;" without which man's being is all misery, and chaos, and darkness; without which it had been better for us if we had never been born, or that we had been born insects to flutter with the breeze, or cattle to graze upon the mountain-side; rather than rational, intelligent, immortal beings, without hope here or hereafter. Brethren, "read, mark, learn, and inwardly digest" God's Holy Scriptures. You know there must be digestion in order to nutrition. In vain the appetite if there is no digestion. It is often a sign of disease, and not of health; for if food is taken, and it is not changed by the process of digestion into aliment, all the functions of life will fail. It will be just so in spiritual life in the new man, the Word must not only be read, but it must be pondered over, and meditated upon, and digested, and this will turn it into food and sustenance for the inner man; just as it is beautifully said in that holy sacrament of which you are about to partake, "Feed upon Him with your hearts, by faith with thanksgiving." There must be the inward feeling in the heart—the digestion, and it is by this digestion only that you can grasp and grapple the heavenly anchor and hold it fast, and so become strengthened day by day. It is by the Spirit of God alone a man is able thus to digest. Yet it is through and by the Word that God nourishes and cherishes, for in vain the food without the chyle that enables the digestion to take place. A man must take the food into the body if he would digest it, but he must have the soul as well; he must look for the Spirit, and in seeking for the Spirit he will honour the Bible. We should look therefore for "comfort and patience," not simply by looking to the Spirit of God, but by looking to Him through and by His blessed Word.

XX.

VAIN SPECULATION.

"What is that to thee? Follow thou me."—St. John xxi. part of 22.

The scenes and sayings of our beloved Master during the interval that elapsed between His resurrection from the sepulchre and His ascension to glory challenge and reward the minutest attention. They present a new phase of the blessed history of our Lord, a phase which represents Him to us not as altogether yet ascended and glorified, though He said, "Touch me not; for I am not yet ascended to my Father: but go to my brethren, and say unto them, I ascend unto my Father, and your Father; and to my God, and your God;" but yet a phase in which He appeared not so much as "a Man of sorrows and acquainted with grief," "enduring the cross and despising the shame," but as a triumphant victor, who had "led captivity captive," and who was at the very vestibule—or, rather, on the first step of the throne on which He now sits as the ruler of the universe. There is, therefore, a certain reserve in His intercourse with His disciples,—not that there was less of tenderness and sympathy, but there was less of humanity, and more of the shrouding of solemn dignity, thus weaning them from walking by sense and sight, and accustoming them to walk by faith in an unseen Saviour, rather than by visible perception of His bodily presence amongst them; and leading us too to see that we are not to know Christ "after the flesh," in a carnal and sensible manner, but "after the Spirit," in a vital and believing perception of the Saviour. The lesson this morning brought before us a beautiful picture of Christ's latter intercourse with His followers, and His tender sympathy, for He still provided for their bodily wants, and taught them that those wants were not yet beneath His notice, though He was Lord of all. His first miracle at Cana of Galilee, and His last miracle, proclaimed Him to be truly the Son of man, whilst at the same time the Son of God. His reproof to Peter too, full of tenderness and faithfulness, must have aroused their attention, and it is beautiful to see the modest humility and obedient spirit of the apostle. He had just been restored by His Lord, having showed a prying self-sufficient spirit, but almost immediately afterwards he received the reproof, and had the commission renewed to him. He had turned, and seeing John, who was the beloved disciple, he said, "Lord, and what shall this man do?" when Jesus had warned him of His own approaching sufferings. To this prying inquiry the Redeemer gave a gentle and yet seasonable reproof, and showed the true way to avoid such temptation. "If I will that he tarry till I come, what is that to thee?" Is it thy concern or mine? Does it pertain to thee or to me? "Follow thou me," that is thy business, and that is thy grand duty. I conceive the passage is appropriate to any time, and especially appropriate to a day when so much of vain speculation and presumptuous inquiry is abroad in the professing Church, when men are daring to ask of God what He has not revealed, and when many of them, as we have seen, are smitten with blindness and leprosy.

The subject then presents these three points:—*The spirit checked:—the check to the spirit:—and the antidote prescribed to that spirit.* May God, by His Spirit, be amongst us, that we may receive His Word, and that we may lean on it in such wise that we may be "as a child that is weaned from his mother."

The spirit checked is evidently *a spirit of meddling* with what does not immediately concern us, or rather, with what we have no right because we have no duty requiring us to meddle, turning our attention to thoughts that do not profit, and exist from idle curiosity and the desire to shelter ourselves from something that we do not quite like. On that account we allow our minds to be diverted from our own proper duty, from our own clear and plain path of obedience, to vain speculations on matters with which we have no immediate concern, and into which, because our Lord has thrown a shield around them, we have no right to pry. Perhaps there is no spirit to which man is more prone than this. One of the main incentives to the original transgression was this spirit of curiosity. What was in the original type, man is still prone to, and there is the same inclination to transgress. It is clear that one main motive on the part of our first mother in violating a plain and solemn command, was presumption. She saw the tree, and fancied that it was good, and she was informed by the tempter, "Ye shall be as gods, knowing good and evil." Now what right had she to wish to know evil? She knew good, was not that enough? Was not ignorance of evil her happiness and her perfection? Why then should she desire to perceive and know this? You will find, if you read the history of the world with care and keep this point before you, that in very many instances we have that spirit and inclination cropping out continually from the corrupt heart of man. Man does not compare spiritual things with spiritual, but with carnal; and by doing so carnalizes them, robs them of their grandeur, and strips them of their dignity. This is the case with the rationalizing philosophers and professors of Christianity, and is the result of pride of understanding, of self-confidence, and of self-sufficiency. The idea of a man being able to master everything within the Almighty range! After all, man's highest attainment is to know well how narrow is his own range, and to bring his mind down to submission to the oracles of God. If a man does not learn this, with all his learning he has but little hope in the things of God, for he fails to learn the first lesson in the divine school, which is that if he thinks he knows the things of God, he himself knows nothing. The first grand elementary lesson in the school of Christ is, "If any man amongst you seemeth to be wise in this world, let him become a fool, that he may be wise; for the wisdom of this world is foolishness with God." "I thank thee, O Father, Lord of heaven and earth, because thou hast hid these things from the wise and prudent, and hast revealed them unto babes. Even so, Father, for so it seemed good in thy sight."

This disposition to pry into what does not belong to us, not only arises from a presumptuous spirit but from a *disinclination to be taught* and to attend to what does belong to us. "They, measuring themselves by themselves, and comparing themselves among themselves, are not wise." This want of wisdom we find continually in people. Instead of seeking to come up to the right standard themselves they are finding fault with others; they are perpetually trying to alleviate their own consciences by inquiring about others. For instance, to take one example, many men, 'instead of asking what is the duty of a Christian, and what is his measure of responsibility, and how he will answer at the bar above, begin to ask, "What is to become of the heathen? what is to happen to them? what shall they do?" "What is that to thee?" The care of a man, and the attention of a man, should be concentrated on his own eternal destiny, and he should say, " I must be lost or saved not as a heathen but as a Christian. Each man will be judged according to what he has, and not according to what he has not; therefore let me take heed to myself." Besides, we must revere the silence not less than the voice of the lively oracles of God; and that man is flying in the face of the Bible who wants to know what the Bible does not tell him. He should respect the line of demarcation, he should accept what God has given him, and receive it with profound and humble submission. He is not to wish, Oh, if God had given more light, if He had told us this secret and explained that difficulty, if He had removed the darkness and made it light, if He would satisfy us and give us more assurance, then we should believe. " If they hear not Moses and the prophets, neither will they be persuaded, though one rose from the dead." A voice heard from the glory above would not bring a man to repentance and salvation, who is not brought by the simple testimony and teaching of God's Word. Be assured of it, the fault is not in having too little of the Word, but in not making a right use of the great amount we have. Never let it be forgotten that the horizon must be placed somewhere. Suppose these vain inquirers and presumptuous speculators were to have to arrange where it should be, where would they put it? Place it farther off, and you have more difficulty, as you have more extent; just as a man climbing, as I have seen, up the Alps; when he has ascended a little distance he thinks, " what a wide and vast prospect I have, but there are bounds within which the horizon confines the view, I wish it were wider." He still ascends, and the horizon widens; but he does not see more plainly, but less plainly. So it is in the horizon of God's heavenly Word; place it where you will, it is still limited, and I believe that the revelation of God is limited in heaven. The loftiest archangel cannot by searching find out God; and so reason must be mixed with faith, and what we see, and seeing cannot believe, here, we should not believe in heaven amidst the blaze and light of the eternal throne.

And, brethren, the inclination to speculation arises from another point. It is not from presumption only, but from a *want of earnestness*. If a man is in good earnest, difficult things become plain; but if a man wants just to get rid of conviction, and to silence his conscience, he cannot do better than inquire how it is such a thing is not made clearer. Until a man is in earnest about his own salvation, he will never make progress, he will never be able to get on.

We have seen the spirit checked, and now we see *the check:* " What is that to thee?" Life is far too short, man's power of judging and reflection is far too precious, the destinies at stake are far too stupendous, and the interests trembling in the balance of man's life are far too momentous, for man to be wasting his time in idle speculation and vain curiosity. " Whatsoever thy hand findeth to do, do it with thy might; for there is no work, nor device, nor knowledge, nor wisdom in the grave, whither thou goest." Yet a little while and it will be impossible to speculate, for it will be all real. It will no more be, " What is he to do?" Man will know what has passed that it is gone for ever, and eternity, that knows no change, will be stretched before him. This thought ought to enforce upon man the solemn admonition, " Awake, thou that sleepest, and arise from the dead, and Christ shall give thee light." There is, perhaps, no cure that is more effectual to man's vain speculation and imagination than the check, " What is that to thee?" If thou didst know it, would it further thy salvation? would it help thee in the path of happiness? would it give thee more of the peace of God? A man must bring his desires and inclinations down to the footstool of Jesus, and receive the voice that says, "Be still, and know that I am God." "What I do thou knowest not now; but thou shalt know hereafter." A man may go on knowing more and more, and not know all; and it will be so in the ages of eternity. "Canst thou by searching find out God? canst thou find out the Almighty unto perfection? It is as high as heaven; what canst thou do? deeper than hell; what canst thou know?" "What is that to thee?" "Secret things belong unto the Lord our God." Beloved, mark the question. What right have we with the property of the Most High? What right have we to meddle with what He has chosen to keep to Himself? Even the earthly monarch can hardly be insulted more, than by having a subject coming to pry into his secret purposes; and if a certain shroud curtains the earthly monarch, how much more is it idle and presumptuous of man to rush into the thick darkness that pavilions the throne of the Almighty! "Clouds and darkness are round about Him; righteousness and judgment are the habitation of His throne." "The things which are revealed belong unto us and to our children." God has lifted the curtain up in a certain measure, so far as to meet our necessities, not to meet our inclinations; so far as to satisfy our faith, but not our curiosity. That is a most important line of demarcation. All that a man needs to know for his life's health is contained in God's Word; and "whatsoever is not read therein, nor may be proved thereby," is of no force for man's condemnation or for his salvation. When you have got all that is in God's Word, you have got all that is good and necessary for you. Here God stops, and here you must stop. You have no right to see even if the curtain were lifted, and much less right to put forth your hand to try to lift the curtain. Is there no need of the check? As far as I have had any room for observation and experience in the universities, in our halls of learning and of science, I have found this, that the men who are always starting novelties and running about with strange notions, seeking to originate novel views in the things of God and in theology, are for the most part men of an irregular turn of mind—men who look upon religion more as a science, and as a part of their round of education, than as the awful throne on which is placed their eternal destiny in hell or in heaven.

The grand antidote for this spirit is supplied by Christ himself:—" What is that to thee? follow thou me." I remember, when at Oxford, seeing a poor foolish sheep; the shepherd was in sight with his flock following him at a short distance, and he was leading them in the pathway of safety; but this one foolish sheep scampered up the sides of the road to graze, and would not follow the shepherd, but would run up and down and crop the grass. By-and-bye, the shepherd got a great distance off, and the rest of the sheep followed him with diligence and with delight; but soon this poor foolish sheep got worried by a dog that took advantage of its defenceless state. This is no inapt figure of us, who are as a fold of sheep that are lost. Christ says, " My sheep hear my voice, and they follow me, and I give them eternal life;" but the foolish sheep will turn aside out of the right and safe path. Instead of looking at the shepherd's footsteps honestly and diligently, marking them, and going after them, the stray sheep says, I will graze where I please, I will be no slave, and the consequence will be the same as it was with that poor foolish sheep; and that case was but a picture and emblem of what such stray Christians will be. I have seen it often with men, and young men especially; seeking to be wise above what is written, they have sunk into the grossest errors and fallacies. Therefore, brethren, the great check to man's rambling in his mind, and wanting something strange and novel, and asking about others, and what is to become of them, and how are they to be saved—for, say they, "surely so many can never be lost"—is this, "What is that to thee? follow thou me." This is the voice of Christ to those who are indulging in vain speculations, and wasting their precious time and imperilling their souls, until they get into an ocean of doubt and difficulty, who, if they had listened to Christ's voice, "Follow me," would have been at the haven of quiet and peace, where they would hear His voice as the dark clouds are driven away, and where we shall see Him, and there will be no more room for doubt. Ah! brethren, how much there is in a quiet subdued mind! Christ himself tells us, "Except ye become as little children, ye cannot enter the kingdom of heaven." And the psalmist David takes up this very point so beautifully in that short psalm: "Lord, I am not high-minded: I have no proud looks. I do not exercise myself in great matters: which are too high for me. But I refrain my soul, and keep it low, like as a child that is weaned from his mother. Yea, my soul is even as a weaned child." Ah! that is true wisdom, that is the height of philosophy and science, for a man to know what he can know, and not what he cannot know, and does not know, and ought not to know, and what does not concern him. There is no one point on which man needs more to be cautioned than this at the present day, when man wants something novel and strange, and is not content with the old simple faith, sealed with the blood of ten thousand martyrs. If he does not simply follow Christ, he will get more and more perplexed and bewildered. And yet, on the other hand, how clear and how plain it is if we follow Him! "Then shall we know, if we follow on to know the Lord." "If any man will do the will of my Father, he shall know of the doctrine whether it be of God." "I am the light of the world : he that followeth me shall not walk in darkness, but shall have the light of life." If you earnestly follow Him, you will have little time and less inclination to meddle in matters that do not concern you. Do your duty earnestly ; and the more earnestly you do it, the more will the rough places become plain, the more will the darkness become light, the more will the crooked ways become straight; not by your comprehending them, but by your submitting to the mind and to the teaching of God.

The whole passage is peculiarly appropriate at this juncture. If you want to trifle, and speculate, and waste your time with religion, as if it were a mere thing of this life, you have no hope ; but if you are in good earnest, and feel, " What shall it profit me if I gain the whole world and lose my own soul ?" How can I meet death and God? then there is good hope if you are setting about it in the right way. You are not to ask, " What shall this man do ?" but, " What must *I* do to be saved ?"

If you are thus in earnest, you must, as far as you know, do God's will, and He will give you more light. " If ye continue in my Word, then are ye my disciples indeed ; and ye shall know the truth, and the truth shall make you free." I have known many who have seemed to be in earnest for a little while. They have set about it to try to seek God ; the young after their confirmation have done so, but by-and-bye they have become faint, and have stumbled over difficulties and darknesses. They have not set to work earnestly and honestly, and did not come with a fixed and a blessed hope. Be assured of it, no Bible, no minister, no man can make all clear and plain ; but the Spirit of God can make all so assured and so satisfying to your minds that you can go on your way without looking to the right hand or to the left, assured that you shall know all when you reach God in that sky that hath no cloud.

Then, brethren, one thought more, which surely is a delightful one, and it is this: "Whatever comes to or befalls others, we should do our duty, warning them and teaching them, knowing that " each man shall bear his own burden," and that every one of us shall give an account of himself to God. Therefore, "what is that to thee? follow thou me." Seek first thine own salvation, be useful as thou canst, and do not vex thyself or trouble thyself with many things you never can control or comprehend.

XXI.

THE VISIBLE CHURCH.

"And, being let go, they went to their own company."—ACTS iv. part of 23.

I HAVE more than once watched with lively interest the bearing and conduct of a flock of sheep. I have seen some of the flock chased by a furious dog, and running far away to escape attack, and separate altogether from the fellowship of their fellows; and I have marked how, no sooner had they escaped from their foes than with marvellous and prompt instinct they were back again and sought the company to which they belonged. There was in the instinct in the animal that which beautifully told them that they were designed by the Creator to be what we style gregarious—that is, they love to be in a flock, and delight in the companionship and unity of those to whom they are allied. Such was the Creator's design in the family that interesting animal, the sheep, is so often employed in the Holy Scriptures to represent to us. How we should be united if we are one in Christ. People give many fine, grand, and imposing descriptions of the visible Church, but, after all, the true secret of the Church of Christ is its fellowship and union that is unseen, and is spiritual, imperishable, and eternal. All else in comparison with this is as the scaffold to the building, as the shell to the kernel, as the body to the soul. When Christ himself addressed His little Church while He was yet bodily amongst them, what could be more beautiful and simple than the language He used? Looking upon them as a little flock in the midst of wolves, as a lily amongst thorns, as a garden in the midst of a wilderness, He said, "Fear not, little flock, for it is the Father's good pleasure to give you the kingdom." And in the words before us what a beautiful and artless, yet grand and expressive, description we have of the little early persecuted Church of the Redeemer! Peter and John had wrought great miracles, and they had been persecuted and had been brought, as their Master had told them to expect, before kings and rulers for His name's sake; but their time was not yet come, and their adversaries let them go. Then, like part of a flock, when no longer chased by their persecutors, they went to their own company; and that was their Church, that was the little body of the faithful. We have been dwelling upon our mutual relationship and union as a flock, because, remember though there is one great fold, there are many small and separate flocks; yet all who are truly called to the one flock, God makes them households, like a flock of sheep. Therefore, we must not go on in a kind of vague generality, or like individuals in a special compartment in the mansion; we must not forget that those who are brought together, more especially in the worship of God, should have a special faith, and fellowship, and regard, and care for each other's present and eternal well-being. The passage, therefore, seems specially suitable to us, and I shall detain your meditations on it a little while, looking to the Great Shepherd and bishop of souls to pour out upon us as a flock much of His Holy Spirit, much of His divine and heavenly grace, that we may abide together in holy unity and fellowship, till we are transplanted to the blessed fold above, where there will be union and fellowship that can never be interrupted.

Let us, for a short time, fix your thoughts on this beautiful and simple *portrait of the Church of Christ*—a company of believers—" they went to their own company :" and then let us lead your thoughts to *the natural and necessary tendency of the hearts of members of a flock to mutual fellowship, and love, and union.*

"Being let go, they went to their company." It is "a company," not a set of detached and separate individuals, having no connexion, no union, no regard for each other. You perceive the difference between a company and a mere scattered crowd. A company means a number of persons, joined together and keeping companionship with one another, having bonds of mutual attraction, and centres of union, and bands of fellowship and regard. Less than this can hardly come up to the spirit and meaning of a company. And how does this company come to be a company? Just as we saw it was the case when Jesus was on earth. Two or three listened to His voice when He called then to follow Him, as He went up and down and called one and another, and those He called obeyed the heavenly calling. They attached themselves to Him as if attracted by a magnet from heaven, they were drawn by His own grace and love. It was so in the case of Matthew the publican, who, when he heard the voice, left all and followed Him ; and by so following Christ as his main object, he joined himself to that little flock that was following Christ, and became united to it, forming one of the company. And this company is thus formed because it is separated from the world, not called out of the duties or relationships or necessary pursuits of the world, for religion was never designed to interrupt the ordinary progress of social life, but separated—if separated in Him—in hope and in affection. They that are after the world follow the world and the things of the world, and this world is their lord and their leader : but not so those who have been called out of the world and called into the flock of Christ; they confess themselves strangers and pilgrims on earth, and look for a city and kingdom to come; they have therefore before them an object unspeakably higher and holier than any the world can ever give; and therefore they are a separated people, and, in a certain sense, while in the world, they are not of the world. "Know that the Lord hath set apart him that is godly for Himself." The word sanctified means in the Greek set apart, separated out of the fallen family of man, and brought into the ransomed family of Christ. There was a separation in the profession of the name of Christ in baptism; those there dedicated have the mark of the flock set upon them; but they only who are effectually living up to that mark, who are in their hearts and affections and conversation separated from the world as their portion and joy, they only are this little company that has a common centre, and that centre Jesus; the branches meet in the stem, the flock knows the voice and follows the steps of the same blessed Shepherd that laid down His life for them, and has purchased them to be His chosen flock for ever. All therefore of the company have their eye steadily and habitually turned to the Great Head and Leader, their ears are open to hearken to His voice. My sheep, says He, know my voice, and follow me. As we have seen a flock of sheep in the broad pasture in a setting sun follow the shepherd, in a long single line indeed, but not to be driven from the well-known familiar sound of the shepherd's voice, they follow after him whithersoever he will lead them, and he brings them to the still waters and green pastures, even so all Christ's faithful people have a perception of His voice; they can tell His "gentlest whisper," whether in providence or grace, whether in chastening or solace, whether in rebuke or in cheering; and they love the voice, because it is the voice of Him their souls love—love because He has first loved them, and therefore they cannot but love Him.

Then, brethren, *this blessed company have all supreme in Him.* They have many little companies here below, they go into different pastures and different scenes, but they all form, as He says, "one fold, under one Shepherd." They shall come from the east and from the west, from the north and from the south, and shall sit down with Abraham, Isaac, and Jacob, where the pasturage never fails, and the water never ceases, in the kingdom of their Father. And so, brethren, it is a company, because, however discouraged they may be, they are true to their companionships; they have common sympathies, common hopes, common joys, common fears, a common Lord and a common fold; and therefore it is no mere dream of enthusiasm, it is no vague impression, that there is a company of the faithful. There has never been a period in this lost world, but there has been some little flock at least of those that Christ has ransomed for Himself, and called effectually by His truth and grace, that He is leading to His own prepared place above.

I can but rest for a few moments upon *the nature and tendency of this little flock.* "Being let go, they went to their own company." It is not an exclusive or selfish or sordid feeling; they did not follow their own aim, but they went to their brothers and sisters. This does not narrow a man's heart. Men can love their own families, they have friends and chosen companions of their own, but they have a special love for those of the household of faith, and they ought to have many ties to bind and knit them together. "By this shall all men know," said the Good Shepherd, "that ye are my disciples, if ye have love one to another." And again He says, by the disciple whom He loved specially, "We know that we have passed from death unto life, because we love the brethren." A special endearment and attraction which exists between them when in Christ, is indeed one of the most apparent and palpable evidences that they belong to the flock.

We oftentimes find this to be the case in times of darkness and doubt and dread, as an aged Christian who worshipped with us, and long knelt at that holy table, said to me once, when he was in much doubt and dread—"Well, there is one thing at least that I am conscious of, that if I am not all I ought to be to go to heaven, I could not endure the society of hell, of the profane, of the scoffer, of the covetous, of the impure, of the blasphemer, of the proud, of the rebellious against God; how could I bear it? That would be hell enough to me, without any torment besides, for God knows that I wish to be with the purest and the holiest and the best, and therefore I cannot think that He has left me altogether without a token that I belong to His little flock." "We know that we have passed from death unto life, because we love the brethren." How natural it is, if a man has been abroad—as we saw it in the son of our beloved queen the other day, when he returned from a distant journey, to whom did he first go? whither did he first repair? To the mother that gave him birth, to the home that cherished him, to the endearments that surrounded the fireside of that home. It must be so, if a man has any natural feeling. If he has been afar off, or detained from home, the first place he naturally hastens to is his home. "And, being let go, they went to their own company." Ought it not to be so? And was it not so in this case? And when they came together to their own company, what was the result? They broke out at once with blessing and praising God, who had allowed them to suffer for His sake; and they were brought to cling closer together, and to feel protection and encouragement in the trial of their faith. They lifted up their voices to God, and they were filled with the Holy Ghost. There was an immediate answer vouchsafed, and they continued together, blessing and praising God; and so they "went to their own company." If they had gone to the world, if they had fled for safety, they would have disgraced themselves and dishonoured their Lord; but they did the right thing, they did not fly to the wilderness, they did not go to the world, they did not seek the arm of the civil power to defend them, but they went "to their own company," and they found sympathy and tenderness. It ought to be so in our sorrows, our difficulties, and our distresses. We should not go to seek comfort where it cannot be found; we should seek it first through the Lord, and next through the channels of His ordinances and in the fellowship of His flock, and they will not disappoint our hope.

What a beautiful simplicity in this description of the Church of Christ! People talk about going to the middle and dark ages to learn what ought to be the character and the ornaments and the accompaniments of the Church of Christ; but certainly the best way is to go at once to the fountain-head, where the water gushes forth from a fresh spring. As it passes along the channel, it must mix with the soil in some measure; but go to the fountain, and you will find what it was in the beginning; and here you have the simple account, "Being let go, they went to their own company." I do not mean to say that times may not alter and circumstances change; there may be many changes in the forms and ceremonies of the Church, but, after all, the more she observes the simplicity of the early Church, the more she is constituted in the bonds of the love of Christ.

Then, in the next place, "follow after things whereby you may edify one another." "Look not every man on his own things, but every man also on the things of others. Let this mind be in you, which was also in Christ Jesus," the great Shepherd, who left the throne of glory for the manger, the cross, and the sepulchre, to take upon Himself the sins of others.

Surely there is another thought. If a man is never brought into this company, he cannot belong to it. Christ gave Himself for us. He redeemed us from all iniquity, and purified us even as He is pure. Then they that are His people must be purified and separated, and brought into this fellowship. "There are diversities of operations, but the same Spirit;" and so some are called in early life, some are called, I believe, from the cradle, some at the font of regeneration in baptism, for we are told, "The promise is to you and to your children," and we there, in baptism, behold the outward sign of an inward grace—others are called in after life, some at one time and some at another; but, sooner or later, every man must be effectually called that shall attain to eternal life. Therefore remember how it is said, "As many as were ordained to eternal life believed;" and again it is said, "There were added to the church daily such as were saved"—the original Greek is "the saved ones." not as many as should be saved, as we translate it, but "the saved ones." Now, brethren, you must be "the saved ones," in order that you may be members of that body. You have all the mark of the Shepherd, and "the foundation of God standeth sure, having this seal, The Lord knoweth them that are His. And, Let every one that nameth the name of Christ depart from iniquity." He that hath both these seals must be a member of this chosen company.

Brethren, how ought we to pray more and more to God to increase the number of that holy company, to beautify that company with the beauty of holiness, to increase the work of grace, that so, in the grand and beautiful language of the Book of Solomon, our branch of the Church may be "fair as the moon, and terrible as an army with banners," to the glory of the Great Head, the Shepherd and Bishop of the Church, Jesus Christ our Lord.

XXII.

THE CHARACTERISTICS OF SPIRITUAL WORSHIP.

"For we are the circumcision, which worship God in the spirit, and rejoice in Christ Jesus, and have no confidence in the flesh."— PHIL. iii. 3.

MAN looketh at the outward appearance, but God looketh at the heart. Yet if man could look at the heart, he would judge by the heart, for the outward appearance is but the shadow. It is true, where there is the reality there will be the shadow; but if there be the shadow and there be not the substance, it is a mockery and a lie. It is, however, because man doth not discern the spirit that man doth not judge according to the spirit. If we had a friend that showed us affection, and could we read his heart and discover there was no truth in the appearance of love, that there was no regard for us, but rather apathy or evil antipathy towards us, should we value the semblance of his friendship, should we regard the outward expression of affection? I trow not! The father wants the inward love of his child, and without that, external regard would be rather an insult, when he sees that the affections of the heart are wanting. The God with whom we have to do in our religion, and in our worship, and in whatever constitutes worship and religion, knows us, He searches us, He tries the reins, and requires truth in the inward parts. How strange that in all ages—strange, were it not for the alienation of the heart from God and its spiritual death—strange it yet must seem that men should continually forget this great principle, and be so prone to substitute the shadow for the substance, the outward observance for the inward spiritual disposition, the attitude, the form, the language, the semblance of devotion for the worship of Him who "is a Spirit, and must be worshipped in spirit and in truth." Yet we have only to read the history of the visible Church, we have only to look around at the present day, as men might have done every day since the visible Church had an existence, to see how intense and strong is the tendency in man's nature to keep back from God, and to mock Him with outward observances, at what cost will men incur sacrifices and make efforts, and what self-denial will they not practise, if only they may satisfy God by these things external; but God still reiterates His inalienable right: "My son, give me thine heart." It must require but little reflection for a man to perceive that nothing is more unwise, nothing is more unphilosophical, nothing is more irrational, than to think to substitute the mere external, outward homage for the homage of the heart. He who is a Spirit, who is omniscient, omnipresent, and omnipotent, knows every desire, every thought, every motion, every spring of the complicated mechanism He himself has constructed for His own service. It is no marvel, then, that the great apostle with such earnestness exhorted his children at Philippi against the danger of falling into the snare of those Judaising teachers, who make so much of outward forms and sacrifices that they would supersede the inner and corresponding spirit of the mind. Supposing God were such a one as themselves, He might be imposed upon and contented with this mere bodily and fleshly exercise, but the apostle speaks thus with a holy zeal: "Finally, my brethren, rejoice in the Lord. To write the same things to you, to me indeed is not grievous."

He had to reiterate the same truths—first to speak them, then to write them, and then to preach them, line upon line, and precept upon precept. This was not irksome to him, because it was his duty—" to me indeed is not grievous, but for you it is safe"—to guard them against the various temptations that were around them. "Beware of dogs." These proud Judaising teachers branded the Gentiles as dogs, and Jesus used the current expression when He addressed the woman whose daughter was vexed with a devil: " It is not meet to take the children's bread, and to cast it to dogs;" and she answered with the pathetic plea, "Truth, Lord: yet the dogs eat of the crumbs which fall from their master's table." The outside of the cup and platter may be clean and polished, and yet the inward part be full of uncleanness; therefore "beware of dogs, beware of evil workers," whatever their semblance to outward devotion and conformity to ceremony and form, " beware of evil workers, beware of the concision." These men exulted in their circumcision as possessing a claim and privilege beyond the poor Gentiles, who were called uncircumcised dogs, and they were rather like that Pharisee who looked askance upon the poor publican; and therefore the apostle said, with a severity and irony not common in the New Testament, " Beware of the concision," forming a word just the reverse of circumcision, or cutting off, cutting out; so that he says with regard to similar false teachers, " They would exclude you, that ye might affect them;" beware, then, of the concision, of those that would cut you off from your faith in Christ; and then come in the words before us, in beautiful connexion. Whatever they pretend to, whether Jew or Gentile, it matters not, " for in Christ Jesus neither circumcision availeth anything, nor uncircumcision, but a new creature. And as many as walk according to this rule, peace be on them, and mercy, and upon the Israel of God;" "For we are the circumcision"—the true circumcision; for that is not circumcision which is outward in the flesh, but true circumcision is that of the heart, in the spirit, and not in the letter; and he is not a true Israelite who is merely one in name and inheritance, but he who is one in deed and in truth; therefore " we are the circumcision, *which worship God in the spirit, and rejoice in Christ Jesus, and have no confidence in the flesh.*"

These, then, are the three distinguishing characteristics of acceptable and spiritual worship. It cannot but be profitable to dwell upon these characteristics, and ascertain how far through grace they are ours; and that we should see how important it is that we should possess them, especially when we are about to partake—as many of you have already done—of the holy supper of Christ, which is the most palpable, as well as the most spiritual, of all the ordinances of the Christian Church, for it behoves us to see that our hearts be right with God when we are about to receive the bread and wine which represent "the body and blood of Christ, which are verily and indeed taken and received by the faithful in the Lord's supper." May God by His Spirit teach us, and give us a spiritual appreciation and enjoyment of His truth.

The first distinctive feature of spiritual and acceptable worship is, that *we worship God in the spirit.* Man, we at once perceive, is made up of two parts, the body, which is the dwelling-place or tabernacle of the man, and man himself, the soul—for man is the soul, and the soul is man. What can be clearer to the rational man than that the soul is the thing that constitutes the man? What he thinks and feels, that is the man; it is not what he does with his body. The act is the outward and visible sign, but it ought to be the outward and visible sign of an inward and spiritual feeling, disposition, and state of mind. As far as it is so, it is true and natural; and so far as it is not so, it is untrue and unnatural. Can it be otherwise than that the great God, when we are engaged in prayer and praise, has his attention directed to our hearts, to what is passing within us, and not merely to what is the appearance outwardly? The words of prayer may be, and often are repeated, and the heart be all the while away, the thoughts fixed upon the things of the world, sometimes on wicked things, while the lips are uttering solemn language, or sending up songs with sweet melody. The voice unites in true concord, as far as the noise goes, as it would in a concert-room or at an oratorio, but the mind is engaged on other things. You may go through the whole of our admirable liturgy, which expresses such contrition, such humiliation, such faith, such devotion, such wonderful and beautiful praise; but is there a correspondence between the outward and the inward praise, or is it merely a using of the language, without the inward humiliation, and deep self-abasement, and fervent intercession, and earnest desire, and deep longing after God, and to see His power and glory? After all, there may be no thirsting after Him, " as the hart panteth after the water-brooks," yet the language may be all sound and true. But is that spiritual worship? And as in the sanctuary, so in the closet and in family prayer. Does a man, when he bows the knee in prayer, seek to draw near to God? Does he try to draw near in spirit and in truth? Does he stir himself up to lay hold upon the Lord? Is there indeed an exercise of the inner man? "We are the circumcision, which worship God in the spirit," and that is spiritual for a man to have intercourse with God, to have communion with God, to draw near to God. In order to do this, a man must worship God by the spirit if he worship Him in the spirit. But such is the carnality of our natural mind, so does our heart and soul cling to the dust, so indisposed are we to spiritual exercise, so dead are our spirits within us, even in the best, that it is not earthly fire that can kindle the sacrifice, and make it ascend to heaven; there must be the heavenly fire provided, and we must look for it coming down from heaven, as the prophet did. It is of no use having the beautiful arrangements of the altar, and the wood, and the victim on the wood, if there be no fire to kindle the sacrifice, if there be no internal spirit, no living fire. "What is it then? I will pray with the spirit, and I will pray with the understanding also." Remember, you must look to the Spirit that you may have the spirit. It is only as the Spirit enables you that your praise will be grateful, your confession contrite, your adoration elevated, and your intercession fervent. "Likewise the Spirit also helpeth our infirmities: for we know not what we should pray for as we ought; but the Spirit itself maketh intercession for us with groanings which cannot be uttered." We never know what to ask or how to pray until the Spirit teaches us. Come then to the house of God, go into your closets, kneel down there, lift up your ejaculations to God as you are on your way to business; do this in the help of the Spirit of God, and He that heareth prayer will give you the mind and the Spirit. This, then, brethren, is the first primary distinctive feature of spiritual worship: "We worship God in the spirit."

And the next is like unto it, *we rejoice in Christ Jesus*. And this, in some sense, must be said to be more discriminating still, because we can conceive a certain earnestness and attentiveness on the part of the heathen in their worship, where they have got a little light, so that sometimes unconsciously the spirit may give the fire, and kindle a very imperfect sacrifice. I have asked the question of many missionaries, if they have ever met with anything of the kind, and in one or two cases they have. It is clear that in those cases a clearer light has been afterwards given, and we are told that the prayers and alms of Cornelius, who was but a proselyte at the gate, went up for a memorial before God. But, however a man may, to a certain extent, worship God in spirit without any clear or distinct knowledge of the way in which the Spirit is to be approached, no man can " rejoice in Christ Jesus" to whom Christ is not revealed; for "no man can say that Jesus is the Lord, but by the Holy Ghost." Therefore the distinguishing feature of a true Christian is that he calls on the name of the Lord Jesus. " Whosoever shall call upon the name of the Lord shall be saved." To call upon Jesus is to invoke Him as the incarnate God, to worship Him as our Saviour and Deliverer, who is " exalted to God's right hand to be a Prince and a Saviour, for to give repentance to Israel, and forgiveness of sins." To " rejoice in Jesus Christ" is distinct from the false carnal joy of the bigoted Judaising formalist, of the Pharisee, who rejoiced in his own works; for forms and ceremonies are of no avail, because of the imperfection with which we do them, and are not to be a ground of trust and confidence. If any man had a right to think he had much to trust in, surely it was St. Paul. He was "circumcised the eighth day," and was brought up a strict and rigid Jew; but what things were gain to him he counted loss when he saw Christ his righteousness, and found that all must be built on Him, and all built to Him—not that we may merit Christ, but we come to Him through His merit. Then, indeed, he said, " God forbid that I should glory"— rejoice, boast myself, be exalted—" save in the cross of our Lord Jesus Christ, by whom the world is crucified unto me, and I unto the world." " What things were gain to me, those I counted loss for Christ. Yea doubtless, and I count all things but loss for the excellency of the knowledge of Christ Jesus my Lord: for whom I have suffered the loss of all things, and do count them but dung, that I may win

Christ, and be found in him." This, therefore, is to "rejoice in Christ Jesus," when He is a man's hope and comfort and joy for time and for eternity—in all his services, in all his various trials, in all his joys, in all his sorrows, in sickness, and in death. All his joy comes from that fathomless fountain of God's grace, through Christ's atonement, and it is the one source of all his consolation, all his hope, and all his thankfulness. And Christian men ought to rejoice, they ought always to rejoice, but always in the Lord. "Rejoice in the Lord always: and again I say, Rejoice." Yea, though I should be left desolate, "yet I will rejoice in the Lord, I will joy in the God of my salvation." One who, if any, should have been expected to have confidence in the flesh, said, "My soul doth magnify the Lord, and my spirit hath rejoiced in God my Saviour." Therefore, brethren, whatever the outward signs of devotion, whatever the outward character and conduct, still the name of the Lord Jesus is the one ground of our glory and our joy. "We rejoice in Christ Jesus our Lord."

Then the crowning characteristic of all. All before has been a negative, as it were, a shadow, but this is the substance:—"*We worship God in the spirit, and have no confidence in the flesh.*" If a man worship God in the spirit, he will have no confidence in the flesh. The word "flesh," in the ordinary sense, admits of a natural and carnal signification; but the word flesh is used in the Word of God, and St. Paul uses it here, in contradistinction to the spirit. It means, therefore, outward bodily exercises—things that are merely secondary, and may be subservient means of grace, such as churches, ministers, services, all ornamentations, the various ceremonies of any one church; all these things may be good servants of the spirit, but they are not to be substituted for the spirit, they are not to be regarded as part of the spirit; they are of the flesh, the body without the soul, the altar without the fire, the shadow without the substance, and, therefore, he says, "have no confidence in the flesh." Therefore our hope towards God is not built on anything we have done or can do; it is not built upon anything, however fitting and proper, and even ordained of God, as far as outward good goes; neither fasting, nor prayer, nor hearing the Word, nor alms-giving, nor even obedience itself, is confidence to us. We thank God for them, and we know these things follow in their place; but we do not substitute any of them, or all of them, for Christ, or unite them with Him, as being our ground of confidence towards God; "we rejoice in Christ Jesus, and have no confidence in the flesh." We have no hope because of our good doings, because of our devotions, or because of anything else merely external; our hope hangs on Christ alone, we glory in Him, and in Him only. "Other foundation can no man lay than that is laid, which is Jesus Christ."

Now, beloved brethren, what can be more clear or plain than this? One marvels that men, who make much of forms and ceremonies, and external observances, and pride themselves upon them—one marvels that their reason and common sense does not assent to all this. It is truth manifest, it is truth obvious, it is truth no man can calmly and coolly deny, because it is to deny his own sense and reason. Ah! men will and may deny it in their conduct. What a man wants, unrenewed, is a religion that will satisfy the conscience and the soul, and take away the fear and dread of death and eternity; and yet, at the same time, not demand of him that spiritual heart, that sacrifice, that spiritual submission to God, that life in the soul which man shrinks from and dislikes. You may be assured of it, therefore, that all men who have any sense of religion, and yet do not give the heart to God, will verge into one of these two extremes—latitudinarianism, on the one hand, so as to explain and rationalise away all that is distinctive and vital in godliness, or, on the other hand, content themselves with doing certain things, with performing certain services, and then think to make their peace with God, or, at all events, to make up what Christ has left for them to do. Therefore beware of the snare on the right hand and on the left hand. On the one hand, do not explain away vital truth, nor, on the other hand, make up for the want of it with hay, stubble, and outward observances. Be in earnest in all the duties of religion, as if you had to save yourselves, just because you are saved in order to these things—not on account of them, but in order to them. Everything in its proper place, the root downward, and the fruit upward, the foundation under the building, and not upon the building. Build in order to perfection, and be trees of righteousness, in accordance with the Lord's planting, and ye shall never be rooted up. Then, however sometimes it may be objected to you that you make so much of the spirit, you may answer without pride or presumption, "We are the circumcision, which worship God in the spirit, and rejoice in Christ Jesus, and have no confidence in the flesh."

XXIII.

GOD'S BLESSING WITH RICHES.

"The blessing of the Lord, it maketh rich, and he addeth no sorrow with it."—Prov. x. 22.

Few things on the face of society are more fitting to strike a man than the mighty power which that thing we style money exercises on the human mind. In civilised society, it may be said to be the mainspring of universal activity, effort and desire. The mass of mankind, and especially in this commercial and manufacturing land, and not less in this day of high-pressure in competition and trade, seem to live for this one object. There are many other things by the way that they may regard, but the supreme thing is the attainment of wealth, or the increase of it, if they have already attained it in large proportion. The appetite grows on that which it feeds upon; like a man with the dropsy, the more he drinks, the more it deepens his thirst. Yet men, if they reflect a little, must come to the conclusion that as a supreme object it is a very poor one. No doubt it can procure comforts and conveniencies, it can procure many things that naturally we desire, it can gratify and pamper "the lust of the flesh, the lust of the eye, and the pride of life;" but, after all, when all is gained, what is gained? Man goes to his grave, he has a more pompous funeral perhaps, he has perhaps the richer trumpery of woe; but it is mockery, the man has gone, naked as he came from his mother's womb, into the presence of his Maker and his judge. There it will not be asked what a man died worth, in the popular sense in which the miserable language is used by mankind; but what will he be worth when weighed in the balances of eternal deserts? what will he answer when summoned before the bar of eternal justice? what will he have for his fortune for eternity? what is his wealth to last for ever? There is, nevertheless, a use of wealth as well as an abuse of it; there is a legitimate desire to attain it, but a very subordinate one it should be. The words before us seem to present us with both these views, at all times appropriate, and especially so at the present day, when trade seems to be almost running loose from the bounds of restraint. The wise man, speaking as directed by the Spirit of God, uttered this memorable aphorism; and it has often struck my mind, though I have not taken it for our subject of discourse before: "the blessing of the Lord, it maketh rich, and he addeth no sorrow with it."

A man rich without riches: and *A man having riches, and not having sorrow and remorse and grief with them.* These are the two points presented by the words, and though at first sight it looks as if it had but one point, we shall find that, like the double cord, you can easily untwist it, and it presents these two subjects:—The blessing of the Lord, that, if man has nothing more, makes him rich; and, in the next place, the blessing of the Lord sometimes makes His children rich, and then adds no sorrow with those riches. May His Spirit direct us and lead us to view these things in the light of eternity, and with the eye of faith, and not in the mist of the false atmosphere the world throws around us, and which often suffuses even the servants of God.

The blessing of the Lord maketh a man rich, though he may

be externally, and as it regards this present life, a very poor man. That is the first point, and it is one of very deep importance and interest. The mass of mankind will be poor for ever. Ever since mankind have been upon this earth a fallen race, the wealthy have been the exception and the poor the rule, and we are told "the poor shall never cease out of the land;" still, I think the word poor is often misapplied. No man is poor that gets the honest bread of industry, sufficient, wholesome, and good. If a man has sufficient food and raiment for himself and his family, it is wrong to style him a poor man. In the true sense of the word, he is not poor, he has enough, and having enough he may be said to have so far sufficient. If he has contentment with it, it will suffice, and nothing will be sufficient for a discontented man. Very little will content a meek, humble-minded man, and the blessing of the Lord maketh that man rich, though he has not what the world would call riches. After all, what is the purpose of wealth? What will it do for a man at the best, but give him enjoyment, and position, and quietness, and rest, and add to his comfort and happiness; but it can do no more. It cannot bribe pain, it cannot stop sickness, it cannot stay death for one moment. In men's agony and distress it is very little it can often do; in cases of remorse, distress, despair, and disquiet of the mind, it is as a breath upon the troubled ocean to make it calm. There is no power in a man's wealth to keep his mind in quietness and peace, but there is that which can do it without wealth, and that is true riches. "Godliness with contentment is great gain. For we brought nothing into this world, and it is certain we can carry nothing out. And having food and raiment, let us be therewith content." Let a man have godliness, and the blessing, and presence, and peace of God, and it is great gain. God never says that of wealth, but, on the contrary, He calls it filthy lucre, and He calls the love of it idolatry, He brands the man who sets it before him as his main object as an idolater, and few things are more detestable, few things are more degrading, few things are more contemptible than idolatry. He does not say so with regard to those who have the blessing of God, but, on the contrary, He says, "All things are yours, whether Paul, or Apollos, or Cephas, or the world, or life, or death, ... all are yours, and ye are Christ's;" and the reconciled believer can say of His Father in heaven through his Redeemer, "The Lord is my portion," choose ye what you will; boast as you will of what you have made, of your riches, of your attainments, of fame, of renown, of distinction, "the Lord is my portion, therefore will I trust in Him." "One thing have I desired of the Lord, that will I seek after." "Seek first the kingdom of God and His righteousness, and all these things shall be added unto you." Now if a man has the blessing of God, then in his cottage, though it be not a mansion, or his hard bed, though it be not a downy one, in his daily toil, though he has no equipage to convey him to and fro, if a man has the blessing of God, he is not a poor man. He may have the simplest fare, and yet not be poor; as a poor woman said to one who visited her, and marvelled at the thankfulness and joy with which she blessed God for her scanty meal—she showed the remnants of a barley loaf and said, "This is my fare." "Coarse hard fare," said he. Said she, "I have enjoyed my crust with my Saviour, and my Saviour with my crust; is not that rich living?" And was it not so? Do you not think that such a soul was happier ten thousand times than many who are "clothed in purple and fine linen, and fare sumptuously every day?" So that even apart from eternity, the blessing of the Lord maketh rich, for He gives a man what riches cannot give, He gives him more than riches can give, a peaceable, quiet, contented, submissive, patient mind. Then how sweet to feel, too, that that portion, which is the portion of the

Lord, is not at the mercy of fires, or storms, or bankruptcy, or bad debts, or cheating, or roguery, or change of circumstances, or revolutions of nations, or wars, or peace, or national engagements of any kind, but that it stands independent; it is above, and therefore cannot be reached, or overtaken, or moved. Therefore, my dear brethren, as there are many of you who never will be rich, do not hanker after it, do not long for it, do not be restless about it, do not torment yourselves, for you will never reach it, and if you did, you would not be one whit better than you are. Be assured of this, though people won't believe it until they have tried it, you may go on and go on as the drunken man does, reeling to the brink of the precipice, and never believing that he is in danger till he falls down and is crushed. "The blessing of the Lord maketh rich." Give me thy peace, and then though I have but little I have much, and I am satisfied. Thy will be done.

And, brethren, the more we meditate on the proverb, the more we see that it has, to a certain extent, the converse bearing upon which we intend the more largely to dwell. The blessing of the Lord, it maketh rich, and then when it is so, He addeth no sorrow.

Here are riches obtained with the blessing of the Lord:— here are riches got, and He does not add sorrow with them.

There are very many men who seem to leave God altogether out of business. They think that to be reminded of Him, and to look to Him in their business, is enthusiasm and fanaticism, if not weakness. They think the man never succeeds who is so weak as to look to God in the temples of trade, upon the exchange, and in the counting-house. That noble man, the late Prince Consort,—whom we trust and believe feared God,—selected for the motto for the great London Exchange, "The earth is the Lord's, and the fulness thereof." All it contains, all its good gifts; and, therefore, if all, then God is over all and in all. There are, however, many instances in which men cannot but see that the Lord has to do with the things of this world: famine, pestilence, inaction, loss of trade, war; these things do not come without God; and it is seen more perhaps in a commercial land, in the dislocation of commerce, than in an agricultural land, where it does not seem as if God were so much to be looked to. Yet the clouds and the sunshine are His. "He maketh His sun to shine on the evil and on the good, and sendeth rain on the just and on the unjust." We have instances of agricultural countries where great distress has prevailed, and the labours and efforts of men have proved abortive. And why? They did not look higher than the earth, they did not look to Him who sitteth above the heavens, who says, "Ye looked for much, and, lo, it came to little; and when ye brought it home, I did blow upon it. Why? saith the Lord of hosts. Because of mine house that is waste, and ye run every man into his own house. Therefore the heaven over you is stayed from dew, and the earth is stayed from her fruit. And I called for a drought upon the land, and upon the mountains, and upon the corn, and upon the new wine, and upon the oil, and upon that which the ground bringeth forth, and upon men, and upon cattle, and upon all the labour of the hands." "Prove me now herewith," saith the Lord afterwards, "if I will not open you the windows of heaven, and pour you out a blessing, that there shall not be room enough to receive it." *There* is the curse of the Lord, making poor in the face of all the efforts of industry and diligence; and *there* is the blessing of the Lord, making rich as soon as God is sought first in His kingdom and righteousness. Then, all things are added. The blessing of the Lord, that maketh rich, if a man seeks it humbly, and does as God would have him, and as God intends him. That is God making rich. I have seen families that did not fear God, and had no regard for Him, all confusion and disorder; the father a drunkard, the mother slatternly and unthrifty, the children all rebellious and turning out against their parents; I have seen grace enter the family, and the father has become sober and diligent, the wife thrifty and faithful, the children obedient and orderly, for the blessing of God has been there. I have seen it produce temporal prosperity, and the man has become rich in the truest sense of the word; comfort has taken the place of disorder and trouble; kindness, affection, and mutual co-operation have taken the place of chaos and dislocation, and the man has become comparatively prosperous and rich. When we see such a man fearing God, prosperous, and becoming one of the princes of society, not merely in wealth but in other things; when he is faithful in small things as in large, making a liberal use of his wealth, we see that to be rich in heart is better than to be rich in pocket, and poor and miserable in spirit; so that you see the blessing of the Lord often manifestly conduces to a man's own faith in God, though, as we have heard this morning, "if riches increase, set not your heart upon them." He that knows the heart gives us that caution. When riches increase they are more apt to become a snare than when a man is poor, for when a man is comparatively poor, he says, "I have very little to care much about." Increase of wealth is unlike other habits, such as indulgence at the table and in wine; they leave a man as he gets old, but covetousness grows upon a man; as Christ in the parable tells us when He says, the lust of riches cropping up, " chokes the word, and he becometh unfruitful." So that you see the possession of the blessing of the Lord puts man into temptation to a certain extent, and thus God will try him as He did Job.

But, brethren, the great thing is this—the grand result of it. The blessing of the Lord maketh men rich, *and adds no sorrow*. That is saying a great deal. I have known many men in my time comparatively happy when in possession of a small competency, what the world would not call wealth; and when they have become rich, I have known them to become unhappy, just in proportion as they have become rich. I have known a man's mind so set on the world, that instead of feeling more content and satisfied, he has craved, and craved, and craved for more, and feared losing what he had got; he has felt uncertainty hovering over him, and the man was literally a richer man when poor than when rich. Why was that? Because riches were sought as an end, and not as a means; because the man had determined to become rich come what would. "Rich I must be, come what will," was what he said, when he should have said, "Saved I must be, come what will." If a man does so become rich he has his portion, "he has his reward;" he turns his back on God, and will not God be just and turn His back on him? Be assured of this, a man has only the blessing of God in getting riches, when God is above the riches in his mind. "They that will be rich"—the Greek is, that set their hearts upon it, "fall into temptation and a snare, and into many foolish and hurtful lusts, which drown men in destruction and perdition." As a heathen poet, writing of the Romans, said, "Money, money, honestly if you can; but at any rate, money." Is it not so? Look about you, money at any rate. Then, when it is so, is not money-making supreme? That which a man loves most, that which he fears most, that which he thinks most of in his heart at night, in the morning, in the counting-house, at the church, or the Exchange, is not that his god? Then is it not clear that such a man cannot get rich with God's blessing? And it is "the recompense of their reward." Christ says, let them have it, "they have their reward." And then, brethren, alas! how often is God left out altogether in partnerships, in schemes of business, in purposes for which men enter into certain schemes! Should not men pray for God's guidance and blessing, and look for it in such things? In his conscience a man knows that it should be so, and then it is only that he has a right to expect the blessing of God upon what he does. You see continually men conducting certain business as a company,—the names are not mentioned,—and the company is, after all, but a shelter for what is done. Men allow to be done in a company what they would never permit in their individual capacity, as if they could be like a man lost in a crowd. Ah! dear brethren, it is the grand thing to acknowledge the Lord in business, whatever it be, in companies, or in partnership undertakings. If you cannot ask the blessing of God honestly and conscientiously in any step in business, give it up altogether. Only let the helm be set aright to the needle, guided by the compass and the chart of inspiration, and a man won't be far wrong; even his mistakes will be forgiven, because they are done from error of judgment. Thus the blessing of God will be in his prosperity, for he giveth wealth and no sorrow with it. Oh, what sorrows are often added with wealth; how some who are revelling in wealth have remorse and disquietude of mind! What a different thing to have wealth and no sorrow with it; what a different thing for a man to be able to look back and say, " I have served God honestly, and I look for the mercy of His dear Son, who knows that herein I have exercised myself to have always a conscience void of offence toward God and toward men; therefore, this is my rejoicing and the testimony of my conscience, that in simplicity and godly sincerity, not with fleshly wisdom, but by the grace of God, I have had my conversation in the world; and if I have got riches, it has not been by cheating others, it has not been by taking advantage of others, it has not been by making articles look shining that would not bear inspection, and that I should be afraid and ashamed to tell men all about." In the present day, men in the pressure of trade think it fair to take advantage of dishonest manœuvres, as if anything would justify them in doing wrong! The blessing of the Lord, *that* maketh rich—and other riches a man should never desire or wish to have—and He addeth no sorrow with it. Remember the sorrow that will at last befall the man that hath not the blessing of God upon him; remember the poor wretched man who lifted up his eyes in hell, being in torment; he was reminded, "Son, remember that thou in thy lifetime received thy good things, and likewise Lazarus evil things;" thou madest choice of thy portion, and thou hadst it, and "now he is comforted, and thou are tormented."

Ah! dear brethren, the subject you see is one of a very practical and a very searching nature. The man who wishes to be honest to himself and to his God should search himself, and examine himself; for certainly in a mercantile community like this the snares of wealth are the snares that most beset us, and therefore the snares of all others that men should be guarded against, that men should watch against. And therefore, with all affection and faithfulness, I speak plainly to you, as I would desire to be spoken to myself if I were in the midst of prosperous trade.

Do not let the poor man say, this is a sermon for the rich; do not let them say, "Oh, that is true of many men who oppress the poor hireling in his wages." You will never get any good by speaking thus of others, you must think of yourselves. There are men as much bent on getting rich who have not £5 beforehand, as men who have £5,000 or £50,000. It is the state of the heart, and not the state of the fortune, that must be right with God. I have known a man getting in business for himself think things were not going right, and desert God. The poverty that leads to true riches is better than the wealth that leads to eternal bankruptcy. I believe it is not wrong if a man gets on, if it is with the blessing of the Lord, with a right mind and with consistency, if he does not "gain the world and lose his own soul," for what profit is it then? If he gets rich, let it be so, if God blesses him in his wealth. But what will make amends for the absence of God's blessing? It may be said of many of you that are in comparative poverty, as it was said of the Church of old, " I know thy poverty, but thou art rich ;" and again, as St. Paul beautifully said, "As poor, yet making many rich ; as having nothing, and yet possessing all things." Blessed paradox! That is to have true riches.

Then, brethren, " seek first," whether you are rich or poor, " the kingdom of God and His righteousness." That is, do not merely seek first at the beginning, as I wish all young men would do, but set out with this principle, " I am not going to lose my soul, and incur the curse of God to get wealth; at any rate, I want it honestly, fairly, and righteously, if I have it; seek first the kingdom of God and His righteousness, not only first in the order of time, but in the order of degree; let the first be first, let the highest be highest, let the supreme be supreme, and the rest all subordinate. Oh! seek first, in business and out of business, seek everywhere the kingdom of God as the glorious goal, and His righteousness as the divine highway to that goal; and then, all things—whatever is best and good—will be added. If the blessing of the Lord make you rich, be it so, He will add no sorrow; if the blessing of the Lord suffice, and if, instead of riches, He give you poverty, what matters what you are here? When you reach heaven you will forget all, in the presence of eternal thankfulness.

XXIV.

GOD'S BLESSING WITH POVERTY.

"Ye shall serve the Lord your God, and He shall bless thy bread, and thy water."—Exodus xxiii. part of 25.

It is possible for a man to serve only earthly objects while he professes to be serving God. That man is a hypocrite; he deceives himself, and would deceive others. But it is possible to seek eternal life regardless of man, even in this world; and though "the recompense of the reward" is reserved to eternity, there are the firstfruits of that reward vouchsafed to men in this pilgrimage, amidst our sorrows, our strifes, and our trials. It is not that God takes away trials and sorrows from His people, but that he intermingles with the cup of sorrow such heavenly consolations, that it is even sweet to drink it. "Godliness is profitable unto all things, having promise of the life that now is, and of that which is to come." If we "seek first the kingdom of God and His righteousness," we have the assurance that all other things that are needful and good "shall be added thereto." What God said to Israel of old He says to us; what He said to His believing people then, He says to His believing people now; and He calls upon those who have ears to listen to it. Beautifully in accordance with the remarks I have been making is that simple and impressive passage before us. God was telling His people what they were to do when they were established in the land sworn to their forefathers, and He tells them what He will do to them if they are faithful to Him. "Ye shall serve the Lord your God, and He shall bless thy bread, and thy water." It is a passage particularly appropriate for those whose bread and water are scanty, and who have but little prospect of gaining influence, or perhaps even competency; who pray literally, "Give us day by day our daily bread," who know not what shall be on the morrow,—to them especially this promise comes with heavenly consolation to their hearts.

The text presents to us *what our duty is in this life:* and *what is our privilege in the discharge of that duty.* Our duty is to serve the Lord our God. Our privilege is, "He will bless our bread and our water." Let us look to His Spirit, that His words may be effectual for our profit.

Very simple, very short, and very plain is the description here of what is man's whole interest. It is summed up in one short portion of a sentence:—"Thou shalt serve the Lord thy God." Man was made to serve, and he cannot help but serve. His pride and his vain notions of independency lead him sometimes to boast like the fool, "How sayest thou, Ye shall be made free?" that "were never in bondage to any man." What resentment they feel against any attempts to enslave them by their fellow-men, but how utterly regardless they are of the wretched thraldom in which their own souls are held by their vile lusts and passions! Every man serves something; many serve wealth, or lust, or pride; and that which they so serve is the devil, for the devil is lord and god of those who serve sin. They that keep his commandments are his subjects. His commandments are, love of the flesh, love of the world, love of mischief; this is Satan's law, and every man who keeps it is Satan's slave. The chain that is bound round the spirit of man has its last link in the hand of the great enemy of souls, the god of this world that worketh with the children of disobedience, and urges them on to their everlasting ruin. Every man is a servant. Those who boast of their liberality while they promise liberty to their dupes, they are slaves to their own corruption; and to whom a man is brought into subjection, to the same is he enslaved. The apostle Paul says—"Know ye not, that to whom ye yield yourselves servants to obey, his servants ye are to whom ye obey; whether of sin unto death, or of obedience unto righteousness?" Either we sin unto wickedness, or are holy unto God. Every being is a servant; from Gabriel down to the lowest existing being, all obey. Our great Creator did not make us to be slaves to mean debased things, He did not put us in a dependent position that we should become subject to vile things, that we should become subject to a lying world, to a deceitful temper, to a corrupt and fallen nature. No. He made us to serve Himself, to serve Him as the perfection of our nature. Look at all things that have not fallen from God;—angel and archangel, cherubim and seraphim, do His commandments, and hearken to the voice of His word. Gabriel stands before Him with outstretched wings and upturned eye, catching His every word and His every look; the stars in their courses, the sun and the moon, all obey their Creator's laws, and own their dependence on Him. The beasts of the field, the birds of the air, the fishes in the sea, the clouds, the storms, the seasons, all obey the great God; and yet there is order, there is harmony, there is beauty. But God found that man, as amongst His dependent subjects, soon fell from Him, and served Him no longer. The heart was betrayed, the mind was beclouded; and sorrow, and sin, and shame followed, and death came as a consequence, and all our woe. But the blessed gospel of Jesus Christ comes to us, and offers again to us admission into His blessed service. Christ came to call us back to God, to win us from the masters who have no right to us to our rightful Lord. He came to break the chains that bind in bondage, and to bring us into the glorious liberty of the sons of God. Beautiful is the description given by the apostle of this wondrous change. We have it in the 6th of Romans, and it is so full and to the point that we pray you, beloved, hearken unto it with all earnest attention:— "Reckon ye also yourselves to be dead indeed unto sin, but alive unto God through Jesus Christ our Lord. Let not sin, therefore, reign in your mortal body, that ye should obey it in the lusts thereof." "Awake thou that sleepest, arise from the dead, and Christ shall give you light." Do not go back to your old drudgery. "Neither yield ye your members as instruments of unrighteousness unto sin: but yield yourselves unto God, as those that are alive from the dead, and your members as instruments of righteousness unto God." You have received the blessed doctrine of Christ, and Him crucified, you have seen its effect and its power, you have been renewed in the spirit of your mind. "For sin shall not have dominion over you: for ye are not under the law, but under grace. What then? shall we sin because we are not under the law, but under grace? God forbid. Know ye not, that to whom ye yield yourselves servants to obey, his servants ye are to whom ye obey, whether of sin unto death, or of obedience unto righteousness? But God be thanked, that ye were the servants of sin, but ye have obeyed from the heart that form of doctrine which was delivered you. Being then made free from sin, ye became the servants of righteousness. I speak after the manner of men, because of the infirmity of your flesh,"—to make it plain and clear to you. "For as ye have yielded your members servants to uncleanness, and to iniquity unto iniquity; even so now yield your members servants to righteousness unto holiness. For when ye were the servants of sin,"—when ye were not the servants of God but the servants of sin, what a wretched master that is! what a debased despot!—" ye were free from righteousness." You might have some convictions, you might have some good desires, but sin was master, and you served your master.

"What fruit had ye then in those things whereof ye are now ashamed? for the end of those things is death. But now being made free from sin, and become servants to God, ye have your fruit unto holiness, and the end everlasting life." Thus it is that a man becomes Christ's as he becomes the servant of God, the old yoke is sundered, the old master is dethroned, the old law binds him no more, he is strong and mighty to do the will of God, and he becomes the servant of God. Such was the beautiful language of St. Paul.

It is the glory of a being like man to be able to say, I serve my God. "Choose you this day whom ye will serve." "As for me and my house,"—if I can have them with me,—"we will serve the Lord our God." Oh! the dignity and self-exaltation of a man who is thus free to serve God. He is a man that can do as he likes, for he likes to do as God likes, his will is in harmony with the omnipotent will, all is harmony, all things work for his good, he is a fellow-worker with his God, God "worketh in him both to will and to do of His good pleasure." O beloved, try what a thing it is to serve God. What a satisfaction, and freedom, and tranquillity, and sense of conscious dignity, accompanied with the deepest humility, it brings, what a blessed confidence for time and eternity, when we can look up to our blessed Master and say, "Lord, what wilt Thou have me to do?" This is indeed "perfect freedom;" this is the secret and sum of that "peace of God which passeth all understanding." No man should despair of breaking the laws of the usurper. I heard lately of a young man, who had many good convictions and desires, falling under the wretched drudgery of drunkenness. Though he prayed to be kept from his besetting sin, his companionships came on and he forgot his prayers, and fell again. At last he was led to abandon himself in hopelessness. A holy man told him to try this one prayer, and to use it as often as his tempter came upon him with his seductions:—"O God, fill me with thy Holy Spirit." In beautiful fulfilment of that admonition we heard in the lesson this morning, "And be not drunken with wine, wherein is excess, but be ye filled with the Holy Spirit." He had grace given him to offer that prayer till a strong temptation came upon him, and he continued praying, the fiend lost his power over him, the thraldom that had ground him to the dust left him, and he became not only a sober man, but a holy man, and a servant of Jesus Christ. Oh then, beloved, ask God for His Spirit to make you free in dependence upon the strength of Omnipotence. There is your hope. If you have never yet tried it, break the fetters, do not be held in bitter bondage, but serve the living God who made you, who redeemed you, who called you, and who will accept you. Oh then, join yourselves fully to the Lord, come to His table, own Him your master, feed upon His heavenly food, bind your hearts "with cords, even to the horns of the altar," and be not ashamed of it; then it shall be said, as Joshua said of Israel of old, "Ye are witnesses against yourselves that we have chosen you the Lord, to serve Him." Yes. He chose me, and I have chosen Him; He apprehended me, and I have apprehended Him; He said to me when following the world, "Follow me," and now I find His service the joy of my heart and the strength of my life. A new privilege will your blessed Master give you, even in this poor, sinful world, you shall have your wages out of the grave, for "the wages of sin is death; but the gift of God is eternal life through Jesus Christ our Lord." What hath the man who knows the service of Christ? What satisfaction, what comfort did he have in the Bacchanalian hour? what in the dark scene of criminal indulgence? what in the indulgence of corrupt pleasure? Did he find satisfaction, or rest, or pleasure, or peace within him? I trow not! And what says his Master now? "I will bless thy bread, and thy water." Here is the promise for all God's servants—every one of them. No one is so poor but he will have some bread and water, and Jesus says if you serve Him, He will bless your bread and your water. You may say, "Will He not give us wealth? will He not give us the good things of this life? will He not gratify our passions and our desires? No, beloved brethren. The people of this world He may make rich, and they may have no sorrow with it; but it is not often that it is so. The just man, the honest man, the sober man will be a prudent man, a wise man, and an economical man, and he will be more likely to succeed in this life; yet this is not the promise. He does not promise wealth, but He rather says, "Seekest thou great things for thyself? seek them not." If wealth comes, take heed, for it is more perilous than poverty. Do not covet it. They that get rich heap to themselves many sorrows. Be assured that a man has more reason to pray in prosperity and wealth, "Good Lord, deliver me," than he has in times of adversity, for "where your treasure is, there will your heart be also." A man has more reason to tremble when wealth is pouring in upon him, than when he is approaching to poverty. Ay, it is not abundance that He promises, but He promises to give bread and water, and to bless it. "I wot that he whom Thou blessest is blessed, and he whom Thou cursest is cursed." Splendour, grandeur, wealth, will not make a man happy if God's curse is upon him. No, he must have the blessing of God. God can make the smallest meal one of feasting, and joy, and gladness, and He can sow grief and mourning at the table of luxury. Oh, how often have we seen how little will suffice with God's blessing. "Having food and raiment, let us therewith be content." If more comes, well; if it does not, we have food and raiment, and let us be content. Cannot God make a little go a great way? As Matthew Henry said:—"My children, the blessing of God can make a little go a great way." You see men receiving large wages, but in their houses all is desolate, filthy, and disorderly; their table is empty, and their wages are devoted to drunkenness and sinful indulgence. There is a leak in the vessel, that keeps it under water; and what is the secret? They lack the blessing of God, there is something wrong between them and God. "The curse of the Lord is in the house of the wicked; but he blesseth the habitation of the just." I have seen the houses of people with small wages, where all is cleanliness, and decency, and order, though there is comparative poverty. Their small table is decently spread, the little food they have is clean, all is orderly, and they sit down to their meal with the blessing of God, and thank Him for the crust. That food is as much as the rich man's, for it is all-sufficient, and if a man has a stalled ox, he cannot look round with more satisfaction, and a greater measure of comfort upon the meal; for God is amongst them blessing their table; He presides in their hearts, and thus their little meal is a sacrifice of praise and thanksgiving. As a poor man once said to me, "I go home on Sunday, and I get a little, sometimes I wish I could get more, but I am thankful for what I have here, and I think of the world where we shall hunger no more, neither thirst any more, and I feel as satisfied as if I had had more abundantly." How beautiful an illustration that those who serve Him, He will bless their bread and water, and will make it go far to satisfy and fulfil their desires! Yea, brethren, and how will God make it give peace and quietness of mind with a little provision, and a small and scanty lot! How beautifully it is said, "His bread shall be given him; his waters shall be sure." They shall have it. As Matthew Henry quaintly says:—"The difference between a rich man and a poor man who serves God is this: the rich man is his own banker, and God is the poor man's banker; and that is a bank that never dishonours the cheques that are drawn upon it in prayer." They are always honoured, therefore His people eat their meals with confidence, because they know their store will not fail them: they know that He feeds the raven; and shall He forget them? He cares for the sparrow; He clothes the lily with a beauty that casts the splendour of Solomon in all his glory in the shade; and if the Father cares for them, will He not provide for the morrow? "The morrow shall take thought for the things of itself." What a sweet seasoning it is when we receive what we have with thanksgiving! How it satisfies! then, indeed, an ordinary meal becomes a sacrament, a living sacrifice of praise and thanksgiving. God says, "I will bless thy bread and thy water;" and if He bless it, then it becomes a feast. Men of this world are far too apt to look at outward appearances; they see a man living in a splendid dwelling, driving in his chariot, provided with everything to administer to his comforts, and people think he must be happy. Perhaps, if you could look into his heart, if you could look into the interior of his family solitude, there would not be the best prospect before you. And why? Because he has not the blessing of God? and instead of desiring his lot, and envying him, you would perhaps thank God that He has made you to differ. It is your own fault if you are not led indeed to say, as St. Paul said of himself, "As poor, yet making many rich; as having nothing, and yet possessing all things" in Christ, if blessed of God, for that alone is satisfaction to an immortal soul. One smile from His face can make the poorest fare to be a luxury, and the lowliest dwelling to be the gate of heaven. Why should we suppose we must have splendour and grandeur to make us happy? The poorest man on earth may be envied by those possessing riches and grandeur; for if, by the blessing of God, he has opened up to him the bright prospect of that kingdom where they shall hunger and thirst no more; angels shall attend him, and wait to waft his spirit to his Father's mansions. Yes, if God bless a lowly dwelling with humble fare, it will not be desolate. God can give satisfaction and peace when all is desolate around. Would to God that every man, rich or poor, whatever be his lot, would lay to heart that this is the "one thing needful," to serve God, no matter in what condition, no matter with what measure of talents and advantage, whether little or much. We must serve Him who hath bought us with His blood, who hath redeemed us from sin and Satan, whom we are pledged in our baptism to serve; that is "the one thing needful." Secure that, leave the rest, and it will follow. As the substance follows the seed, so will prosperity and peace accompany the honest service of God.

And if you are to serve God, you must break loose from the service of other masters. "We are debtors, not to the flesh, to live after the flesh. For if ye live after the flesh, ye shall die: but if ye through the Spirit do mortify the deeds of the body, ye shall live." Therefore, take up arms against the tyrants that would usurp dominion over you, resist your angry tempers, your envious and hateful passions, your tendencies to indulge the flesh, resist impurity, resist drunkenness, resist uncleanness, and every other evil spirit, take up arms against them, be free, maintain your freedom, struggle earnestly for it, it is a glorious conflict—and glory, honour, and immortality are your reward. Do not be dragged back to serve the devil, and the world, and the flesh; but be true to your God and serve Him, and you will find His service "perfect freedom," and perfect happiness. And, dear brethren, I would entreat the poor in this world to pray to God to give them this spirit. It may be they cannot get rich, it may be they must be servants all their lives; but men, if they serve the Lord, are free in His service; and though they are poor, they are no more than their Master was when on earth. It is not what it is for a few fleeting years, but what it will be for everlasting ages. Let them realise that "a man's life consisteth not in the abundance of the things which he possesseth;" a man's true dignity, and happiness, and greatness, is to enjoy the favour of God, that is the "peace which passeth all understanding." If calm contentment pervade the soul, it will make the cottage bright; and without it the palace will be desolate. This will satisfy with the meanest fare, and without it the stalled ox has no flavour. "Better is a dinner of herbs where love is, than a stalled ox and hatred therewith." Therefore I entreat you, my friends in the lower ranks of life, do not give way to that wretched delusion, that a man is to be measured by what he has, or that his happiness is graduated by his possessions. A man's soul in peace with God, and having His blessing, that alone makes a man blessed, and that alone can make a man happy. That made Paul and Silas happy in the dungeon; it gave peace to Daniel in the dismal lions' den; and it made Shadrach, Meshach, and Abednego undismayed in the burning, fiery furnace.

XXV.

THE EDUCATION OF THE YOUNG.

"Suffer the little children to come unto me."—St. Mark x. part of 14.

Not to help in the work of the Lord is, in some sort, to hinder it. It is to be feared that very many who fear God rather hinder than help to bring the little ones to the good Shepherd of Israel. They do so through their unbelief. They are apt to think, as the apostles probably thought, that to bring very young children to the Saviour was rather to intrude upon and interrupt His holy work, than to do that which is pleasing in His sight. There exists very extensively an impression in the minds of many, that a child at an early age is inaccessible to the work of grace and the service of God; and the consequence is that very many look upon such a scene as that before and around us with comparatively little interest. If they take any interest, it is in the effect produced for this world, and not in the effect produced for the next world; it is in these young folks being prepared for the ordinary occupations of life, and not in the preparation for the life everlasting. And there are very many who in their own families, alas! bring up their children with very little interest or attention to their everlasting interest, because they deem it too soon to interfere with their thoughts of God; they do not believe that the work should be begun so soon, therefore, they put it off and delay it, and alas! it is sometimes never begun. When the Redeemer, who pillars the universe with His everlasting arms, was on earth, He showed us an example that rebukes all such unbelief and want of faith in the power of His grace and extent of His love, for He not only forbade those who would have forbidden the little ones, but, "by His outward gesture and deed He declared His goodwill toward them, for He embraced them in His arms, He laid His hands upon them, and blessed them." And our Church, very scripturally, and, as we conceive, echoing the spirit and sentiment of our Lord, says, "Doubt ye not, therefore, but earnestly believe, that He will likewise favourably receive these infants"—that are presented to Him—"that He will embrace them with the arms of His mercy, that He will give unto them the blessing of eternal life, and make them partakers of His everlasting kingdom." Surely, if we will not believe, we shall not be established; but if we believe His promises, we shall have good hope in following His steps.

I have taken these beautiful and simple words of Jesus, as specially appropriate to this occasion.* *"Suffer the little children"*—not merely those that are getting into mature age, whose intellects are unfolding, who are capable of reasoning upon the truths revealed to us in God's Word, but even the very young ones, into whose hearts we can only drop little grains of instruction and heavenly wisdom—"Suffer the little children to come unto me."

My simple endeavour will be to prove this point, that *little children should be converted to Christ, and brought to Him for salvation in their early days.* May the Spirit attend His Word, that we may ourselves receive that Word as little children, and so enter into the kingdom of heaven.

One argument that has always appeared to me to be of much weight in this discussion is, that *children are, at a very early age, capable of doing wrong;* and, if they are, they must,

* School anniversary, Sunday morning, May 14, 1865.

by a parity of reasoning, be capable of doing right—for they would not be capable of doing wrong if they were not capable of doing right—the one implies, necessarily, the other. Where is the individual that has watched children, even from their mother's womb, who can deny that children are capable of doing wrong, and that, at a very early age indeed, they discover the taint and tendency of their evil minds and hearts? At a very early age indeed, they have a consciousness of when they are doing wrong, and surely they have also a consciousness of when they are doing wrong in God's sight. There are early indications of moral responsibility in the child, in the actings and strivings of conscience; and, the more they are watched, the more surely and certainly we are convinced that they exist—though it is as the twilight, when things are indistinctly seen in the shade—but still there is sufficient of the dawn of light to make the child partly responsible. Then, if the child has a conscience that tells him he is doing wrong, he should have that conscience cultivated to tell him that he has a moral responsibility in him. There would be some excuse for neglecting and slighting this if our offspring were mere irrational animals; but when we know that the child has a soul, is a rational being, and that rational being is discovered in the first germ and bud of its moral nature, we ought not to doubt that such little ones should be suffered to come to Christ, and we should attempt from the very beginning to train the young tendrils of their convictions and affections to the root of the tree of life, and not leave them to run riot, and to waste amid the thorns and briars around them.

Another argument, still more powerful, is, that *the diseased and disordered state of the child shows itself at a very early period indeed.* Before, probably, reason dawns, or conscience is called out, the child indicates that all is not right with it; there is a restlessness, a peevishness, a perverseness, a contumacy, there are little passions and indications of pride and self-indulgence. How very early these young weeds begin to sprout up in the soil of the unrenewed and evil heart! I remember well on one occasion visiting a gentleman, who had been brought up in the heresy that denies the corruption of our nature, but who happily was led to God, and his family with him, though still there mingled with him some of the early prejudices of his unhappy education. I remember well, that on one occasion he repelled with distaste, and almost disgust, the idea of corruption being in the young heart, even from the mother's womb, and, pointing to his own infant, sleeping in the room, he said, " If you could make me think that lovely babe of mine, with its cherubic and innocent looks, had the little seeds of evil implanted in it, I should almost shrink from it." I said, " Whatever may prove to be the effect, I am certain the cause is there ;" and I added, " we will leave it to one who has far more opportunity of judging than you have, she who has nursed the child in her lap and cherished it at her breast;" and she replied earnestly, "If you saw it as I do, you would see that underneath all, and through all, the lovely innocence, as we esteem it and regard it, there are the little germs and indications of pride, passion, self-will, rebellion, and restlessness." Oh yes, we *must* come to the truth after all, the child *is* born with a heart naturally deceitful and desperately wicked, prone to evil, seeking what is wrong, having a distaste for what is right and good. It needs, therefore, diseased as it is from its mother's womb, a remedy; and it needs that remedy as soon as it indicates the disease. If your child is poorly, you do not say it is too young to have recourse to a doctor, but you send the more anxiously and earnestly for the doctor because the child is too young to seek for medical advice itself. And if you seek for medical advice for the mortal body, should you not seek for the heavenly medicine that alone is fitting for the immortal? Should you not, as you see that the child is disordered from the cradle, seek that it may from the cradle be led to Him who came to heal all our diseases and to make us whole?

Then, further, I would argue that we should suffer and encourage the little ones to come, *because grace, the work of God, is not so much a thing of the head as of the heart*, not so much in what we learn as in what we love, not so much in clearness of our creed as in our moral disposition. He that loves much serves much. He that simply knows much does not love. Of what avail is his knowledge? It is but the cold moonshine that will never cause anything to grow. There must be warmth as well as light, there must be the sun if there is to be life. And so with regard to a child. He cannot perhaps learn much, he cannot perhaps comprehend the mystery of the Trinity in Unity, or conceive of the wondrous mystery of the Incarnation; he cannot comprehend in the fulness and grandeur of its adaptation the atonement; —this is not needed, it is not natural, it is not possible that he could;—but a child may love and trust, and what he trusts he loves and obeys. Perhaps there is no love more natural and tender and true than that of an affectionate child for its parent; there is no service more spontaneous and sweet than the service that springs from the loving trust a child has for its parent; and if a child can trust an earthly father, cannot a child trust a heavenly Father? You say, "Yes, but a child sees the earthly parent, and it cannot see the heavenly Parent." Are we such creatures of sense and sight, even as children, that we cannot have some apprehension of the Great Father and loving Saviour that loved us even as a mother loveth her children, and did for us even what a parent cannot do? Cannot a child, therefore, have a sense of gratitude to God, of trust in God, of desire to please God, of fear to offend Him? cannot he have a sense of His surrounding presence, and feel that He encompasses us, and His eye is over us by night and by day.

And further, and more especially, it appears to me children may be brought to Jesus in confidence, they may become the lambs of His flock, and the children of His grace, *because the work is not the work of man, but the work of God the Holy Ghost.* If it were alone man that were to turn and influence them, we might indeed abandon the task in despair, and say there is no hope; but when the Saviour of sinners bids us suffer them to come to Him, when it is the Spirit of God that we know can fill the smallest heart as well as the largest, and that, like the waters of the deep, that deluge and engulf the earth, and fill with limpid water the little shell, can descend to the least and lowliest, as well as overmaster and control the mightiest and most exalted, surely it ought not to seem a thing incredible that God who made the child should remake it. We know that the God that moved on and fashioned chaos moves also upon the little chaos of the infant heart, and cleanses it; so that, the fountain being purified, the stream shall be pure, and the child shall be born again. Why bring we our children to baptism even to receive the seal and sign of Christ, expecting that God will receive them, if we think it in vain to seek a child's salvation, if we think the Spirit of God cannot turn the heart of a little child into a temple of the mighty God, in which he deigns and delights to dwell?

Let us add one argument more. *The result of Christian experience has ever been, as it cannot but be, in favour of our bringing the little ones to Christ.* Do we not read of Samuel, who, from his infant days, was taught to hear the voice of God, to know it, and to say, " Speak, Lord, for thy servant heareth?" And what do we read of him? That " the child Samuel grew on, and was in favour both with the Lord and also with men." Then, again, was not Timothy taught from his mother's knee the Scriptures, that were able to and did make him wise unto salvation? And do we not find, that most blessed exemplar of all, Jesus, who condescended to become as a little child, and "increased in wisdom and stature?" Did He intend this as an example for His young disciples, as lambs of the flock? Assuredly he did. Then, is not "the promise unto you and to your children?" and does not God say, "I will pour my Spirit upon thy seed, and my blessing upon thine offspring?" and did not Jesus, when He would teach us to be humble and meek, set a little child in the midst and say, "Except ye be converted, and become as little children, ye shall not enter the kingdom of heaven?" Did He do this, and is it impossible that the little child should become a recipient of His grace, and a follower in His footsteps? Was He not foretold as the good Shepherd gathering the lambs in His arms, and gently leading them? Did He not, as the first test of His almighty love, say to Peter, "Feed my lambs," and then add, "Feed my sheep?" Did He not intend that we should begin with the lambs, and feed them ere we feed the sheep?

The subject is so deeply interesting, and one so little thought of, that we would gladly enlarge upon it if time and strength permitted. Sufficient has been said to teach us to believe that a child may be made a child of God from its early age. Do we believe this? Many of us act as though we did not, we have so little faith. Surely there is enough to encourage us to believe that a child may be saved. What a beautiful thing to have a child saved, holy, happy, and blessed. We may have—as some of us have had—dear children taken away in early life, going away in the sweet and calm apprehension of a child's faith to rest in Jesus, going home without terror or fear; and if we are to believe, so should we have hope for our children, and seek to train them up for God. Sunday-school teachers, remember that it is not on account of goodness in the past that you take pains with your little ones, and seek to win them to the Lord. Who shall say what efforts may fail? You are not to look to results, but leave them to God, doing your duty faithfully, and trusting Him earnestly; and then you shall find that "your labour shall not be in vain in the Lord."

Then, again, surely it teaches us that we ought to pray for these little ones. Here is the great instrument of grace indeed, for it is the work of God pre-eminently; and it is by drawing down, as it were, through the golden pipes of devotion the heavenly dews and the divine rays upon the tender plants that we may hope to see them spring up "as willows by the watercourses;" and then "our sons may grow up as young plants, and our daughters may be as the polished corners of the temple;" and beautiful will it be if it leads them to seek, "not that outward adorning of plaiting the hair," but the adornment of "a meek and quiet spirit," which is the jewel that will sparkle in heaven.

Let us then cherish our Sunday-schools and our day-schools, and pray for them; and not merely once a year give, as you have been accustomed to do largely, but foster and cherish them by sympathy, by influence, and by prayer; and doubt not that there will be many plants from these nurseries of the Lord that, after flourishing in the garden of the Lord on earth, at last shall garnish the garden of the Lord above. If we present no other motive to you than that of love to Him and gratitude to Him in the encouragement you have for your own dear children, that should constrain you, as it is a most grateful and graceful motive, to give what you do in the spirit of love and liberality, "not grudgingly, or of necessity," for "God loveth a cheerful giver."

XXVI.

THE WISDOM OF WINNING SOULS.

"He that winneth souls is wise."—Prov. xi. part of 30th verse.

So far as is revealed to us, there is no world in the infinitude of worlds that the great God hath called into existence to which there attaches so profound an interest as there attaches to this little speck of ours. The reason is, that it is, if we may so speak, the battle-field of the moral universe. It is here the mighty conflict is waged between the powers of darkness on the one hand, and the powers of light on the other. Heaven is moved from above, hell is moved from beneath, the scene of the mighty struggle is this little ball of clay, the prizes at stake are the deathless souls of men; and each weighed in the balance of immortality and priced by the blood of God Incarnate, may well awake the most thrilling and intense interest above, beneath, and it ought to be here amongst ourselves. But, alas! whilst heaven is so earnest to save, and hell so bent to destroy, how often do we see souls steeping themselves in stupor and death, and but little alive to these illimitable interests which arouse such awful and deep and profound sensations in the world of truth and in the light of eternity. It pleases God that in this mighty battle there should be used not only omnipotent powers unseen and often unrecognised, but human powers; that men themselves should be commissioned for the strife. It is to this the wise man seems to refer, when he says in these few and most striking words, "He that winneth souls is wise." It has pleased God to commission His unworthy servant now addressing you to be one of the messengers of His truth, to give him a commission in the army of His grace, and for thirty-nine years (with how much weakness, and sinfulness, and unfaithfulness!) it has pleased God to allow him to testify to His truth in this town; and for thirty-three years within these walls, with scarcely an interruption of any kind. It seems, therefore, peculiarly appropriate that I should not omit our wonted appeal to you on this anniversary,* but choose a subject that will appeal to the hearts of each one of you; reminding me, on the one hand, of the solemn charge committed to me, and you, on the other hand, of how profound is your interest in the work which has assembled us together within the courts of the Lord.

The glorious enterprise—to win souls :—*The wisdom of him who achieves it*—"He that winneth souls is wise." May God the Holy Ghost be amongst us, enabling me to speak, perfecting strength in weakness; and enabling you to hear as you will wish you had heard when we meet before the judgment-seat of our common Lord.

The glorious enterprise is to win souls. They need to be won. If they were not lost, they would not require to be won. If they had not been "led captive," they would not have required to be rescued. We are led, therefore, to the great fundamental point to which we are continually drawn.

What has the soul to be won from? From *Satan*, the "god of this world," "the prince of the power of the air, the spirit that now worketh in the children of disobedience," that leads fallen man captive at his will. While man abides under his dark despotism—the despotism described as the kingdom of darkness; because, full of ignorance, and blind-

* Sunday, November 6, 1864.

ness, and confusion, and disappointment, and death, we come under his power. Under the wondrous mystery and awful economy that placed the father of all mankind in the foils of Satan, all our race fell through the solicitation of Satan, and, having fallen through his solicitation, we became so far under his power; and hence it comes to pass that, "born in sin and shapen in iniquity," we are under the control, and instigation, and embrace of him that walketh about, "as a roaring lion, seeking whom he may devour." His mighty arm is bent for our destruction. He influences and tempts the whole human family, so that there is not a man that liveth that is not tempted from Satan.

One of the old fathers fancifully, but fearfully, supposes that as every man rescued by Christ has his guardian angel to watch over him, so has every man not delivered by Christ his accusing and tempting angel to betray him, and, if possible, secure his destruction. Under the power of Satan what can man have of hope, or happiness, or peace? From Satan he must be delivered, or he never can be delivered from his ruin. But Christ Jesus was revealed "to destroy the works of the devil." He hath "led captivity captive," "despoiled principalities and powers," and opened the kingdom of light in antagonism to the kingdom of darkness, and every one that is translated from that kingdom of darkness into that kingdom of light is won from Satan's grasp, and the stronger than the strong man armed has come upon him and rescued the victim from his grasp; then a man is free when the Son makes him free, then a man is at liberty when the truth hath set him at liberty.

And man has to be won, not only from the power of Satan, but from that which gives Satan his power—*sin*. Satan could have no power against us if it were not allowed by God as a righteous retribution for man's sad defection from his Creator, Preserver, and Benefactor, in whom he lives and moves and hath his being, to that "father of lies," that murderer from the beginning." While sin is upon man unforgiven, he is in the grasp of the prince of darkness; it is by sin he leads him captive, and leads him into his sad snares; but Christ came that sin might be forgiven—that man might be renewed. To win a man's soul, therefore, is to win it from the love, and service, and bondage of sin, to win it out of the dread guilt that rests upon it, to deliver it out of that control of corruption which keeps a man under guilt and keeps him a slave.

But it is not only from sin that a soul is to be won, it is to be won also from *corruption and death*—eternal death. The consequence of man's subjection to Satan, of his lying under the guilt of his habitual transgression, is that he abides under the sentence, "The soul that sinneth, it shall die," "The wages of sin is death," and abiding in that condition a man abides under the frown of God and in the vestibule of hell, with only the breath of his nostrils between him and the death that never dieth. Never dieth! Who can tell what that is? Such as the soul is—such is the man, it is himself; and the soul lost—the man is lost. And, brethren, who can tell what that is—a lost soul! He who knew it best gives us an awful glimpse of it when He says, "What shall it profit a man, if he shall gain the whole world, and lose his own soul? Or what shall a man give in exchange for his soul?" The poorest, the meanest, then, has something compared with which everything besides is dust and ashes.

And now, brethren, what has a soul thus won from Satan, and sin, and corruption, and death, to be won to? It has to be won to Christ, won to reconciliation, won to holiness, won to happiness, won to heaven. What a glorious triumph! What a splendid victory!

Won to *Christ*. The seed of the woman destroyed and crushed the serpent's head; He came into a guilty world and bore our guilt; He has borne the burden of our iniquity; He is the mighty preserver of our race; He went down to the battle-field of death, and proved triumphant over him, openly making an end of him in "His agony and bloody sweat," in "His cross and passion," and in "His glorious resurrection." The reconciliation is complete on His part, and all that is wanted is reconciliation on our part. It is a hard thing to win the soul to Jesus; for it has to be won from blindness, self-infatuation, perverseness, self-delusion, self-deceit, and the thousand stratagems of Satan, and the snares of the world. Ah, brethren, it is not an easy thing to win the soul. Jesus can do it with His own omnipotent grace; but without that the whole universe is powerless to do it.

The soul has to be won to *reconciliation* and acceptance. All that come to God by Christ are "freely justified from all things," and being accepted in His righteousness, stand amongst the children of light, the saints of God, the chosen of His own love that He sets apart for Himself. What a glorious transformation! From enmity to friendship, from rebellion to adoption, from being far off from God to being brought nigh to Him through the blood of Christ.

And then, the soul thus won from condemnation and corruption is won to *holiness*. Sin shall not have the dominion over him; his mind is ever led by the Spirit of God, and that wicked one shall not have power over him. "Whosoever is born of God sinneth not." There may be, and will be, still the corrupt inclination in the heart, but we shall be more than conquerors through him whose precious blood gives us the victory. A man, when he is won from corruption, from wretchedness, and from misery, is free to serve God; he finds liberty of the soul, a peace and a joy the universe cannot give or take away; he finds that in Christ all things are his, for he is God's. His sorrows, his trials, his disappointments—what we call accidents—are all in the hands of unerring wisdom and infinite love, and that which seems against us we may be sure is for us; for "if God be for us, who can be against us?"

Then, he is won *to heaven*, the ground and triumph of all. If rescued here by Christ, he is rescued for glory hereafter. Nor will the soul that is thus won ever fall or come short of eternal life, for in the hands of Jesus he is safe against all trials, and Christ will at the last crown his work, "when this corruptible shall have put on incorruption, and this mortal shall have put on immortality," when "death is swallowed up in victory," when man, consecrated in body, soul, and spirit, shall awake up in the presence and after the image of the God that made him, the Saviour that redeemed him; when "fulness of joy and pleasures for evermore" shall complete the wondrous triumph; and "thanks be to God which giveth us the victory through our Lord Jesus Christ," shall a multitude of won souls sing as their everlasting anthem of praise for ever and ever. Beautiful fulness of the glorious enterprise!

And as a consequence of it, is the wisdom of him that achieves it. He is a fellow-worker with God, a fellow-soldier. Jesus said, "As my Father sent me, even so send I you." Why was Jesus sent? "The Son of man is come to seek and to save that which was lost." "I am not sent but unto the lost sheep of the house of Israel." Then, brethren, the humble, faithful minister who desires nothing in comparison with winning souls may feel that he has Christ with His banner waving over him, the sword of Christ—"which is the sword of the Spirit, which is the Word of God"—in his hand, and the armoury Christ has armed him with—faith, truth, wisdom, courage—around him. There is his confidence and strength. He cannot be too profoundly doubtful of his own strength, or too confident in the Lord. He might as well try to create a world as to win a soul without Christ, but through Christ's strength with him, the words from his lips shall not "return void," but God will glorify himself in many souls saved.

Brethren, is not this heavenly wisdom? It requires a wisdom that we have not ourselves to speak the truth in simplicity, and plainness, and faithfulness. We must "know nothing but Christ and Him crucified;" we must apply the sword of the Spirit with such skill that it may reach every heart, so that "in manifestation of the truth we may commend ourselves to every man's conscience," and so be able to plead with Paul, "I am pure from the blood of all men, for I have not shunned to declare unto you all the counsel of God." It requires wisdom, as it requires faith, to do this. How then should you pray for your ministers, that God may give them wisdom in rich abundance, that they may "preach Christ crucified, unto the Jews a stumbling-block, and unto the Greeks foolishness; but unto them which are called, Christ the power of God, and the wisdom of God."

Then, brethren, oh, what wisdom there is in so high a name! I sometimes think, Oh, if I were merely a man of merchandise or literature! Still every other pursuit seems dull and insipid in comparison to this. Men seek to win fortunes, they have ambitions and schemes, they seek to win a good name and renown; but what are all these when a man looks upon them from a sick-bed, and much more from a death-bed? Then all his fond affections depart, and how little remains! What has he but a costlier coffin or more gorgeous monument, or what is perhaps a lying pageant that attends him to the grave. And what then? Passed, passed as a dream! But the architecture with which the builder together with God has to do, is immortal and unchangeable;

the enterprise with which he has to take up is not here, of the earth, earthly, but of the heaven, heavenly; and the souls that are won are won to Christ, and they will be His best trophies and dearest joys in the great day. May we not say of many of you, "What is our hope, or joy, or crown of rejoicing? are not even ye in the presence of our Lord Jesus Christ at His coming? For ye are our glory and joy." For what can be such an unspeakable source of deepest thanksgiving to a minister of God as to win souls to Him who loves souls, to travail till Christ be formed in them, that there may be many sons and daughters, many whom he knows not in this world, but whom he shall meet in the great day, in the world of life and light, as won through his testimony, won to salvation, won to heaven! What an unspeakable privilege and honour to be engaged in the very work that awakens all the interests of the unseen world, that brought the Eternal Word from the bosom of the Father to the manger, the cross, and the sepulchre! Oh, the privilege of being a fellow-worker with God in such a work as that! Where is there any work in comparison that is not foolishness, mere dust and ashes, shadow and unreality, when brought into contrast with that higher work? Men and brethren, I thank God that I am permitted to stand before you once more at the close of another year of my ministry, to appeal to you earnestly that, as my work is to win your souls, so you yourselves may waken, every one of you to the great work. O brethren, "examine yourselves," "prove your own selves. Know ye not your own selves, how that Jesus Christ is in you, except ye be reprobates?"

Can we commemorate the glorious deliverance that Christ has wrought for us more touchingly, or affectionately, or intelligently, than in partaking of those blessed memorials of His blood-shedding, of the agony and struggle it cost "the Captain of our salvation" to win our souls? Why do so many neglect to come? Let your own consciences answer. Soon you will have to answer on the bed of death.

Dear brethren, I beseech you, seek to know the worth of your soul, not by its eternal loss, but by its eternal gain. Be assured of it, the rest you pursue is but as dust and ashes in comparison with this great object. First seek for yourselves, and then seek for others, the salvation of the soul. And for the ministers of Christ, may it be our prayer—as it was beautifully given in counsel by St. Paul to his son Timothy—" Take heed unto thyself and unto the doctrine; continue in them: for in doing this thou shalt save both thyself, and them that hear thee."

XXVII.

TREES OF RIGHTEOUSNESS.*

"Those that be planted in the house of the Lord shall flourish in the courts of our God. They shall still bring forth fruit in old age; they shall be fat and flourishing; to show that the Lord is upright: he is my rock, and there is no unrighteousness in him."—Ps. xcii. 13-15.

THERE is a peculiar beauty and gracefulness in the spreading and shadowing trees of the East, more particularly the green-tree. When these trees are planted in some moist soil near to water, they attain a height, a strength, and an altitude very imposing. The green and bright tree is often employed in the inspired page as an illustration. From the beginning of the creation, the almighty God himself seems to have regarded trees, for when He made all things, and pronounced them very good, every tree was pleasant to the sight and exceedingly graceful; and we read of the heavenly Husbandman himself planting in His chosen garden "the tree of life," to be to man the representation of those who are from nature's wilderness translated into the garden of grace, where they are endowed with heavenly fruitfulness. Among the representations of this kind there are none more affecting than that which the psalmist uses, when he says that the blessed shall be "like a tree planted by the rivers of water." The same figure is frequently and beautifully used in the book, bringing

---

* Portions of this sermon, having special reference to a deceased member of Mr. Stowell's congregation, are omitted.

them up higher and higher, until at last they are called "trees of righteousness" of the Lord's planting. The sweet singer of Israel, in describing God's seed and God's servants, takes up the same figure in the psalm before us. "The righteous," he says, "shall flourish like a palm-tree, he shall grow like a cedar in Lebanon;" and then it follows—"Those that be planted in the house of the Lord shall flourish in the courts of our God. They shall still bring forth fruit in old age; they shall be fat and flourishing; to show that the Lord is upright: he is my rock, and there is no unrighteousness in him."

TREES OF RIGHTEOUSNESS, then; these are our subject:— *Their planting and their flourishing: their fruitfulness and their freshness even to the end: the ground and the purpose of the whole.*

First, we shall consider *their planting and their flourishing:* "Those that be planted in the house of the Lord shall flourish in the courts of our God." Secondly, *their freshness and fruitfulness even to the end:* "They shall even bring forth fruit in old age, they shall be fat and flourishing;" and thirdly, *the ground and purpose of the whole:* "to show that the Lord is upright."

. . . .

May the Spirit of God accompany His word, that we may be trees of His planting, bear much fruit, and afterwards be glorified with Him.

The planting of the trees of righteousness. They are "planted in the house of the Lord, and flourish in the courts of our God." The temple had around it an outer court exposed to the sky, and it is recorded that in that outer court there were planted beautiful evergreens, and palm-trees, and cedar-trees, spreading their green branches around. These trees are strikingly emblematical, and therefore had their proper place in the courts of the house of our God. It is a delightful picture. It is in the nature of man to flourish and to fade; and yet it is not his nature, it arises from his fallen condition. Men talk about the "debt of nature" as if men were made to die. They were not made to die. They were made to live; but death came as a curse and a calamity, and they brought it upon them by their disobedience. "The wages of sin is death;" no sin, no death—and therefore I correct myself: it is not man's nature to die, but it is the lot and fallen condition of every man born into the world. He has the seeds of decay, and withering, and death within him, and it is every man's doom to decay, and waste, and dissolve. The strongest man, the most intellectual man, the most prosperous, the mightiest conqueror—all are conquered at the last by the king of terrors. Decrepitude and decay seize upon the mightiest prince as upon the lowliest peasant. It is the law of our fallen state, and it has become so through sin, and, therefore, the trees of nature, flourish as they may, and bear fruit as they will, shall soon fade away. There must be transplantation, there must be grafting again, to use a kindred figure, used by Christ himself, and beautifully foretold by the prophet—" Instead of the thorn shall come up the fir-tree, and instead of the brier shall come up the myrtle-tree: and it shall be to the Lord for a name, for an everlasting sign that shall not be cut off." There is, therefore, the transplanting out of nature's arid and barren soil into the heavenly soil of grace in Christ Jesus ere there can be vigour conveyed. Our blessed Lord himself tells us, except the branch take root in the vine it cannot bear fruit. And so we must be grafted into the true Vine; and if we are not so grafted we wither and die; but if we are grafted in and united to the true Vine we bear fruit. It is in this wise only that any of nature's trees can be made fruitful and flourishing. And this is done ordinarily by the operation of the Word of God, by His ordinances, and by His Church. When, therefore, it is said, " They that are planted in the house of the Lord," it is intended they that are transplanted out of the soil of nature by the ordinances of Christ's own appointment, who by the power of the Spirit are transplanted into a new life, and have given to them a new sap, so to speak, and these shall flourish in the courts of the Lord. The baptism of a child is a sign or mark of its being transplanted into the garden of the Lord, and we are to endeavour to bring up children to their calling, and to plant them in the courts of the Lord God, where they shall grow "as willows by the watercourses" of God's teaching, of God's influence, of God's ordinances, and of the various channels of His grace; and they that are so planted shall spring up as willows. I have never known a faithful and devoted servant of God that did not love God's house, I have never known one that did not take pleasure in communion with Him, I have never known one that did not love His Word, for there, in His Word, is He made known to His people, and there only can He be known as the God of grace; therefore there is no infidel, there is no contemner of God's Word that can be said truly to be transplanted into the courts of grace, that can be said to have the Spirit of God through Christ Jesus, and that is made a new creature. We find that holy men of old, who flourished in the courts of the Lord, did not neglect the duties of life; we find that they did not live the life of the hermit, they did not live the life of the recluse, they did not hide their light under a bushel, but they placed their light in a candlestick. "Let your light so shine before men, that they may see your good works, and glorify your Father which is in heaven." "Herein," said Christ, "is my Father glorified, that ye bear much fruit; so shall ye be my disciples." Planted in the house of the Lord, they are planted there by the heavenly Father. Many may seem to be planted and be like a graft of the gardener, attached to the tree with all care, not knowing whether it will come to anything, and after all bear no fruit. The graft must take effect if it is to bear fruit and live. And so when the plant is not planted by the heavenly Husbandman, it withers and fades, and must be rooted up, because "every plant which my heavenly Father hath not planted shall be rooted up." But they that are planted by the heavenly Husbandman in the house of our God shall flourish and give forth fruitfulness in works and labours of love, and have their leaves still spreading forth, as the prophet Jeremiah describes, leaves spreading by the river, deriving from it heavenly fruitfulness and fitness to go forth in the courts of our God, living in union and in connexion with Him, and bearing fruit abundantly. Beautiful expression! And, brethren, this is no inapt picture of a holy life, united to Him, growing up in Him, deriving all their beautiful blossom and fruitage from their union with Him. And just "as the branch cannot bear fruit of itself, except it abide in the vine; no more can ye, except ye abide in Christ." All is from Christ. It is most important that we should bear this in mind, for when we come to our last hours we shall see that it is the only ground of all fruitfulness and righteousness.

In the next place, we have *their freshness and fruitfulness to the end.* "They shall still bring forth fruit in old age; they shall be fat and flourishing." There shall be no drawback, but they shall grow and flourish. The grace of God in the child of man is a very beautiful thing. "We have this treasure in earthen vessels, that the excellency of the power may be of God, and not of us;" and every believer in Christ says, "By the grace of God I am what I am; all that is good in me is of grace, all that is in me is of heavenly sending." I have often thought, whether is the work of God more beautiful in the old and tried pilgrim or loving and attractive in the young and tender child just beginning to lisp the name of Jesus, and deriving the answer of the blessed

Spirit, as he calls to Him, "Speak, Lord, for Thy servant heareth?"

It is beautiful to see the young retaining the early lessons of simplicity, and receiving the kingdom of God as a little child; beautiful it is to see the youth kept unspotted from the world, to see the bud unfold in the gardens of grace, and to exhibit the beauty that never comes from the soil of earth; it is beautiful to see the young man and the young woman adorning the doctrine of God their Saviour—lovely and beautiful it is to see it: "Remember thy Creator in the days of thy youth;" thou mayest never have a youth again. But beautiful as this is, there is something more lovely in the sight of "the hoary head," when it is found in the ways of righteousness; then indeed it is a "crown of glory." Beautiful things are written and said of the young, but nothing so exalted as this is said: "A hoary head is a crown of glory, if it be found in the way of righteousness." How lovely when you see the hoary head, as it is here described, bearing more fruit and flourishing. It is natural in youth to be fair and to bear fruit; and the natural trees are more fruitful when they are young, and their first fruits are the sweetest and the best: and here is nature reversed, and when all in nature would be decay, "the trees of the Lord are full of sap." When all in nature is aridness around, when the trees are aged, and the boughs are broken, and moss is covering them, and they are budding forth but a few trembling leaves and scattered blossoms, when there is no fatness or sap in them: so oftentimes it is in old age, when after a long life the energy has departed, the mind and the spirit are trembling, there are complainings and murmurings and repinings, and the poor wretched tree, when about to be torn from the roots, cleaves closer and closer to the soil, and grasps at health, and the paltry and pitiful wealth to the last. Therefore the more marvellous and signally beautiful is it when we see the order of nature reversed, when we see the tree of righteousness unlike the tree of nature, when we see not the withering leaf and the scattered blossom and the shattered bough, but all fresh, and fat, and fruitful. Often do we see the aged Christian realizing this picture, and when about to flee away, kept by the Spirit of God from becoming sour and unprofitable. God does sometimes so manifestly give to his children, as they are departing unto his presence, the spirit of gladness and the spirit of praise; and I have known aged Christians hardly cease from praising God when about to depart. They have felt so deep a love to God, and joy in His people's interest, and in His work, and in anticipation of a happy home, and a bright and glorious communion with Him in another and better world, that when the seeds of decay have come upon them, they have longed to depart and be set free, and they have looked forward to the unseen future with cheerfulness and patience, and contentment, and hope, longing to be with God, to be praising Him for His mercies, to be in fellowship with His dear Son Jesus Christ, and in the full and perfect enjoyment of His Holy Spirit. How beautiful it is to see the order of nature thus reversed, to see while the old trees of this world are fading and perishing, the aged trees of righteousness are fat and flourishing, and bearing more fruit! How beautiful to see the aged, as the venerable Simeon and Zacharias, praising God and flourishing in the courts of the house of our God, their work accomplished, and nothing left to do but to depart in peace, for their eyes had seen the fulness of the salvation of God! You may perhaps think they are to be admired and to be envied, and to say, Would that we were like them! They are not to be envied, for what had they that we have not received?

Now we come, brethren, to *the blessed ground and purpose of the whole,* " to show that the Lord is upright: he is my rock, and there is no unrighteousness in him." There is the sum of the whole. God has made a covenant with His people, and never fails. The psalmist's house was not with God, as he would have it; his children were to him a bitter and a sore trial, piercing his soul with many sorrows, but he could say, "although my house be not so with God, yet He hath made with me an everlasting covenant, ordered in all things, and sure; for this is all my salvation." There was the rock on which he was planted, there was the secret of his dependence. And as he foretold it, so was it in himself, he brought forth more fruit, and was fat and flourishing. Yes, brethren, never to man should be any praise, all the praise should be to God. When we think of the infirmities that beset and wait for men, and what men would have been if left to themselves, we see that it is owing to the sovereign mercy of God's goodness in Christ that we have pardon and salvation; and it is to Him alone that the praise must be. I have never known an aged Christian, faithful to God, that would not say with the aged Paul, that all he ever was was through the grace of God. " By the grace of God I am what I am : and his grace which was bestowed upon me was not in vain ; but I laboured more abundantly than they all : yet not I, but the grace of God which was with me." You see he takes the ground and purpose of all, and, casting himself before the cross, says, "Thou art worthy." Be assured of it, God visits His poor creatures that He may manifest in them the mightiness of His power, and the riches of His grace; and the world itself, when it sees this in the freshness of bright youth, or in the fulness of hoary age, must say, "This is the finger of God." "Let me die the death of the righteous, and let my last end be like his." Oh that the sacred fruitfulness that does not fade may be mine! Oh that I may have that abiding life, that glory and that honour that cometh not from above, that lasts for ever, and never dies! The Christian never dies; it is not death when he departs, it is life. He does not cease to bear fruit; he bears it often with his last breath, and it appears in the world everlasting and without end.

. . . . . .

What a consolation to Christian mourners when they can have the blessed assurance that can only be enjoyed fully when the tree has been long planted in the courts of the Lord. "Show me thy faith without thy works, and I will show thee my faith by my works."

. . . .

The great lesson taught us is that we should strive to be planted in the house of the Lord, and bearing fruit in the house of God. What have you that you cannot leave behind you? There are two things that are never taken from man when he dies,—his sins and his righteousness—his sins will never leave him if he dies in them; and his righteousness—yet not his, but Christ's in him—will never be taken from him. It is but a little time, and we shall have nothing but sin or salvation. Which is ours? If we were called away this night, which should we take with us? Let this be put by every man to his own conscience, let him not put it away, for "the night cometh when no man can work." Let us glorify the faithfulness and the grace of God in Christ. "I will never leave thee, nor forsake thee." "The Lord is my light, and my salvation; whom then shall I fear? the Lord is the strength of my life; of whom then shall I be afraid?" Heart and flesh may fail, friends may forsake us, but the light of His countenance never fails, for "all the promises of God in Him are yea, and in Him amen, unto the glory of God." Heaven and earth shall pass away, but not one jot or tittle of His precious promises shall pass away till all be fulfilled.

My young friends, would you wish for a bright and happy

old age? set about it now. Be assured of it, you will find it is for the most part those that were planted early that flourish in the courts of the house of God; it is they for the most part that bring forth most fruit in old age. God may convert the aged sinner; but that is not the order of God, it is not the order of grace, it is not the order of nature. Plant the young tree now. Oh, then, " remember now thy Creator in the days of thy youth." Cry now, " My Father, Thou art the guide of my youth." And let us pray that in the end, when we are transplanted from below, it may be to the courts above, where we may be like those of whom it may may be written, " The memory of the just is blessed."

XXVIII.

READY AND WAITING.

"Be ye therefore ready also: for the Son of man cometh at an hour when ye think not."—St. Luke xii. 40.

"Therefore be ye also ready: for in such an hour as ye think not the Son of man cometh."—St. Matt. xxiv. 44.

The opening of the following chapter in St. Luke is this: "There were present at that season some that told Him of the Galileans, whose blood Pilate had mingled with their sacrifices. And Jesus, answering, said unto them, Suppose ye that these Galileans were sinners above all the Galileans, because they suffered such things? I tell you, Nay: but, except ye repent, ye shall all likewise perish. Or those eighteen, upon whom the tower in Siloam fell, and slew them, think ye that they were sinners above all men that dwelt in Jerusalem? I tell you, Nay: but, except ye repent, ye shall all likewise perish." When God then speaks in His providence, His people ought to speak by His Word, and the echo of His voice in providence should be found in His own divine oracles. As I have heard in the grandeur of the Alps, when the thunder has been raging, there have been echoes awakened all around from every dell and every hill, repeating back the grand sound; and when some sudden explosion took place, there were reverberations on the other side. It ought to be thus when God visits any neighbourhood or any nation with some very solemn, fearful, and startling visitation. It is not a vain curiosity, it is not even provocative judgment, as though those that suffer were worse than those that are saved from sudden death, or, as some would argue, that some more guilty than others are suffered to escape; it is not even sympathy for the sufferers and succour as far as human aid can avail—though that ought to be the result; but there should be a solemn awakening of every individual to prepare to meet his God, and to be pardoned and found in Him in peace, so that whether He cometh "at even, or at midnight, or at the cock crowing, or in the morning," they may watch, that come when He may it may be well with them, that His footsteps may not alarm them though they be heard from afar off, that they may not shake and quake at His approach, and that when He comes He may not be a terror, because He comes not as an enemy but as a friend, He comes not to destroy but to save.

May it be so, beloved brethren, with us in relation to that awful catastrophe with which it has pleased God to visit a neighbouring city and its environs,* than which, within our recollection, none has been so sudden, none so tremendous, none so desolating, none so deadly. It would be unaccountable if we stretched not forth our hands in kindness to succour so far as we can, and, above all, if we did not lay it to heart, that it is not at all improbable that some such sudden visitation may befall ourselves. Each individual man is liable, at any moment "the silver cord" may be "broken," and he be before his Maker. The voice of Jesus, then, comes home with peculiar and touching solemnity, "Be ye therefore ready also; for the Son of man cometh at an hour when ye think not."

* The Inundation at Bradfield, near Sheffield.

The solemn admonition; "Be ye also ready:" and, *the most impressive argument to enforce that admonition:* "The Son of man cometh at an hour when ye think not."

Let us look to His Spirit to open our hearts to receive His word with solemnity and with submission, that we may hear His voice, and so may attend to that "peace which passeth all understanding," which "neither death, nor life, nor things present, nor things to come," can take away from those who enjoy it.

"Be ye also therefore ready" for the great end of life. Ready to stand before your Maker; ready to be accepted of Him, and admitted by Him into His holy and happy family. What is life save that? What is life for but that? What is all that we are pursuing and thinking about in comparison with that end and purpose? "Oh that they were wise," says God himself, "that they understood this, that they would consider their latter end"—to be ready to meet God. You are familiar, brethren, with the theory; would that each would experimentally set it with his seal, and so wait as to be ready! If we are to meet God in peace, we must be at peace with God. No man is ready to meet God who is not at peace with Him; peace made with Him, peace made also by Him—for it never would have been made had not the Lord, the blessed "daysman," the Prince of Peace, made peace by the cross. God was in Him "reconciling the world unto Himself, not imputing their trespasses unto them," so that now we, His ambassadors, "beseech men in Christ's stead, be ye reconciled to God." It is the atonement that makes the sinner and the Judge to be at one, the blessing is completed, the meeting-place is ready, the covenant is sealed, the everlasting righteousness is finished, and we are invited to "come, for all things are ready." But man is not ready. The peace does not profit unless it is entered into; the covenant does not avail unless a man is engaged in it; the lamp is of no use unless we receive light out of it; the ark will not avail in the flood unless man has entered into it and God has shut the door; the meeting-place is in vain prepared unless man goes to it; the fountain rises in vain in all its covenant efficacy if man is not washed there. If a man does not avail himself of Christ, whatever he may know, however he may have been baptised, if he has not entered into personal reconciliation, if he has not "fled for refuge to lay hold on the hope set before him," if he has not been—as the word is in the Greek—turned round, if he has not been brought back from sin and Satan, and from nature's fallen state, into acceptance with God in the Beloved, if he has not, by "repentance towards God and faith towards Jesus Christ," become another man and entered into new relationship with God, not merely of the creature to the Creator, of the subject to the sovereign, of the culprit to the judge; but the relationship of the sinner to the Saviour, of the rebel in reconciliation with his sovereign; if he is not in Christ, having cast down the arms of rebellion, and laid hold, as it is beautifully said, of His "strength," "how shall we escape, if we neglect so great salvation?" how shall we meet Him on the judgment throne, if we are forced then to acknowledge, I rejected my Saviour, I preferred sin, I preferred to serve the world, the flesh, and the devil, and when peace was pressed upon me without money and without price, I would not accept it, I did not embrace it? "He that believeth not shall be damned." If a man dies unbelieving, he dies at variance with God, and the peace that was purchased by the blood of Christ will be but an aggravation of his guilt and of his sin.

To be ready to meet God we must be at peace with God, and be made meet for Him, and fit to be in His presence. Every man of thought, of sense, of conscience, must know that it would be impossible for an impure being, such as man is by nature, ever to come into the blazing light and overwhelming presence of the Lord God Almighty. How would he find himself, what concord would there be, what kindred feeling between Him and those holy, holy, holy saints around the throne? Would not man feel that he had got into the wrong place! Put the question to your own hearts. "Holiness, without which no man can see the Lord." "What fellowship hath righteousness with unrighteousness? and what communion hath light with darkness? and what concord hath Christ with Belial?" Must not purity here be man's preparation for perfect purity? Must not delight in the things of God be man's preparation for the things of God? Must not willingness to do His will here be meetness to do His will hereafter? As are the first-fruits, so is the harvest; as is the grace, so is the glory; as man lives, so he dies; as he dies, so he stands before God; and as he stands before God, so will he be judged in the last day, and either take his place on the right hand and go into life everlasting, or on the left hand, and go into everlasting fire; and "who amongst us can dwell with everlasting burnings?" Therefore, brethren, no man can be meet for the presence of God that is not in Christ, that is not a new creature, old things having passed away. His affections must be drawn heavenward by the magnet of a Saviour's love, his heart must be where his treasure is. If heaven is to be his portion, heaven must be his choice.

Then, brethren, to be ready to meet God, we must also be willing to meet him. Ah! when the summons suddenly comes upon a man, it will test him, and search him to his heart's core. He will not then be able to throw it aside and get rid of it; he will not be able to drown the thought in drunkenness. If he does, what a fearful summons it will be! When the summons comes, a man *must* attend to it whether he will or not. Who shall be able to live one hour, who shall be able to breathe one breath beyond the moment fixed by God? Then, brethren, that which a man has to do, that which he has to pass through, surely he should be familiar with, and count upon. Surely such a journey ought to be packed up for, and provided for; for if a man lays up so much for his old age, how much more ought he to lay up for eternity? That is the one thing: no matter how else it is, if it is peace at the last, for his soul goes to glory, and he may look down upon the kings and princes of the earth, and the rich man clothed in purple and fine linen, when he is in torment, will see the poor man in Abraham's bosom, and he will ask in vain for a drop of water to cool his tongue. "Be ye also ready."

What an awful and solemn consideration it is, that "the Son of man cometh at an hour we know not of!" No man can deny it, for he sees it continually, that the "wise men also die and perish together, ... and leave their goods for others." There is no exception. No man is mighty enough to withstand the last enemy; all must bow before the king of terrors. This it is that makes death so dreadful to the sinner, and so calm though solemn to the saint. It is beautifully said, "The Son of *man* cometh at a day and an hour that no man knoweth." The Son of *man*. If it were said, the Son of *God*, there would be something more awful in the sound; but it is the Son of *man;* one that shared our sorrows, bone of our bone, and flesh of our flesh, He has travelled through that dark valley before us, He has crossed that rapid flood, and He it is that comes to us. "This is our God; we have waited for Him, ... this is the Lord,—we have waited for Him—we will be glad and rejoice in His salvation;" for He hath overcome the power of death, and hath made us more than conquerors. "The Son of man cometh at an hour we know not of." Death is not the mere debt of nature, as some vaguely say; it is not a mere necessity of our constitution; it could not have been but for sin. It is the Judge of all the earth coming to acquit, or to condemn; to receive to everlasting blessedness, or to sentence to righteous punishment; it is God's officer sent to drive the culprit away from God's anger, or to convey His dear children to His everlasting bosom. Look upon it steadily, as you all must ere long; bring it before you, take it by the hand, ask it what it is, whether it is to come to us as Satan to bind us, or as Christ to save us; whether as an angel of mercy, or as the angel of destruction. God grant that we may ever bear it in mind that "the Son of man cometh at an hour we know not of," that "the Judge standeth at the door."

We know that the hour of our death is fixed; there is no uncertainty with God. Those two hundred and forty-eight fellow immortals that were submerged into eternity, most of them in the twinkling of an eye; it was all arranged—it was fixed. Not fatalism, not destiny, but purpose. Does nothing happen without God? are "the hairs of our head all numbered?" cannot "even a sparrow fall without God's permission?" and can this be accident merely, as some profanely say? What we know not now we shall know hereafter; but remember, I pray you, that there is no uncertainty, there is no chance, there is no accident with God. And it is a comfort to a Christian man to feel that there is no uncertainty, and that he need not take anxious thought. He should only seek to be ready to die, and *when* the messenger shall come to him God must decide. How much anxiety and vain fear and bitter sorrow would it save us if we walked by faith and not by sight, if we could realize that God's coming to us is fixed and certain, and if we could wait for our appointed time as the tried patriarch of old did. But though these things are fixed and certain to God, there is no certainty to us. Do you think that those two hundred and forty-eight persons, when about in the midnight hour to close their eyes in sleep, did they, at that dread and solemn hour of their visitation, think that they should never see the sun again? Did they think that they would never have one opportunity of falling down again and asking God to be merciful to them? Did they think that they would not be able to breathe out perhaps even a dying cry for mercy? Did they think when they last closed their eyes in time, that when they awoke up it would be never to sleep again, in that place where there is no more night? Alas! do you suppose they imagined it was their last night upon earth any more than we do now? And yet they were called in a moment, in the twinkling of an eye. Who amongst us shall say that even this night they shall not be summoned by some sudden stroke, or by disease? These may seem simple and familiar truths, but they are most solemn and most important. Let us then take them to heart as we ought, let us realize them as we ought, for "we know not the day nor the hour when the Son of man cometh." What may happen at any time should be prepared for at every time; we should be ready always for what we always know may be, and for what we cannot too much keep ourselves looking for, "the glorious appearing of the great God and our Saviour Jesus Christ." We cannot be too much in the beautiful attitude described by Himself, so that when the bridegroom cometh to the bridal chamber our loins may be "girded about, and our lights burning, and we ourselves like unto men that wait for their lord, when he will return from the wedding; that when He cometh and knocketh, we may open unto Him immediately. We should be thus ready; and the poor man, when aroused from his sleep, to find himself submerged in an overwhelming deluge; if that was his happy state of preparation he would open immediately and welcome the bridegroom with the cry, "Come, Lord Jesus, come quickly."

It is not my intention to enter into particulars of the tremendous and desolating scenes of that destructive flood. What I am anxious to press upon you is the deep and solemn lesson it teaches us. I need not remind you how unexpected and how overwhelming it was. That beautiful and populous valley, which consisted of scores of houses and miles of gardens, of fair trees and lovely streams, is now a wide-spread desert, full of desolation and wrecks of houses, and furniture, and gardens, and trees, and flowers, and the wrecks too, alas! of those that once dwelt in those houses. I need not remind you how many have been extricated dead cold corpses from the mass of ruin and destruction; how many aching hearts, and weeping eyes, and breaking spirits there must be surviving; how God, in His providence, snatched one of a family from the ruins, and left others to perish: "one shall be taken and the other left." That providence, without which one sparrow dieth not, ruled over the raging waters, and singled out whom He would. And I need not, but in one short sentence, remind you that the voice of the Almighty has been heard in the waters. "It is the glorious God that maketh the thunder." He hath spoken to that neighbourhood, and the echo of His voice should reach us, and we should take our Master's message to heart, "Be ye also ready, for in such an hour as ye think not the Son of man cometh."

I need not, brethren, impress it further upon you. My whole sermon has been a personal application. Now, I simply say, if you have never begun the mighty work of life, let not to-morrow's sun arise without a diligent attention to it. Seek earnestly to be ready to die. Go to the Saviour for peace, for pardon, and for grace, without which you can never be ready to die; for none can be ready without Jesus, none can be ready but through the atonement of His blood, none can be ready but through the work of His Spirit renewing the soul after His image. If this be the case with you, then, indeed, this solemn season of Easter, when we trace the Saviour in the garden of Gethsemane, to the hall of judgment, on the cross, down to the sepulchre, and up to the throne of glory, shall be to us a bright and a blessed season. This will be so if we are able to date from this Easter our beginning to be found in Him who by His death hath destroyed death, and by rising to life again hath restored His believing people everlastingly.

XXIX.

THE JUDGE AT THE DOOR.

"Behold, the Judge standeth before the door."—JAMES v. part of 9.

THE Church of Christ has had from the beginning to look forward. It is of the very nature of faith that it looks to the future; not exclusively, for it looks to the past; but as our grand hope is ever before us, we are ever to be turning to what has to come, rather than exclusively to what has gone by. To the coming of Christ as at this time,* in great humility the eyes of all the faithful were directed; and for that event, the coming in lowliness and love, seeking to save the lost, the faithful waited. He was "the messenger of the covenant that they had waited for, hoped for, prayed for, and looked for. Now the eye of faith looks backward on the agonies of the cross, and sees that He has made a full, perfect, and sufficient oblation, satisfaction, and atonement for the sins of the whole world. There it is that all His true followers are to plant their feet, and upon that rock they are to stand. They are to bring there all their dangers and sorrows in their journey through the wilderness, watching and praying and feeling that they are under the shelter of His mighty protection, under the shield and banner of His cross. Thence, therefore, they are to

* Advent Sunday evening, 1864.

turn their eyes forward; their great prospect is before them, and therefore their attitude is to be "looking for and hasting to the glorious appearing of the great God, even our Saviour Jesus Christ."

This morning we endeavoured to show you the practical influence of that great truth upon the spirit, and temper, and words, and inward thoughts of every one who realizes and anticipates it as he ought. This evening surely there is peculiar force and emphasis in the words we have selected for our attention. It is *a solemn truth:* "Behold, the judge standeth before the door." And then there are *the solemn lessons that flow from that solemn truth:* Prepare each soul to meet Him.

I say there is peculiar emphasis in the words, for I have often observed that as one year is coming to a close, and we are called to remember that He who came to save us is coming to judge us, God seems to send home the solemn admonition by special providences. It is a solemn thought that that fellow worshipper we prayed for this morning was just entering into the presence of the Judge as we prayed for him; probably within a minute of the very time we prayed he was gone whither prayer cannot avail us, and is now safe in God's keeping. It is also a solemn thought that another worshipper was called away from this place to witness probably the last breathing of an eldest son. These things are going on up and down, and they are intended to echo the important warning, "Behold, the Judge standeth before the door." May God solemnize our minds and impress our hearts whilst we seek to realize this great truth, which can only be realized in efficacy as the Holy Spirit gives His testimony. May He do so now, for Christ's sake.

The simplest truths are oftentimes the most vital and the most sublime. What can be more simple, and yet sublime and intensely interesting, than this brief declaration—"Behold, the Judge standeth before the door?" We behold many things. The world says, "Behold this wonder;" the thoughtless and vain say, "Behold this prodigy;" the covetous and the grasping say, "Behold this plan, this fine scheme or speculation by which a fortune may be realized." But all these things are vanity. "Vanity of vanities, all is vanity." We invest things with a grandeur and an importance which do not belong to them. "Man walketh in a vain shadow, and disquieteth himself in vain: he heapeth up riches, and cannot tell who shall gather them." When *God* says, "Behold," there must be something indeed to behold. There is nothing that excites wonder or astonishment in heaven but what is invisible, and spiritual, and eternal; and, therefore, when the Spirit of God says by His servants, "Behold," ought not every eye to be turned in deepest anticipation and earnestness, every ear to be opened in solemn patience, every heart to be awed and subdued before what God must disclose?

"Behold, He cometh, and every eye shall see Him." Behold who is it that stands before the door. He stands there in a twofold aspect—as a Redeemer and as a Judge. Throughout life we may see Him as a Redeemer—at all events, throughout the day of grace; and it is not for us to limit it, though God knows its limitation. "Seek ye the Lord while he may be found, call ye upon Him while He is near." "The night cometh when no man can work," and therefore it is our joy and confidence to proclaim it. "Behold, I stand at the door and knock; if any man hear my voice, and open the door, I will come in to him, and will sup with him, and he with me." How beautiful the two "beholds!" They may be placed side by side. Behold a Saviour waiting, behold a Judge impending. Oh, blessed are they that receive the former "behold" in anticipation of the latter, and look on Him whom they have pierced by their sins; and mourn, and have their hearts bound up with the balm of His precious blood, and are renewed and made whole by the power of His Holy Spirit, before they have to appear before Him as the Judge of the quick and the dead.

It is not to the former of these "beholds" that the words of the text direct your attention, but rather to the latter. Behold, *the Judge*. We have seen, brethren, in our own city of late, a judge amongst mankind coming amongst us, and ushered in with solemnity. There is something majestic and solemn in the tribunal of human judgment. With what varied feelings and intense solicitude must the coming of the earthly judge be regarded by many with whom he will have to do! Many doubtless regard it with carelessness, and make it a mere spectacle, a mere scene, a matter of curiosity and excitement; yet it is not the less important, though they disregard it and make light of it. To the man who has to stand at the bar, especially the man who has to stand with his life at stake, to him it must be a most thrilling event; and when he hears the trumpet sound that ushers in the judge, what deep thoughts are at work in his heart as to how he shall face the judge, and what is before him! His thoughts are concentrated upon that one point. The one critical thought is, what will be the issue to him? Now it is indeed meet and fit that *we* should thus realize the Judge before the door. Let us not think of others, and how they are to fare. Let us not say, "Lord, what shall this man do? how shall this man stand? what account shall this man give?" Rather let it be, "There is my Judge; I am one that is to be judged and tried; I am to stand for life or death, heaven or hell; I must be lost or saved for ever—must meet the sound,

'Come, ye blessed of my Father,' or, 'Depart, ye cursed.' 'We must all stand before the judgment-seat of Christ.' 'I beheld the dead, small and great,' gathered before the judgment-seat of God. There was not one exempted, not one could hide himself, not one could escape that Judge." The Judge standeth before the door, and is not far distant, even from any one of us. People think, when they are children, how long the time will be before they are men or women; then, when they have come to their youth and manhood, they still think there is a long life before them; but when they begin to go down into the valley, and the shadows of life are casting behind them, and the twilight is gathering around them, what a dream life seems. It seems like looking back from a lofty hill when a journey has been taken. The traveller sees but a few of the prominent points here and there, as if the valleys—and largely the plains too—had disappeared, they are in obscurity. And so it is with life. What is your life?—behold, what is it? It is even as a vapour, that we behold for a little while, and it vanishes away. And therefore, brethren, it may well be said, "The Judge standeth before the door." Just as if you were without the door. We cannot tell the moment the door opens, and death ushers a man before the tribunal; for a thousand years are but as yesterday, and yesterday as a thousand years, in that world where, if I may so speak, the hands of the clock know no turning and no change.

Is not the Judge before the door, because of the certainty that He is there? Men say, "Where is the promise of His coming?" Men say, "Tush, He delayeth His coming." In the days of our Lord's first coming did not men despair of His coming, as at this time, in great humility? Did not men doubt and deny His coming? But did He therefore fail? Did not God "in the fulness of time" send forth His Son, "made of a woman, made under the law, to redeem them that were under the law?" "In the fulness of time." Is there not as clear an intimation that the date is as fixed for His second coming as it was for His first coming? God "hath appointed a day, in the which He will judge the world in righteousness, by that man whom He hath ordained; whereof He hath given assurance unto all men, in that He hath raised Him from the dead." "Behold, He cometh." How beautiful the expression! It is not, Behold, He shall come, but, "Behold, He cometh," He is on the way. And is He not nearer and nearer in point of time every sand-grain that drops? Surely, then, brethren, what is so certain should be. ever regarded as near. It is not simply the proximity of the Judge, it is the certitude that makes the thing present. Then, ought there to be any doubt, when God has said it, to whom every knee shall bow?

And if the certitude of the event should make us realize it before the time, not less should the hidden certitude make us, while certain, all uncertain. Where are the men who relied upon years to come, and said, "To-day, or to-morrow, we will go into such a city, and continue there a year, and buy, and sell, and get gain: whereas ye know not what shall be on the morrow. For what is your life?" What a vapour! What is it at the best? A mere brittle thread, trembling every moment for its very brittleness. We know not the instant when it may be snapped for ever; and as we die we shall remain, and appear before the tribunal of God. In this sense, then, is not the Judge before the door? Is not the breath in our nostrils the one step to the opening of that door, and lo! we are in the presence of the Omniscient and Omnipotent, we stand before God! Surely every man, woman, and child should say, "Prepare, my soul, to meet Him."

The Judge standeth before the door, because He is there to receive His own, and to deliver over His enemies that they may be justly consigned to darkness and despair. The first martyr prayed, "Lord Jesus, receive my spirit." That was a prayer to his Judge as well as to his Redeemer. How beautiful to the godly man, to think that he is before the bar of God, that he has passed through the dark passage into the bright abode! "Yea, though I walk through the valley of the shadow of death, I will fear no evil: for Thou art with me; Thy rod and Thy staff they comfort me." And how awful a thought to the ungodly, and the unbelieving, and the scoffer, and the mocker, to come to stand before the bar, that He may deliver over the ungodly and profane to a "fearful looking for and waiting" for the coming of judgment! What despair to the wicked! what joy and hope to the good! "Behold, the Judge standeth before the door."

Then, brethren, if such be the solemn proclamation, how solemn the lessons that it enforces!

Now primarily and pre-eminently, because it stands first, is the individual and personal lesson. There is but a step between me and my Judge; how then should I seek to be found in Him in peace when He comes; how should I seek and study to conform my thoughts, and tempers, and words, and ways, and works to Him, and realize His holy law, that I may give an account with joy; how I should study day by day, in my business dealings, in my course of life, in my intercourse with the world, so to form my plans, so to cherish my hopes, and so to shape my purposes; how should I venture into no scene, be found in no pursuit, in no pleasure where I would not wish to meet my Judge standing before the door. He stands before the door, in the ale-house and in the dram-shop, in the theatre, and in the haunts of wantonness and abomination. Why do not men remember this? If they were to realize it, would they go to scenes and places where they would not wish the Judge to come in and find them? Yet come He does, where men brutalize and imbrute and madden themselves, and make themselves insensible. What an awakening! Yet, brethren, it will be so, it is so, often; and no man has a right to say it will not be so with him. We should study to be where we should not be startled if the Judge appeared; we should study to regulate our temper, and thoughts, and conduct, so as to be found in a right spirit, and temper, and mind when he comes. Oh, what a life we should lead when we are habitually thus under the Judge's eyes! Men say, "Why frighten us out of our enjoyment, why seek to make us live continually in terror, and torment, and bondage, and fear?" Suppose it were so for threescore years and ten, what is that to eternity? Anything to be found ready to meet the Judge. But it is a sad mistake to suppose that it is so. It is not a spirit of bondage, it is a spirit of liberty; for it sets a man above the world, above the dread of earthly loss, above being crushed down by sorrows and trials, and makes him full of hope, and liberty, and love, and peace.

Then, brethren, is there not another thought? Should we not urge those who are not doing so, to seek to meet their Judge? Oh, what an awakening and startling thought to those who are living as if there were no Judge, and no soul to be judged; "the Judge standeth before the door!" Alas! the fact comes, whether they remember it or forget it. "Awake thou that sleepest, and arise from the dead, and Christ shall give thee light." *Now* is the time. "Now is it high time to awake out of sleep; for now is our salvation nearer than when we believed," or when we believed not. "The night is far spent, the day is at hand;" the night is far spent, and the day is nigh at hand to the righteous; the day is far spent, and the night is nigh at hand to the wicked. There is the awful converse! It is night to the righteous in comparison with the glorious day; it is day to the wicked in comparison with the blackness and darkness for ever that awaits those who do not prepare to meet their Judge. Surely this should be as a trumpet-blast in the ears of the careless and the thoughtless! Is it not high time to awake out of sleep?

Then, brethren, if the Judge stands before the door, what a lesson it is, following the lesson of the morning: "Judge nothing before the time;" "Judge not, that ye be not judged." It is remarkable, that when my eye fixed upon the passage, I felt it was as it were an enforcement of the words of the morning. It comes in this connexion:— "Grudge not one against another, brethren, lest ye be condemned: behold, the Judge standeth before the door." Do not be anxious to take yourselves to the judgment-seat; wait till the Judge comes, who will right all, and do justice to the oppressed, and none will have to complain, for God will vindicate eternal providence, and justify His ways to man. Every tongue shall be silent, and every mouth dumb before the Judge when He arises to adjust for ever, fully and completely, all the infinitude of the various wrongs, and crimes, and outrages that have marred this poor fallen world, "in the times of the restitution of all things spoken of by the holy prophets since the world began."

And surely this solemn truth should teach us patience and submission—"Wherefore doth a man complain, a living man, for the punishment of his sins?" And yet how many there are complaining and mourning like wild bulls wrestling against the net in which they are entangled! The Judge before the door should silence their murmurings and still their tumult, and they should still wait. Wait a little, "wait, I say, upon the Lord." And surely that little psalm we took part in this evening may well come before us. "Lord, I am not high-minded: I have no proud looks, I do not exercise myself in great matters: which are too high for me. But I refrain my soul, and keep it low, like as a child that is weaned from its mother: yea, my soul is even as a weaned child." For truly does Jesus say to us in our difficulties, and doubts, and trials, "What I do thou knowest not now, but thou shalt know hereafter;" therefore, in all your trials and difficulties refer to His judgment-seat.

Brethren, I need not apply the subject; the whole of the latter part of my sermon has been an application; only, may God grant that it may be so applied to us, that we may learn to live each day as if it were our last, with the recollection ever to our mind, there is the Judge before the door. Oh, young men and young women, you preparing for confirmation especially, remember this. David said,— "I have set the Lord always before me; He is on my right hand, therefore I shall not fall." Set Him before you, not only as a Saviour, but as your strength, and trust, and hope, and joy, and resurrection, and life, and Judge, at whose judgment-seat you must shortly give an account; and may He at the last give you life everlasting.

XXX.

THE SOLEMN MESSAGE.

"Let your loins be girded about, and your lights burning; And ye yourselves like unto men that wait for their lord, when he will return from the wedding; that when he cometh and knocketh, they may open unto him immediately."—St. Luke xii. 35, 36.

There are some events so uncertain and so unlikely, that our wisdom is not to disquiet ourselves. There are some events inevitable, and over which we have no control; our wisdom here again is to let them alone. How much of our sorrow, anxiety, and inquietude arises from intermeddling with things that do not belong to us! We had it from our Master's lips this morning, "Sufficient unto the day is the evil thereof." "Take no thought for the morrow." But there are some few events of such magnitude that they absorb all others in their shadows, things of such certainty that to doubt their coming proves a man to be insane, and of which the Author of all and Ruler of all has placed it so far in our power to forecast and provide for them, to take pleasure with a view of them, that we may give to their character when they come either unspeakable blessedness or unspeakable terror. We may invest them with the smile of an angel or the power of a fiend, we may either have them changed into blessing inconceivable or a curse that we cannot measure. Such an event, beyond all others, is a man's death, his interview with his Creator, his Preserver, his Redeemer, and his Judge. That event is of such surpassing awfulness and grandeur, that nothing else is to be mentioned in comparison with it. It is an event so certain, that however men may wish to forget it, however they would wish to deny it, they cannot. They might as soon deny their very existence. Need I say that it is an event which it is not in man to forecast, but which we may so anticipate as to provide for and prepare against, that it may come to us awfully welcome and solemnly serene, a stern, but a tender friend. I say, that not to provide for it and not to prepare for it, argues that a man is not a prudent man—he hardly deserves to be allowed to be a rational man. Why were reason and understanding given us? why was the Church of God appointed for us? why did the Lord Jesus Christ take our nature and die and suffer in our stead? why is the Spirit of God poured out from on high? why are all these things, but that man may prepare to meet his God? Surely, then, not to prepare is for a man to judge himself unworthy of eternal life, to fling away his birthright and to make shipwreck of his immortality.

I take the words before us as offering *a most solemn message:* "Let your loins be girded about, and your lights burning; and ye yourselves like unto men that wait for their lord, when he will return from the wedding; that when he cometh and knocketh they may open unto him immediately. Blessed are those servants, whom the lord when he cometh shall find watching."

The words present *our Master's coming: our attitude of preparation for His coming: and the reception we should give Him when He comes.* May the Spirit of God be with us, that we may profit by the message.

We talk of death, we talk of judgment, we talk of the decisions of the great day, but, after all, they are summed up in one idea—the Lord returning to judge His people, and to receive His ransomed Church and His bride. The advent of Christ, as it has been styled—Christ's second coming in glorious majesty—this is the great hope of the Church, this is the grand point of expectation, this is the goal of faith, this the pinnacle of hope. Before Christ came into the world, His advent in the flesh was the great hope; but since Christ's first coming and His return to prepare a kingdom for His people, the eye of holy expectation is to be directed steadily and unceasingly to the second coming of the Bridegroom to take to Himself His own blessed ones to sit down with Him for ever in the kingdom of His glory. This is the "consummation and bliss both in body and soul," of the whole Church of God unceasingly serving God day and night till He shall come again in the brightness of His glory. Scepticism assumes this to be an improbability, but the Book of God says, "He cometh, He cometh to judge the world." At the same time, to every individual man his death is to him the coming of his Lord, for then he enters into the immutable moral condition that shall never, never undergo a change, and he abides so until judgment. The moral condition of a man at his death makes his misery or his blessedness; but still, beloved, I love myself to swallow up, as it were, all thoughts and ideas even of the intermediate state, the state of the spirits of the just made perfect—though we know that they are absent from the body and present with the Lord—and to look forward to the final coming of Christ, to the restitution of all things spoken of by the prophets since the world began, when the whole creation that travaileth in pain shall be delivered from the bondage of corruption, when a new heaven and a new earth, wherein dwelleth righteousness, shall appear for ever, and shall cast into the shade the former heavens and earth. This, beloved, is the culminating point to the ransomed Church of Christ. And, brethren, what is it, after all, that gives to that last great crowd its crowning glory? It is that the Master shall appear, that the Lord whom we love, who has given us life through His death, and hope through His atonement, shall then appear, and His saints shall appear in Him with glory.

The Master, the Bridegroom cometh. The Jewish marriage solemnity, from which this idea is taken, is a most expressive one. The bridegroom comes in the evening to the house of his betrothed, and then the final solemnity of the union is completed, and he brings back his bride to his own home and her future home, and the maidens, her fellows, and "the virgins, her companions that follow her," shall be brought, and "they shall enter into the king's palace." Oh, what glory, what liberty, what greatness, what grandeur! Where else is a master so tender, so sympathising, so kind as that! Has there ever been one that has shown such infinite love towards his poor followers as to purchase them with his own heart's blood, who has wrought out their righteousness, and has delivered them from the bondage of criminals to make them—not his servants only, but his friends and brothers, fellow-heirs and partakers of his kingdom? Beloved, what a Master it is that we serve! Would that we felt his service to be "perfect freedom!" would that we longed for His coming! and that we could, in answer to His solemn announcement, "I come quickly," say, "Even so, come, Lord Jesus!"

It is marvellous that the servants of Christ so little long for the glorious day when each will sit on His right hand, and God will vindicate His eternal providence, when, from the ruins of this wretched system, shall emerge a glorious economy such as shall fill eternity with wonder and heaven with praise; it is marvellous that His servants are not more in *the attitude of expectation* for that time. It would be so if we valued our privileges aright; but, alas, how many are only thinking of how to avoid death, of how to forget death, and are calculating upon remaining far from God! and how few are calculating the time that they shall hear the blessed knock at the door, and are familiarising their minds with heaven, so that when it comes it may not be as a terror, but as a smile from an angel's face! Alas! no wonder it comes upon men as a sudden and awful thunderbolt! no wonder that so many are driven and dragged away, not going forth in holy ecstasy! It is because men are not living, and preparing, and making ready for it.

And how are God's children to be ready? "Let your loins be girded about, and your lights burning." There is the figure carried out still. You are all familiar with the fact that in Eastern countries they are not clothed like us. That which with us is close and compact, is with them loose and graceful, and their garments are flowing in folds around them. It may give dignity, but it presents impediments, and in consequence they are accustomed to have leathern girdles, or bands of costlier materials, to brace up their flowing robes, and to press them around them. They are then girded for speed, and the figure is beautifully appropriate, as is also the reference to the lamps to light at the midnight hour. These references are as impressive as they are appropriate, and they convey to our minds the state of preparation we must be in if we would welcome our Master's coming. The affections, and hopes, and desires, and happiness of this present world, what are they but the flowing garments that encumber and endanger a man, and impede his readiness for Christ's coming, and make the thought of it distasteful to him? Take care, young man and young woman, that you do not get your affections so occupied with earthly hopes, and prospects, and affections, that you are not ready to meet your Lord! Take care that you are not so absorbed in secular things, and carried away by affection for earthly objects, and intoxicated by vain pursuits, and hopes, and fears, that death would come upon you as a terrible surprise and find you altogether in disorder and confusion; and instead of the Master's knocking being music in your ear, it would be as a terrible thunderbolt crushing your dwelling and yourself! Pray, then, that you may be living in expectation of Christ's coming. We should never let our loins get loose and flowing, we should never become entangled with the briers and thorns of the wilderness, we should never let the tendrils of our heart's affections wind round even legitimate objects, if those objects draw us away from Christ.

Then the lights must be burning. Our hopes are our lights, they give us joy, and assurance, and confidence, and reliance on Jesus. Do not forget what you were, and that you have been purged from your former sins. Do not let the telescope become dim and dark, but keep the lens bright and clear, and be familiar with the objects. What a blessed thing it is when summoned to be able to say, "I know whom I have believed, and am persuaded that He is able to keep that which I have committed unto Him against that day." If that be our feeling, the Lord, our Redeemer, will banish all the shadows of the valley of death, and will irradiate with His promises our passage to the house of the Beloved. Let our loins then be girded about, and let us be in the attitude of readiness on the watch-tower, waiting and expecting daily our Master's coming.

And then, brethren, *the reception* we should give that blessed Master when He cometh. When He knocketh, we should "open to him immediately." He cometh and knocketh. We all become familiar some time or other with the knock of one we much love; and we do not even need to see the person approaching the door, for there is something in the footfall and in the knock that tells us at once who it is. If it is the knock of one we love it is indeed as music to us, and what feelings of emotion and delight it awakens in us! Jesus knocks sometimes very suddenly, and sometimes amid much physical agony and much mental weakness and trepidation. I have seen death-beds that for physical agony have been very solemn; but still, when the knock comes, as that of a friend who is loved and is known, it should be welcome. If, after you have retired to rest on a cold stormy night, a friend knocks at the door, you do not therefore deny his knock, and refuse to open to him. So, let your Master come when He will, "at even, or at midnight, or at the cock-crowing, or in the morning;" in the swift inflammation, in the stroke of paralysis or apoplexy, or in slow and lingering consumption, it should never be out of place—it should never be unwelcome. Oh no, for it is the knock of Him whom our soul loves, it is the knock of Him who says, "I go to prepare a place for you, and if I go. . . . . I will come again, and receive you unto Myself; that where I am, there ye may be also." Ought such a visitor to terrify or be unwelcome to us? Ought we not to open immediately? There should be no flowing garments to hinder us, no dim lamps to be trimmed; all ought to be ready,—the lamp clear, steady, and bright, the loins girded, and man waiting for the Lord's appearing. Oh for such an attitude in the midst of our mercantile pursuits, in the midst of our business speculations, in the midst of domestic cares and endearments! It is our plain interest in the midst of friendships, and allurements, and enjoyments to be still in that waiting attitude. It is wisdom, it is safety, it is consistency, it is peace, it is happiness. You all feel it—you all know it. Would that it were practically so, that each one of us was prepared to open immediately! It is surely an immediate welcome and a ready expectation that such a Master should receive when He comes as the Blessed Redeemer, to welcome us to the mansions that He has prepared for us and purchased with His own blood. "Blessed is that servant, whom the Lord when He cometh shall find watching," waiting and ready to welcome Him, having "his loins girded" and "his lights burning."

THE END.

www.ingramcontent.com/pod-product-compliance
Lightning Source LLC
Chambersburg PA
CBHW030816230426
43667CB00008B/1239